EMPOWER Moves
for Social-Emotional Learning

Tools and Strategies to Evoke Student Values

lauren **porosoff** • jonathan **weinstein**

Solution Tree | Press

Copyright © 2023 by Solution Tree Press

Materials appearing here are copyrighted. With one exception, all rights are reserved. Readers may reproduce only those pages marked "Reproducible." Otherwise, no part of this book may be reproduced or transmitted in any form or by any means (electronic, photocopying, recording, or otherwise) without prior written permission of the publisher.

555 North Morton Street
Bloomington, IN 47404
800.733.6786 (toll free) / 812.336.7700
FAX: 812.336.7790

email: info@SolutionTree.com
SolutionTree.com

Visit **go.SolutionTree.com/SEL** to download the free reproducibles in this book.

Printed in the United States of America

Library of Congress Cataloging-in-Publication Data

Names: Porosoff, Lauren, 1975- author. | Weinstein, Jonathan (Jonathan H.), author.
Title: EMPOWER moves for social-emotional learning : tools and strategies to evoke student values / Lauren Porosoff, Jonathan Weinstein.
Other titles: Exploration, motivation, participation, openness, willingness, empathy, and resilience moves for social-emotional learning
Description: Bloomington, IN : Solution Tree Press, [2022] | Includes bibliographical references and index.
Identifiers: LCCN 2022023258 (print) | LCCN 2022023259 (ebook) | ISBN 9781954631595 (Paperback) | ISBN 9781954631601 (eBook)
Subjects: LCSH: Affective education. | Social learning. | Emotional intelligence. | Motivation in education. | School environment--Social aspects.
Classification: LCC LB1072 .P67 2022 (print) | LCC LB1072 (ebook) | DDC 370.15/34--dc23/eng/20220926
LC record available at https://lccn.loc.gov/2022023258
LC ebook record available at https://lccn.loc.gov/2022023259

Solution Tree
Jeffrey C. Jones, CEO
Edmund M. Ackerman, President

Solution Tree Press
President and Publisher: Douglas M. Rife
Associate Publisher: Sarah Payne-Mills
Managing Production Editor: Kendra Slayton
Editorial Director: Todd Brakke
Art Director: Rian Anderson
Copy Chief: Jessi Finn
Senior Production Editor: Tonya Maddox Cupp
Content Development Specialist: Amy Rubenstein
Copy Editor: Madonna Evans
Proofreader: Sarah Ludwig
Text and Cover Designer: Abby Bowen
Associate Editor: Sarah Ludwig
Editorial Assistants: Charlotte Jones and Elijah Oates

Acknowledgments

● ● ● ● ●

The authors would like to thank the following people.

Taslim Tharani, for being a compassionate friend and an essential colleague and co-conspirator in this work. Tas helped me see the limitations of Western psychology for addressing community concerns. This book has much more of a focus on relationships and belonging than our previous work, due largely to conversations I had with Tas.

Laurie Hornik, whose brilliance in the classroom continues to inspire me even though we're no longer colleagues. The conversations we had over eleven years of working together and that we continue to have now have their watermark on every page in this book.

Melanie Greenup, whose mentorship lit a fire in me and so many others.

Leslie and Harold Porosoff, who were the first to teach me that learning matters and I matter.

Jonathan Weinstein, my co-everything. Thank you for making this book, and this life, with me. I love you.

—Lauren Porosoff

Many teachers, friends, and colleagues from the University of Mississippi's Department of Psychology—you know who you are. Kate Kellum and Kelly Wilson, who introduced me to the world of contextual behavioral science, behavior analysis, and such B. F. Skinner (1964) quotes as, "Education is what survives when what has been learned has been forgotten" (p. 484).

I have been blessed to be a link in a chain of tradition of caring and love. To this legacy, I owe my everlasting gratitude to my late mother, Eve Jean Weinstein, and my grandparents, Mildred and Alexander Weinstein, all of whom were dedicated educators at public schools in the Bronx and Westchester Counties.

Lauren Porosoff, my sine qua non for this work and this thing I call my life and my family. I love you too.

—Jonathan Weinstein

Solution Tree Press would like to thank the following reviewers:

Nathalie Fournier
K–5 Teacher
Prairie South School Division
Moose Jaw, Saskatchewan, Canada

Ian Landy
Principal
Powell River School District
Powell River, British Columbia, Canada

Craig Mah
District Principal of Schools and Service Projects
Coquitlam School District
Coquitlam, British Columbia, Canada

Luke Spielman
Principal
Park View Middle School
Pewaukee, Wisconsin

Natalie Vardabasso
Assessment Instructional Design Lead
Calgary Academy
Calgary, Alberta, Canada

Dianne Yee
Assistant Professor of Education
Western University
London, Ontario, Canada

Visit **go.SolutionTree.com/SEL** to download the free reproducibles in this book.

Table of Contents

• • • • •

Reproducible pages are in italics.

About the Authors ix

INTRODUCTION
Social-Emotional Learning That Empowers Students 1

    SEL as Empowering Students to Live by Their Values. 2

    Beyond SEL as a Distinct Entity. 5

    How to Use This Book 6

Part I: Social-Emotional Learning Activities That EMPOWER Students 9

    Leading the Activity. 11

    Extending the Work. 11

    Adjusting the Activity. 12

    Addressing Challenges 12

    Your Empowerment. 13

CHAPTER 1
Exploration: Empower Students to Discover How Values Show Up in Their Lives 15

    Shape of My Life Posters 16

    Values Concept Photos 20

    Our Values in Action 22

    Values and Questions Card Game 24

    Your Own Exploration 28

    From Exploration to Motivation 28

    Domains of Life. 29

CHAPTER 2
Motivation: Empower Students to Associate Their Actions With Their Values 31

    Fun and Important Graphing 32

    Values on My To-Do List 35

Four Self Responding 37
Values on My Device 40
Your Own Motivation 42
From Motivation to Participation 43
Things I Need to Do This Week *44*
Four Self Responses *45*
Enacting My Values When I Use Devices *46*

CHAPTER 3
Participation: Empower Students to Create Their Own Ways to Enact Their Values 47

Emotions and Values Audit 48
Enjoyment and Satisfaction 55
Assessing My Classes 59
Value of the Week 61
Your Own Participation 63
From Participation to Openness 64
Noticing My Emotions *65*
Choice Reflection *66*
Class Assessment *67*

CHAPTER 4
Openness: Empower Students to Share How Other People Move Them Toward Their Values 69

Leading With Values 70
The Acknowledgments Section 72
Satisfying Our Needs Together 76
Bringing Our Full Selves to Our Friendships 78
Your Own Openness 82
From Openness to Willingness 83
Values Leaders *84*
People I'm Close To *85*

CHAPTER 5
Willingness: Empower Students to Serve Their Values When It's Especially Hard 87

Guests in Our Houses 88
Freak Out, Act Out, Zone Out 92
Frustration Coloring Book 96
Discovery Drawings 97
Your Own Willingness 100
From Willingness to Empathy 101

  Three Kinds of Out *102*

  Getting Back In *103*

  Four Illustrations *104*

CHAPTER 6
Empathy: Empower Students to Understand and Care About One Another's Values 105

  Storytelling Circles 106

  Common Values and Complementary Strengths 108

  From Conflict to Connection 111

  Building an Apology 114

  Your Own Empathy 117

  From Empathy to Resilience 118

  Values and Strengths *119*

  Compassionate Responding *120*

  Six Parts of an Apology *121*

CHAPTER 7
Resilience: Empower Students to Turn Their Struggles Into Opportunities to Reaffirm Their Values 123

  Feedback Comics 124

  Struggle Portfolio 128

  Failure Timeline 130

  Self-Care Alerts 134

  Your Own Resilience 137

  From Activities to Strategies 139

  Feedback Comic Panels *140*

  Learning Struggles *141*

Part II: Strategies That Make EMPOWER More Effective 143

CHAPTER 8
Designing an Empowering Social-Emotional Learning Program 145

  Integrating SEL Into Existing Programs 146

  Applying Systems Thinking 157

  From Integrated to Responsive SEL 159

CHAPTER 9
Supporting Students Who Struggle to Enact Their Values 161

  Understanding How Avoidance Functions 162

Identifying Avoidance Behaviors 164
Addressing Knowledge and Access Barriers 165
Understanding Why Suggestions Don't Help 166
Evoking Instead of Suggesting 168
Using More Strategies to Shape Values-Based Behavior Change 172
Making Time for One-to-One Conversations. 175
From Students to Families. 176

CHAPTER 10
Inviting Families Into Conversations About Student Values 177

Choosing Language to Describe EMPOWER 177
Helping Families Extend EMPOWER Activities at Home 178
Bringing Families Into Conversations About Student Avoidance 180
Bringing Families Into Conversations About Student Success. 183
Understanding the Qualities of Empowering School-to-Home Communications. 185
From Families to Lifelong Empowerment 187

EPILOGUE
Making the Process the Outcome 189

APPENDIX
Reproducibles 191

Examples of Values 192
Values and Questions Cards 193

References & Resources. 209

Index 215

About the Authors

• • • • •

Lauren Porosoff is the founder of EMPOWER Forwards, a collaborative consultancy practice that builds learning communities that truly belong to everyone, and where everyone truly belongs. An educator since 2000, Lauren taught middle school English at the Ethical Culture Fieldston School in the Bronx, New York, where she also served as a grade-level team leader and a diversity coordinator, and led curriculum mapping and professional development initiatives. Before working at Fieldston, Lauren taught middle school history at the Maret School in Washington, DC, and second-, fifth-, and sixth-grade general studies at the Charles E. Smith Jewish Day School in Rockville, Maryland.

Lauren's commitment to transforming the psychological experience of school has been a constant in her teaching practice, leading her to learn about methods of values-guided behavior change in acceptance and commitment therapy, compassion-focused therapy, relational frame theory, motivational interviewing, and other applications of contextual behavioral science (CBS). Informed by research and practices from these fields, and by her eighteen years as a classroom teacher, Lauren develops tools and protocols that empower students and teachers to bring their values to their actions. Her work includes the instructional design processes she describes in her book *Teach Meaningful: Tools to Design the Curriculum at Your Core*, the professional learning strategies in *The PD Curator: How to Design Peer-to-Peer Professional Learning That Elevates Teachers and Teaching*, and the approaches to social-emotional learning in *EMPOWER Your Students: Tools to Inspire a Meaningful School Experience, Grades 6–12* and *Two-for-One Teaching: Connecting Instruction to Student Values*, both of which she coauthored with Jonathan Weinstein.

Lauren has written for *AMLE Magazine*, *Educational Leadership*, Edutopia, *Independent School*, Learning for Justice (formerly Teaching Tolerance), *Phi Delta Kappan*, the *PBS NewsHour* blog, and *Rethinking Schools* about how students and teachers can make school a source of meaning, vitality, and community in their lives. She's presented on these topics at regional and national conferences of various professional organizations, including the Association for Contextual Behavioral Science, Learning and the Brain, the National Council of Teachers of English, the Progressive Education Network, and various state and regional associations of independent schools.

Lauren received a bachelor's degree in English from Wesleyan University and a law degree from George Washington University.

To learn more about Lauren's work, visit EMPOWER Forwards (https://empowerforwards.com) and follow her on Twitter at @LaurenPorosoff.

Jonathan Weinstein, PhD, is currently a clinical psychologist with the Northport VA Medical Center in Northport, New York. In his eleven years with the U.S. Department of Veterans Affairs, he has served in a number of roles and specialties including general mental health, post-traumatic stress disorder, substance abuse and suicide prevention, and intern and staff training. Before working for Veterans Affairs, Jonathan served in a variety of mental health and education roles in New York, Maryland, and Mississippi, stretching back to 2000.

Given his own experiences as a student with special needs, Jonathan has had an enduring interest in the science of empowerment. As an early contributor to the development of relational frame theory and acceptance and commitment therapy at the University of Mississippi's Center for Contextual Psychology, Jonathan studied behavior analysis and its applications for behavior therapy, social categorization, and education. More recently, Jonathan and his coauthor adapted elements of contextual behavioral science for teachers to empower their students. He has also applied this work to empower veterans who are at high risk for suicide. In addition to coauthoring *EMPOWER Your Students: Tools to Inspire a Meaningful School Experience, Grades 6–12* and *Two-for-One Teaching: Connecting Instruction to Student Values*, Jonathan's publications appear in *Behavior and Social Issues*, *The Psychological Record*, *Salud y Drogas*, and the *Journal of Contextual Behavioral Science*. He has presented on these and related topics at national and international conferences including those of the Association for Contextual Behavioral Science, the Association for Behavior Analysis International, the Association for Behavioral and Cognitive Therapies, Learning and the Brain, and the Progressive Education Network.

Jonathan received a bachelor's degree in history from Vassar College, a master's degree in public administration from New York University, and a doctoral degree in clinical psychology from the University of Mississippi.

To learn more about Jonathan's work, visit EMPOWER Forwards (https://empowerforwards.com) and follow him on Twitter at @jhweinstein.

Lauren and Jonathan grew up in neighboring towns but didn't meet until a mutual friend introduced them in 1992. After many years apart, they reconnected on social media and were married in 2010. As Lauren described her ongoing mission as a teacher—to make school meaningful for students—Jonathan quickly saw connections to his work in contextual behavioral science, which is all about helping people find meaning and purpose in life by connecting their actions to their values, and accepting the pain and struggle that always comes along with living a meaningful life.

Although Lauren resisted at first, she and Jonathan eventually started to discuss the interconnections between her work as a progressive educator and his as a CBS-trained clinical psychologist. Together, they developed a variety of CBS applications for education, in areas ranging from instructional design to social-emotional learning to professional development. Lauren and Jonathan live in New York with their two spectacular children and a cat named Benedict. When they're not nerding out about relational frame theory or arguing about whose turn it is to make the kids' lunches, Lauren and Jonathan enjoy hiking, foraging, cooking, high-concept fantasy shows, and cake.

To book Lauren Porosoff or Jonathan Weinstein for professional development, contact pd@SolutionTree.com.

Introduction

● ● ● ● ●

SOCIAL-EMOTIONAL LEARNING THAT EMPOWERS STUDENTS

In the most-viewed TED Talk of all time, Sir Ken Robinson (2006) remarks on how schools have a hierarchy of subjects, such that no education system in the world has students spend as much time learning to dance as they spend learning mathematics. He cheekily asks, "Why not? I think this is rather important. I think math is very important, but so is dance . . . . We all have bodies, don't we? Did I miss a meeting?" (Robinson, 2006).

We'd make the same point about social-emotional learning (SEL). The goal of SEL—and really all learning—is to empower students to do meaningful work, develop meaningful relationships, and live meaningful lives. Yet we've never seen an education system that devotes as much time to SEL as mathematics or English. Just as we all have bodies, we all have identities, relationships, thoughts, feelings, goals, and values—all of which are rather important. Nevertheless, if there's a hierarchy of subjects, SEL is near the bottom. Maybe—*maybe*—teachers of elementary students can get away with devoting significant time to self-learning and relationship building, but by middle and high school (if not sooner), academics are the top priority. In fact, SEL programs are deemed successful when they boost academic performance (Mahoney, Durlak, & Weissberg, 2018).

That logic strikes us as backward. Of course we want to ensure students leave school prepared with the academic skills they need for college or a career. *Then what?* What kind of lives will college and career be part of? Academic achievement helps set students up to live meaningful lives: to do meaningful work, build meaningful relationships, and contribute meaningfully to their communities. What if, at school, students learned how to live meaningful lives, not only in the future, but also right now?

This book is about an approach to SEL that empowers students to build meaningful lives by connecting their actions—including their actions at school—to their own values.

SEL as Empowering Students to Live by Their Values

Our approach to SEL is informed by contextual behavioral science, whose practitioners seek to "alleviate human suffering and advance human flourishing by developing basic scientific accounts of complex behaviors" (Villatte, Villatte, & Hayes, 2016, p. 4). Core to that work is the concept of values, because when people become aware of their own values and choose to act in accordance with those values—as opposed to choosing what's easy, convenient, comfortable, or fun—they can live more fulfilling lives (Hayes, Strosahl, & Wilson, 2012).

Psychology professor Kelly Wilson (2009) defines values as "freely chosen, verbally constructed consequences of ongoing, dynamic, evolving patterns of activity, which establish predominant reinforcers for that activity that are intrinsic in engagement in the valued behavioral pattern itself" (p. 64). This definition has been widely cited in books by and for psychologists (Bennett & Oliver, 2019; Blackledge, 2015; Dahl, Plumb, Stewart, & Lundgren, 2009; Hayes et al., 2012; Tirch, Silberstein, & Kolts, 2016).

For our purposes, we'll focus on four features of values.

1. Values are consequences of our experiences.
2. Values are freely chosen.
3. Values are not the same as preferences.
4. Values are qualities of action.

Values Are Consequences of Our Experiences

First, values are *consequences* of our patterns of activity. That means our values develop as reflections of, or in reaction to, our various experiences. For example, one of Jonathan's greatest values is curiosity. When he was growing up, he loved to explore the woods behind his parents' house. He played games of manhunt with friends, which would last for hours because he was so well hidden no one could find him. Even a four-month battle with poison ivy wouldn't keep him away. Over time, Jonathan started hiking, camping, and canoeing with friends. Jonathan's value of curiosity is very much a reflection of these experiences, and he continues to live that value today when he hikes with his family and develops his interest in ecology and mycology.

Another of Jonathan's greatest values is compassion, and unfortunately, that is less a reflection of his experiences than a reaction to how he was treated as a student with learning disabilities. He recalls being demoted from the top reading group in the second grade. He got an unexpected invitation to join the music program, only to accidentally break the bridges of two cellos in the same week. He remembers the stern look his mother gave him when the rental store refused to give him accident insurance for a third cello. As a result of getting removed from his school bus for kicking the bus monitor, Jonathan was invited to attend a morning recess group with peers who would one day comprise the starting lineup of his high school wrestling team. Having felt the experience of being marginalized, and at times, dismissed,

Jonathan learned to see potential and possibilities in the people around him. Compassion has become a quality of action Jonathan cares about and cultivates.

Values develop as consequences of any and all experiences. For students, these experiences include their family life, cultural background, geographic origin, friendships, physical and mental health history, and school history. The various and intersecting elements of their identities—including race, gender, sexuality, socioeconomic status, and disability—affect how they move through the world, interact with others who share and don't share their identifiers, and interact with systems that were or weren't built with them in mind. All these experiences inform the values students live by.

Because values are consequences of our experiences, many of this book's activities ask students to notice patterns in their lives and do more of whatever brings them a sense of meaning, vitality, and community. Some activities ask students to notice their struggles, because feeling sad, angry, or disgusted can reveal something important that's at stake.

Values Are Freely Chosen

Even though our values come from somewhere, we get to *choose* when, where, and how we enact them. One of Lauren's values is creativity, and she chooses to bring this value to many domains of her life. She tries to be creative in her teaching, cooking, parenting, and more generally in how she solves problems and approaches difficult tasks. However, she does not try to exercise creatively. She takes the same walk around her neighborhood every day and finds that perfectly satisfying. Even when we can't choose what happens in our lives, we can choose to approach our actions and interactions in ways that match our values.

However, making values-based choices isn't so easy at school, where many rules, expectations, and preferences govern behavior. Students sometimes rigidly adhere to a preference, unthinkingly conform to an expectation, impulsively break a rule, or escape the context in which a rule operates. Values offer a way for students to choose lives they themselves find meaningful.

Choosing values-consistent actions isn't just nice for students to be able to do; it's essential for equity and justice. If we attempt to increase good behavior and decrease bad behavior but do not explicitly state where our definitions of *good* and *bad* come from, we might impose historically dominant cultural ideologies and turn SEL into what educator Dena Simmons (2021) calls "white supremacy with a hug."

Educator and activist Cierra Kaler-Jones (2020) critiques SEL that teaches Black and Brown students to "manage and regulate themselves and their emotions, conform and constrict their identities, and not express their fullest, most authentic selves." When SEL functions to teach behaviors that make white adults comfortable, "we are not asking students to feel, we are asking them to accommodate white supremacy" (Kaler-Jones, 2020). This book's approach to SEL is not about policing student behavior so it better conforms to white cultural expectations; it's about empowering students to make choices that match their own values.

To that end, we *evoke* freely chosen behavior rather than suggest how students *should* behave. Most activities and strategies in this book rely on a perspective-taking tool called *deictic framing* (Hayes, Barnes-Holmes, & Roche, 2001). Everything we experience in life comes from the perspective of *I* (ourselves), *here* (our physical location), and *now* (our present moment). But by imagining our situation from the perspective of another person, another place, or another time, we begin to expand our awareness of what is possible for ourselves, here and now. With that expanded awareness, students can think about how they might bring their values to various situations in their lives.

Values Are Not the Same as Preferences

We act on our values because the actions are important to us, even if they're sometimes difficult or painful. Thus, values are different from mere preferences. Think of any important part of your life—whether it's friendship, partnership, parenthood, pet parenthood, teaching, learning, caring for a loved one, making art, getting exercise, you name it. Chances are that while it's a source of great joy, it also sometimes involves discomfort, pain, and struggle.

We don't have to accept discomfort into our lives, but if we're willing to experience it, we greatly broaden the spectrum of what's possible. Writing a book would not have been possible if we'd been unwilling to accept the frustration of trying to express an idea more clearly, the disappointment of rejections from publishers, and the tedium of editing the forty-third draft. Being parents to our two magical children would not have been possible if we'd been unwilling to be woken up in the middle of the night by a crying baby or a crying teenager, or to experience panic and heartbreak. Our life partnership and work partnership are sources of great joy—and also, at times, of exasperation. Unless we die at the exact same moment, one of us will one day experience the immense grief of losing the other. If we wanted to avoid all that pain, we could, but then either we wouldn't be married at all, or we wouldn't be the kind of partners we want to be.

When something we do matters, the parts we find uncomfortable are not merely uncomfortable. After Jonathan's mother died, he spent hours writing thank-you notes to everyone who'd attended the funeral. Jonathan's mother was a deeply loving person who invested in many relationships, so there were a lot of notes to write, and graphomotor tasks have never come easily to Jonathan. Plus, it's not like he was writing grocery lists; he was concluding his mother's relationships and trying to honor the person she was. So much about this task was painful—cognitively, emotionally, and even physically—but it wasn't merely painful; it was deeply meaningful. Had Jonathan been unwilling to accept the pain, discomfort, and struggle inherent in his task, he never would have gotten to that meaning.

This book is about helping students clarify and commit to their values so they're equipped to find meaning, vitality, community, and purpose in their lives, not only in the future but also right now. That means accepting the discomfort that inevitably comes along with living a meaningful life. We're not saying we like pain or that we want teachers and students to feel uncomfortable. We just recognize that a full and fulfilling life includes pain, discomfort, and struggle.

A values-consistent action is intrinsically rewarding; we're not after some other reward such as money, status, attention, pleasure, or relief. We might get some of these rewards too, but our feelings of satisfaction and vitality come from doing the action itself. Many of this book's activities ask students to distinguish between short-term or extrinsic rewards and the long-term, intrinsic satisfaction that comes from doing something important.

Values Are Qualities of Action

In our work, we use a simpler definition of values than Wilson's more technical one: values are "qualities of action that make life meaningful" (Porosoff & Weinstein, 2018, p. 6). As qualities of action, values describe *how* we do things—in students' cases, how they learn, work, solve multiplication problems, perform chemistry experiments, write persuasive essays, paint pictures, listen to classmates, comfort friends, and so on.

To name qualities of action properly, we need adverbs such as work *productively*, solve problems *resourcefully*, and listen to classmates *respectfully*. However, we find that students and teachers more easily use adjectives such as *productive*, *resourceful*, and *compassionate*, so we tend to use adjectives in this book. We also use nouns like *productivity*, *resourcefulness*, and *compassion*, but keep in mind that these aren't physical things we can get or have; they're qualities we bring to our actions.

The "Examples of Values" handout (page 192), which is in the appendix and which we refer to often throughout the book, has a list of sixty values. It's not meant to be an exhaustive list or prescribe the "right" values for students to have. It provides examples of qualities students can choose to bring to their actions at any time, in a wide variety of contexts. Even when they can't choose what happens in their lives, they can choose how they live. We believe SEL should empower students to make that choice.

Beyond SEL as a Distinct Entity

Dedicating time to SEL shows students that thinking, talking, and writing about their values is important enough to merit dedicated time in their schedule. Students don't leave their emotions at home, stuff their identities in their lockers with their coats, or keep their relationships in their backpacks so they can take them out and put them away as needed.

However, if students only talk about their values during dedicated periods, they might get the message that conversations about values exist in their own realm, separate from everything else they do in and beyond school. They might learn how to *talk the talk* during advisory—eloquently describing values they want to live by and behaviors they claim they'll try—but not *walk the walk* after they leave the room. Why would they? They don't typically speak Spanish in science class, solve equations in history class, or play kickball in music class. Unlike equations and kickball, values are always available and relevant, but if students only do EMPOWER activities during advisory, they might understandably think of them as an advisory thing.

Dedicating time to SEL doesn't mean we can't also embed it into instruction. We take this *both-and* approach with other kinds of learning. Students take writing classes *and* write for their history, science, and mathematics classes. Students take technology classes *and* use various digital tools to perform experiments, make art, and solve equations. If schools can take a *both-and* approach to writing and technology, they can also take a *both-and* approach to SEL.

Different approaches to SEL define healthy relationships with oneself and others in different ways. (That's because what someone considers to be healthy depends on their values!) EMPOWER, as an approach to SEL grounded in contextual behavioral science, defines students' relationships with themselves and others as *healthy* when they can have the capacity to understand and enact their values. Therefore, it's possible to implement EMPOWER in one or more of the following three ways.

1. As an advisory curriculum, through which students learn the habits and skills they need to understand and enact their values

2. As a pedagogical approach across academic classes, during which every lesson, assignment, and interaction becomes an opportunity for students to understand and enact their values

3. As a set of interventions, during which counselors or other trained providers support individual students who experience or are at risk of experiencing mental health challenges by helping them understand and enact their values

This book's activities can constitute an SEL curriculum through which students learn the habits and skills they need to understand and commit to their values. Many activities also work as SEL interventions to support students who struggle academically, socially, or emotionally. In addition, this book can shape how you teach academic content. Using the activities and strategies, you can design academic instruction so that lessons, assignments, and classroom interaction become opportunities for students to understand and enact their values. That is, you can use this book to help you develop an SEL pedagogy.

How to Use This Book

Our EMPOWER model, which is derived from contextual behavioral science, includes seven interrelated ways students can fill their lives with meaning, vitality, and community by choosing values-based action.

Exploration: Discovering how values show up in our lives

Motivation: Associating our actions with our values

Participation: Creating our own ways to enact our values

Openness: Sharing how other people move us toward our values

Willingness: Serving our values when it's especially hard

Empathy: Understanding and caring about one another's values

Resilience: Turning our struggles into opportunities to reaffirm our values

Part I of this book (chapters 1–7) contains twenty-eight activities, aligned with the EMPOWER components, that help students discover and do what matters to them while facing the inevitable challenges that come along with living a values-consistent life. Part II (chapters 8–10) contains strategies to implement EMPOWER effectively by incorporating the activities into existing curricula and programs and by having conversations that help students enact their values more fully. We put the activities first so you can visualize *what* SEL rooted in student values looks like before you read about *how* to integrate it into your school program and amplify its impact. We also expect some educators will want to try out a few activities from part I before reimagining SEL more broadly. However, you might prefer to read part II first, so when you read the activities, you understand how they could be part of a larger whole.

Throughout both parts, we use examples from middle and high school to show how the activities and strategies work, and our prompts and handouts use language we expect middle and high school students to find accessible. Nevertheless, educators in elementary schools, universities, and professional learning spaces have found much of this work useful as written or easily adaptable. We hope that whatever grade you teach, you'll find these activities and strategies easy to understand and use, but that you'll also trust your own expertise and make adjustments to suit your students' needs. Expand or eliminate certain components. Make remixes and mash-ups. Use alternative materials or technologies. Rewrite the prompts so they make sense to your students and sound like you. Repurpose the activities and strategies in ways we, the authors, wouldn't have imagined. We encourage you to approach this book flexibly so it empowers you to empower your students.

PART I

Social-Emotional Learning Activities That EMPOWER Students

Part I offers activities that help students become aware of their values, notice opportunities to pursue their values, practice changes to their behavior, and handle the inevitable struggles associated with making these changes.

- **Chapter 1**—"Exploration: Empower Students to Discover How Values Show Up in Their Lives"
- **Chapter 2**—"Motivation: Empower Students to Associate Their Actions With Their Values"
- **Chapter 3**—"Participation: Empower Students to Create Their Own Ways to Enact Their Values"
- **Chapter 4**—"Openness: Empower Students to Share How Other People Move Them Toward Their Values"
- **Chapter 5**—"Willingness: Empower Students to Serve Their Values When It's Especially Hard"
- **Chapter 6**—"Empathy: Empower Students to Understand and Care About One Another's Values"
- **Chapter 7**—"Resilience: Empower Students to Turn Their Struggles Into Opportunities to Reaffirm Their Values"

Each chapter in part I includes four SEL activities that correspond to an element of EMPOWER.

Several activities in this book are adapted from our previous books. The versions you find here are different in at least one of the following three ways.

1. The activity in this book applies to a broader set of circumstances. For example, Four Self Responding (page 37) is an adapted version of the Rubric Response protocol in *Two-for-One Teaching: Connecting Instruction to Student Values* (Porosoff & Weinstein, 2020a). Soon after developing that protocol to help students think about rubrics in terms of their values, we realized the same process can help students consider how they want to approach assignments, lessons, and many other situations. Similarly, the Emotions and Values Audit (page 48) is an adapted

version of a protocol by the same name in *Two-for-One Teaching* (Porosoff & Weinstein, 2020a), but while that version has students review an academic unit in terms of the emotions they felt while experiencing it, the version here has students review any experience.

2. The activity was originally developed for use with teachers and is adapted here for use with students. For example, *Two-for-One Teaching* (Porosoff & Weinstein, 2020a) begins by asking teachers to fill out a graph based on what they consider fun and important. When we realized students can benefit from doing something similar, we created the Fun and Important Graphing activity that you find in chapter 2 (page 32).

3. The activity in this book better meets students' needs in the time this book was written. For example, the Self-Care Alerts activity (page 134) in chapter 7 of this book is adapted from Self-Kindness Gift Cards in *EMPOWER Your Students* (Porosoff & Weinstein, 2018). Even when we were writing that book in 2015 (but certainly now), few students use physical gift cards, but many use electronic alerts.

We've also included handouts that don't appear in our previous books and simplified the instructions so the activities are easier to use. We encourage you to come up with your own adaptations so the activities you find in this book work for your students.

The first time you introduce an EMPOWER activity, explain in general terms what students will do, but without revealing too many details in advance so the activity doesn't lose its impact as it's happening. We also recommend working up to activities that make students more vulnerable. That might mean starting with low-risk activities such as Shape of My Life Posters (chapter 1, page 16), proceeding to medium-risk activities such as Frustration Coloring Book (chapter 5, page 96), and saving high-risk activities such as Failure Timeline (chapter 7, page 130) for late in the year, when students have built trust in you, in one another, and in the process of doing values work.

In general, activities in earlier chapters involve less risk, and activities in later chapters involve more. How vulnerable students choose to be will depend on how you run the activity, whether you participate in it, what kinds of SEL activities your students have done in the past, and how they relate to you, one another, and themselves.

Each activity includes the following guidance at the start.

- **Suggested duration:** This is a suggested number of minutes, not an estimation of how long the activity takes. The actual duration will depend on your comfort with the activity and with SEL more generally, whether your students are doing the activity for the first time or have done it before, your students' characteristics, group dynamics, the school schedule and calendar, and a variety of other contextual factors. We recommend deciding in advance how long you want the activity to take and pacing it accordingly. Longer activities can be broken up and done over more than one class period.

- **When to use:** This proposes a time of year or situation that would make the activity especially relevant. Again, any activity's relevance will depend on what's happening for your students, so trust your judgment.
- **Materials:** Most activities require simple supplies that are already available in many classrooms. Most also use handouts you can find in the book or online. Visit **go.SolutionTree.com/SEL** for free reproducibles. You can use the reproducibles by printing them or having students open them on their devices as entry-form PDFs, which especially helps students whose individualized education plans (IEPs) or 504 plans call for computer use. But when possible, we recommend using actual paper so students won't be able to see what their classmates are writing but will be able to see that their classmates are writing. Seeing their peers do the activity sometimes encourages reluctant students to try it too.

The following sections also appear with each activity.

Leading the Activity

We provide a step-by-step procedure for each activity, but we encourage you to make adjustments to suit your students' needs and your classroom dynamics. Many activities use writing or drawing as a means of reflection. Even students who don't enjoy writing or drawing have told us they appreciate the opportunity to discover their own thoughts and feelings. That individual reflection is sometimes an end unto itself; other times, students choose what, if anything, to share with a partner or group. Having a private space for reflection and being able to choose whether and what to share is particularly important for people in historically marginalized groups whose safety often is not preserved or prioritized in school environments. Some students might not share very much at first but begin to feel safer doing so over the course of the year. Even if they don't, writing offers the opportunity to share with themselves. The fact that so much of their work is private means they can easily opt out. But it's precisely because they can opt out that they can also opt in.

Also, many activities portion out the work so students won't know what's happening next. For example, when students are drawing what it looks like when they freak out, act out, and zone out, they don't know that the next step will be to consider how other people respond to those behaviors. If they did know that was the next step, they might not be as honest about their own behaviors, or they might depict behaviors that garner positive responses. Knowing the next step sometimes limits students' approach to the current step.

Extending the Work

Extensions help students build on the work they did during the primary activity, so it becomes more than something they happened to do one day in class, but rather, a starting point for values-consistent action in their lives. Most extensions consist of follow-up questions to ask after a few days or weeks so students have a chance to discuss whether they tried values-consistent actions they came up with during the activity itself. For example, after students write apologies, you could wait a few days and then ask whether they delivered their apologies. A student might have felt awkward when apologizing to a friend, but telling her classmates about that apology might make her feel proud of herself. Having felt that pride, she might be more likely to apologize in the future, even if she feels awkward. Follow-up discussions help students who enacted their values experience positive feelings so they'll be more likely to take similar actions in the future. Follow-up discussions also help students who *didn't* take values-consistent action to explore the costs of inaction and think of ways to overcome any obstacles.

Some extensions explain how to repeat the activity so it becomes a meaningful learning routine. For instance, the Values and Questions Card Game (page 24) works best if students play it regularly; they learn the game mechanics and usually start to say more in response to the questions.

Other extensions offer longer-term or higher-stakes versions of the primary activity. For example, after committing to one act of self-care, students could commit to a weekly self-care action, or they could invite a friend to engage in self-care together.

A few extensions are a second activity that requires having done the first one. For example, after assessing how well a class provides opportunities for them to live their values (the primary activity), students could write thank-you notes to the teacher (an optional second activity). Although these second activities take time—possibly more time than the primary activity—they help students make their values manifest in their lives.

Adjusting the Activity

No activity works in every context, so we've offered variations to make the activities accessible to you and your students in your setting. If an activity, or even its variation, doesn't seem like it will work for your students, we encourage you to adapt it so it does. We intentionally do not make assumptions about what disabled or neurodivergent students might need. Your students' IEPs or 504 plans are a better guide than us in helping you make any adjustments, as you would for those students in any lesson. We also recommend partnering with occupational therapists, speech therapists, behaviorists, and special educators in your building as you consider how to use any activity in this book. Most of all, take your cues from the student.

Addressing Challenges

Our values make us vulnerable. As soon as something becomes important to us, we expose ourselves to the pain of potentially losing it. Someone might steal what belongs to us or destroy something we love, or they might make fun of it, diminish its importance, silence it, subjugate it, or refuse to see it at all.

If we realize we've gone against our values, we might feel guilt or shame. Those feelings are hard to face even in private, but students might encounter them while sitting among their peers. No wonder they sometimes resort to avoidance moves such as making jokes, rolling their eyes, complaining, whispering to each other, telling us what they think we want to hear so the activity will be over as quickly as possible, or simply refusing to participate.

For each activity, we anticipate the ways students might be vulnerable and suggest how you can help them overcome their own avoidance behaviors. We recommend validating students' feelings and asking questions to help them observe their own internal experiences so they can then choose how to proceed. But we don't recommend pushing too hard, as that usually just invokes further resistance (Miller & Rollnick, 2013). Even those who steadfastly refuse to engage—or who haven't yet developed the skills to participate in a discussion about values—will see and hear their peers talking about their values, actions, and interactions and learn new ways they can relate to their own. These students might hear a statement that invokes their own values or feel connected to a peer who shares an experience that's similar to their own. It's better when students do the activities, but not doing them doesn't mean they're not learning anything. As long as the student stays in the room, these experiences will have some impact.

If students *do* participate fully in activities that invoke their vulnerabilities, they might get upset. They might realize that an important relationship isn't as mutual or fulfilling as they'd thought, or that they're failing to live up to the person they truly want to be. They might recognize how they've harmed themselves or others, or how others have harmed them. When leading an activity, you might not have the time or training to fully support a student who becomes upset. We recommend working closely with counselors; psychologists; diversity, equity, and inclusion (DEI) directors; nurses; deans; or anyone else who can provide one-to-one support to students who want or need it. When collaborating with members of your school's wellness team, describe the activity and how you'll lead it, discuss potential issues that might arise and specific students who might need support, and establish a plan for when and how the support provider will step in.

Your Empowerment

Each chapter concludes by discussing how you can cultivate that chapter's aspect of EMPOWER in yourself, often by doing a version of that chapter's activities. We recommend that you do the activities alongside your students and go first, thus modeling the behavior you're trying to elicit, just as you do when you show your students how to write a thesis statement or solve for *x*. Education professor bell hooks (1994) explains her own willingness to go first when she asks her students to take risks: "In my classrooms, I do not expect students to take any risks that I would not take, to share in any way that I would not share. When professors bring narratives of their experiences into classroom discussions it eliminates the possibility that we can function as all-knowing, silent interrogators. It is often productive if professors take the *first* risk" (p. 21, emphasis added). Unlike when you're teaching academic content and positioning yourself as an expert, doing SEL activities with your students means positioning yourself as a fellow vulnerable human so students can be vulnerable, too. But using EMPOWER yourself isn't just about modeling behaviors for your students. It's also about making your own work a source of meaning, vitality, and community in your life. We think improving your own psychological experience of school is enough of a reason to do this work.

Chapter 1

• • • • •

EXPLORATION
EMPOWER STUDENTS TO DISCOVER HOW VALUES SHOW UP IN THEIR LIVES

In *Walden*, Henry David Thoreau (1854/1995) famously wrote, "I went to the woods because I wished to live deliberately." The woods do slow us down and get us to pay more deliberate attention to the changes in seasons, the sounds of falling leaves, the tiny movements of spring peepers, and the subtle differences between a delicious chanterelle and a toxic jack-o'-lantern mushroom. Yet it's possible to live deliberately not only in the woods but also at home, at school, at the grocery store, on the train, and in all the other places we go. We can teach deliberately, write deliberately, paint deliberately, spend money deliberately, and listen to music deliberately. We might or might not choose to do these things deliberately, but we can. It might or might not be important to us to be deliberate when doing all these things, but it's possible. Values, as qualities of action, are always available.

This chapter's activities ask students to explore their values—the qualities they want to bring to their actions. None of these activities tell students what they *should* value or ask them to come up with a set of core values. Instead, the work is purely exploratory, asking students to try on different values, almost as if they were trying on different pairs of glasses to see how the world looks through each one. Values are like lenses through which we see our lives; they don't change the world around us but do change how we experience and relate to it, and ultimately how we choose to act. These activities help students discover how different values show up, or could show up, in their lives—and how their lives might look and feel different if and when they enact those values.

 Shape of My Life Posters

Students make posters that reflect how they want to bring their values to their actions in various life domains, such as their academic, artistic, and social lives. The idea of measuring values in various life domains comes from the Valued Living Questionnaire, developed by psychologists Kelly Wilson, Emily Sandoz, Jennifer Kitchens, and Miguel Roberts (2010). Unlike a questionnaire, this activity helps students make sources of meaning in their lives more visible—to themselves and one another—by representing them as colorful shapes on a poster.

> **Suggested duration:** 45 minutes
>
> **When to use:** At the beginning of the year, as a way for students to get to know each other
>
> **Materials:** Copies of the "Domains of Life" handout (page 29); quarter-sheets of paper in eight different colors; full-sized sheets of white paper; scissors; glue sticks; thin, black markers or pens; a list of values such as the "Examples of Values" handout (page 192)

Leading the Activity

The following steps will help you effectively lead the activity.

1. Distribute copies of the "Domains of Life" handout (page 29). Explain that these are areas of life that are important to many people. Some might be very important to them personally, some less so, and some might not be important to them at all. The top four domains—(1) social, (2) academic, (3) artistic, and (4) athletic—tend to intersect with school, while the bottom four—(1) family, (2) civic, (3) spiritual, and (4) physical—represent areas of life outside school.

2. Ask students to write some of the things they *do* in each domain of their lives. For example, a student's artistic life might include painting, baking, or deejaying.

3. Provide the art materials: colored paper, white paper, scissors, glue, and black markers or pens. Assign a color to each domain of life, and ask students to write the colors in the appropriate boxes on their handouts.

4. Ask students to cut each piece of colored paper into shapes that represent that area of their lives. The size of their shapes should represent how important that area of life is to them. After they finish cutting out their shapes, they glue them onto the bigger sheet of white paper, creating a poster that shows how important these areas of life are to them.

5. Inside the shapes, ask students to write some of the things they do in these areas of their lives (which they identified in step 2).

6. Provide students with a list of values, such as the "Examples of Values" handout (page 192). Ask them to write, on the white background of their posters, qualities they most want to bring to the actions they wrote.

7. Invite students to share by leaving their posters on their desks, walking around the classroom to view each other's work, and then discussing what they noticed about themselves and each other.

Figure 1.1 shows an example life poster based on what was important to Lauren during her senior year in high school (although she probably would have used more interesting shapes). We used rectangles to show how the shapes can be very simple, but the poster can still reflect what matters to the student.

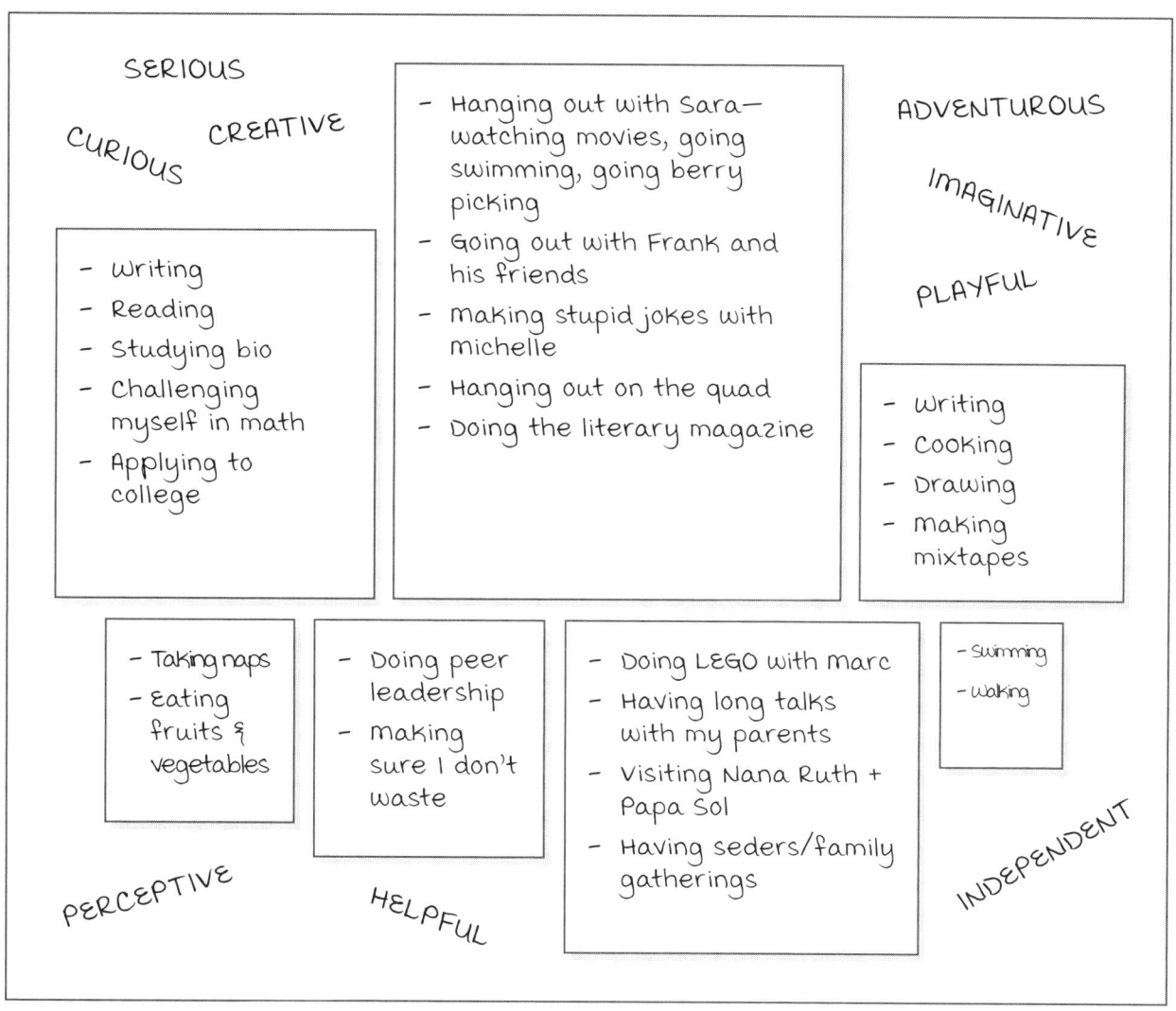

Figure 1.1: Example life poster.

Extending the Work

This activity asks students to consider how important various parts of their lives are. You can ask more questions to help them explore how they approach these parts of their lives.

- "Are there parts of your life that feel very important that you'd like to put more time or energy into? What might that look like?"

- "Are there parts of your life that get *too* much attention? Maybe there's something—or someone—that takes a lot of your energy, and you'd like to save energy for other people or things? How could you set limits in those situations?"

- "Are there parts of your life that you feel pressured to attend to? Where's that pressure coming from? How is that part of your life important to *you*? What do you want to do in that part of your life?"

- "How could you bring some of the important activities from your out-of-school lives into school? For example, are there ways you could read or write about that activity for a class, or start a club so other people could do that activity, too?"

After several months have passed, you could ask the students to talk about how their posters would look different if they were to make them again. Which shapes would be bigger? Which ones would be smaller? What new things would they write on their shapes? If they were going to make posters like these a year from now, or five years from now, what do they hope they'll write in their shapes? What small steps can they take toward those things right now?

If you use the life poster activity as an icebreaker at the beginning of the year, revisiting (or even remaking) the posters midway through the year could help students see how their priorities have changed or stayed the same. Students might be more open and honest with themselves and one another, especially if they've done other values activities in the interim.

You can also help your students bring some of the same values to school-related domains that they bring to their out-of-school interests. Imagine a student who loves baseball and spends hours practicing his batting stance—but who hates writing and rushes through any writing assignment. If he wrote *diligent* on his life poster next to his baseball bat, his teacher could ask him about how it felt to practice his batting stance diligently (exciting, boring, frustrating, or tiring, perhaps) and how he felt when he finally mastered it (happy, proud, or excited, perhaps). From there, the teacher could ask the student whether he'd be willing to be a bit more diligent in editing his writing, which might feel frustrating and tiring while he's doing it but might lead to feelings of pride. Students' areas of interest are usually arenas in which they enact their values.

Adjusting the Activity

Depending on your students, you might omit certain domains and add others, such as work life, financial life, political life, and religious life. You could even consider domains of life within a particular subject area. For example, an engineering teacher might include technology use, invention, and problem solving as domains of life.

Some students might want to make a single composition with the different colors of paper rather than cutting them into unrelated shapes. A student could cut all the papers into hearts of different sizes, form all the papers into one big heart, or make the papers into strips and weave them together. Lauren had a student who cut her *family* paper into the shape of a big kite and made all the other areas of her life into ribbons on the kite's tail; she explained that her family was what carried her and made everything else she did possible. Another student made a sculpture of a person, with the head, face, torso, arms, and legs each made from a different color.

Students who have trouble using scissors can cut or rip their papers into simpler shapes, draw or paint in different colors instead of cutting shapes from paper, or use a drawing program on a computer or tablet. They can draw their shapes on a playground or parking lot blacktop with different colors of chalk or blow up balloons of different colors to sizes that represent the relative importance of their life domains, and then write keywords on their balloons in permanent marker. Anything that comes in many colors and that can be made into various sizes would work for this activity.

Addressing Challenges

Some students might wonder where to put a particular activity if it belongs in multiple categories. For example, soccer might be part of a student's athletic life and her social life. Baking might be part of another student's artistic life, in that he likes to invent new flavor combinations and make ornate decorations, but it also may be part of his civic life if he sometimes sells his cakes so he can donate the proceeds to an environmental organization. In cases like these, students can make a single shape (such as a soccer ball or a cake) using multiple colors, or they can just use the color that represents the domain they primarily associate with that activity.

Some students will want to spend a lot of time making intricate shapes and arranging their posters, while others will slap blobs onto their papers so they can be done. Plan something for faster students to do while they're waiting for their artistic peers, but don't worry if some posters are prettier than others. The point of this activity isn't to make art but to help students notice what matters in their lives and choose how they want to live.

A bigger challenge lies in the emotions this activity can stir up. For example, students might feel guilty if they think they're not devoting enough attention to some part of their lives or if they think some part of their lives should matter more to them than it actually does. Also, students might worry about how their peers will judge them based on what they say is important in their lives. For example, a student who plays soccer but doesn't think it's that important might worry about what her teammates will say if they see a very small ball on her poster. You can't make those fears or judgments go away, but you can acknowledge them—and then move on.

If you're thinking of putting the posters up on your classroom walls, consider the pros and cons. Students might not be as honest and forthcoming if they know anyone who comes into the classroom might look at their poster. On the other hand, it can be tremendously validating for students to put the important parts of their lives on display. Tell your students ahead of time how public their posters will be so they can decide which parts of their lives to include, and give the option of keeping their posters private. In any event, doing the activity is more important than displaying its product.

Even if students aren't totally honest in how they depict their valued domains, the poster will help you and your students know each other better. They might minimize the importance of piano or chemistry in their lives, but if these interests show up on their posters at all, you can ask about them. You can also ask students to share, not about the private aspects of their lives, but about the *experience* of keeping things private: "Does anyone have something that feels too private to put on your poster? Without sharing what that thing is, does anyone want to share how it feels to have something important in your life that you can't talk about? How do you want to approach that part of your life?" Since these questions invoke vulnerability, you might have students respond in writing rather than in a discussion.

Values Concept Photos

Students take photos of people, places, and objects that represent a particular value. Because values are abstract qualities, not physical things they can see or touch, students might have trouble imagining more ways to enact their values. Taking photos of a value in action helps them seek, find, and document many ways a value can manifest in the world.

> **Suggested duration:** 30 minutes
>
> **When to use:** Anytime
>
> **Materials:** A list of values such as the "Examples of Values" handout (page 192), cameras

Leading the Activity

The following steps will help you effectively lead the activity.

1. Provide students with a list of values such as the "Examples of Values" handout (page 192). Give them time to silently read over the list while they notice which values they feel drawn to and less drawn to.

2. Ask students to choose one value to explore in greater depth.

3. Lead a brief discussion on what *conceptual photography* is: the photographer takes photos of people, places, and objects that represent a particular idea. If possible, show students examples of conceptual photos that you've taken or found, and explain how each photo illustrates a particular idea.

4. Ask students to take photos that represent their selected values. Their photos can include the following.

    - People who put their selected value into action (Students should inform their subjects of how they will use the photos and ask permission before taking them.)
    - Places that make it easier for people to enact the value
    - Animals, plants, or objects that symbolize living in accordance with the value

5. Have students take turns explaining their photos in small groups or as a whole class.

Extending the Work

Students can make slideshows to exhibit their photos. After choosing which photos to include in the slideshow, students insert each photo into its own slide that also includes an explanation of how the photo illustrates the value. Students give the slideshow a title that reflects the value the photos represent. Slideshows make the photos easier to share more widely, and students can invite their classmates and family members to leave comments about the ideas they expressed.

Adjusting the Activity

You could introduce the activity in class but then have students take their photos outside school. Students will have to do the assignment on their own time, but they'll be able to take photos of people in their families and communities, places in their homes and neighborhoods, and things they care about but can't access at school. If you decide to have students take their photos for homework, be sure to inform families and discuss privacy concerns with your students.

Addressing Challenges

Even if it seems like every student has a camera phone, not everyone may have one, or have easy access to one. Asking them whether they have cameras might make some students feel compelled to share socioeconomic circumstances or family rules that they'd rather not discuss. We recommend providing cameras for students to use if they want or need to. If necessary, pairs of students can share cameras, and if they do, camera partners can help each other think of things to photograph (or pose for one another).

This activity provides a good opportunity to discuss privacy and consent with your students. Also, be sure to read your school's photography policy before your students do this activity. Many schools give parents and caregivers the option to refuse photos of their children being taken. You might also send an email to your colleagues, letting them know about this activity. If you have too many reservations about your students taking photos of people at the school, you can have them only take photos of places and things.

 Our Values in Action

Students form groups to imagine ways they might bring a particular value to some aspect of their lives at school. The activity helps students see school as a potential site of values-consistent action, and it builds community as students generate ideas together and learn more about what matters to their peers.

> **Suggested duration:** 45 minutes
>
> **When to use:** Anytime
>
> **Materials:** A list of values such as the "Examples of Values" handout (page 192), writing supplies, paper

Leading the Activity

The following steps will help you effectively lead the activity.

1. Ask students to silently and independently make a list of ways they could complete the following sentence: *As part of my work at school, I _____.* You might offer your own examples of things you do as part of your work at school. Set a timer for two minutes and tell students to make as long of a list as they can in that time.

2. Provide students with a list of values, such as the "Examples of Values" handout (page 192), and ask them to choose one value they're especially drawn to.

3. Ask students to turn each item on their list into a question: *How can I be [the value they chose] when I _____?* For example, a student who chose the value *generous* might turn the statement *As part of my work at school, I write essays* into the question *How can I be generous when I write essays?*

4. Have students read their lists out loud, softly to themselves or to a partner, so they can *hear* their own questions rather than only see them on the page. Tell them to notice how they feel as they hear their own questions, because any change in their feelings is a sign that the question is especially interesting or important to them.

5. Ask each student to choose one question to share with the class. You can have each student read the question out loud, write it on the board, or put it into a shared electronic document.

6. Ask students to propose, from the shared pool, a question that they would be excited to discuss with a group of their classmates. Students can propose their own question or anyone else's. Aim to get enough questions that students can sort themselves into small discussion groups.

7. Designate an area of the room for each discussion question, and have students choose a group by moving to that part of the room. Make sure at least one person in each group is taking notes, but encourage everyone to take notes because different people will find different points to be noteworthy.

8. Set a timer for the discussion. (Allow about ten minutes, give or take, depending on how much time you have and your students' capacity to maintain small-group discussions.) Let students know how much time they'll have; tell them when they're about halfway through their time and when they have one minute left.

9. Invite notetakers to share highlights from their groups' discussions.

Extending the Work

Like all the activities in this chapter, this one is meant to be purely exploratory and not necessarily lead to specific action steps. That said, you could ask students to write commitment statements, beginning with the words *I will* and stating a specific action they will take based on their discussion. They might simply continue a conversation with someone in their group, have a separate conversation with a teacher or family member, or brainstorm more ways to bring the value to their various actions at school.

Some students might commit to trying a particular strategy their group discussed. For example, the group that discussed the question, "How can I be generous when I write essays?" might have talked about how proofreading is a form of generosity to the reader. A student in that group might write the commitment statement, "I will proofread extra carefully after I write my history essay."

Adjusting the Activity

If your students are learning remotely, they can do this activity on an online learning platform. They can share their questions in the chat box. As they propose questions for discussion, you can create breakout groups for each question. Then, have students choose their breakout groups based on the questions they want to discuss. Tell students that if they end up in a breakout group with no one else, they should return to the main room and choose a different group.

Addressing Challenges

Like any small-group discussion with no designated facilitator, these can get off topic. If you circulate and occasionally participate in the various discussions, groups that are off topic might get back on topic as soon as you join in. Some groups might need you to intervene, which you can often do just by asking how the current discussion relates to that group's question. Joining groups is a delicate matter, though, because some students might feel like they need to impress you—or will *not* want to share their authentic feelings and opinions in front of you. This activity works best when it's one of many that establish a trusting and interdependent classroom culture. If you feel like your students aren't being as open and honest as they could be, that's actually a sign to have these kinds of discussions *more* often.

 Values and Questions Card Game

Students play a card game that involves answering questions about values they can bring to their learning, their work, their relationships, and other aspects of their lives. Games provide a playful yet structured context for students to discover their values and connect with one another. We recommend playing this game *with* your students. If you have a large class, you might introduce the game by showing example cards from both the Values and Questions decks and asking for three volunteers to play the game with you while everyone else watches. That way, you can take the first turn and show your students that you're willing to take the same risks you're asking them to take. This game is adapted from our Values and Questions card game (Porosoff & Weinstein, 2020b) and used here with permission. You can find the decks and variations (page 193) in the appendix.

> **Suggested duration:** 20 minutes
>
> **When to use:** A few months into the year, once students have started to get to know each other
>
> **Materials:** At least one deck of Values cards and one deck of Questions cards for every twenty students; we recommend printing the cards on two different colors of cardstock to make it easier to tell the decks apart, and laminating them for durability. If possible, make enough decks so each group of four or five students has its own. If students can shuffle and deal out the cards themselves, the activity will feel less teacher-directed—but making more decks is more work for you.

Leading the Activity

The following steps will help you effectively lead the activity.

1. Break students into groups of four or five.
2. Shuffle the Values deck. Deal three Values cards to each student, placing the cards in front of them, face up. (If you've made enough decks, have one student in each group shuffle and deal the cards.)
3. Shuffle the Questions deck. Deal three Questions cards to each group, placing the cards in the center of the table, face down. (Figure 1.2 shows what the table will look like at this point, when all cards are dealt but before play begins.)
4. Explain that the game has three rounds.
   - *Round one*—The first Questions card is flipped over. Players take turns responding to the question with their choice of their three values. After responding to the question, the player flips over the Values card they chose so it's face down, signaling that they're finished

responding and that the card is no longer in play. (Figure 1.3, page 26, shows what the table will look like during this round after three players have answered the first question.)

- *Round two*—The second Questions card is flipped over. Players take turns responding to the question with their choice of their two remaining values. Again, after responding, the player flips over the Values card they chose so it's face down.

- *Round three*—The third and final Questions card is flipped over. Players take turns responding to the question with whatever value they have remaining.

5. Invite students to share how it felt to play this game.

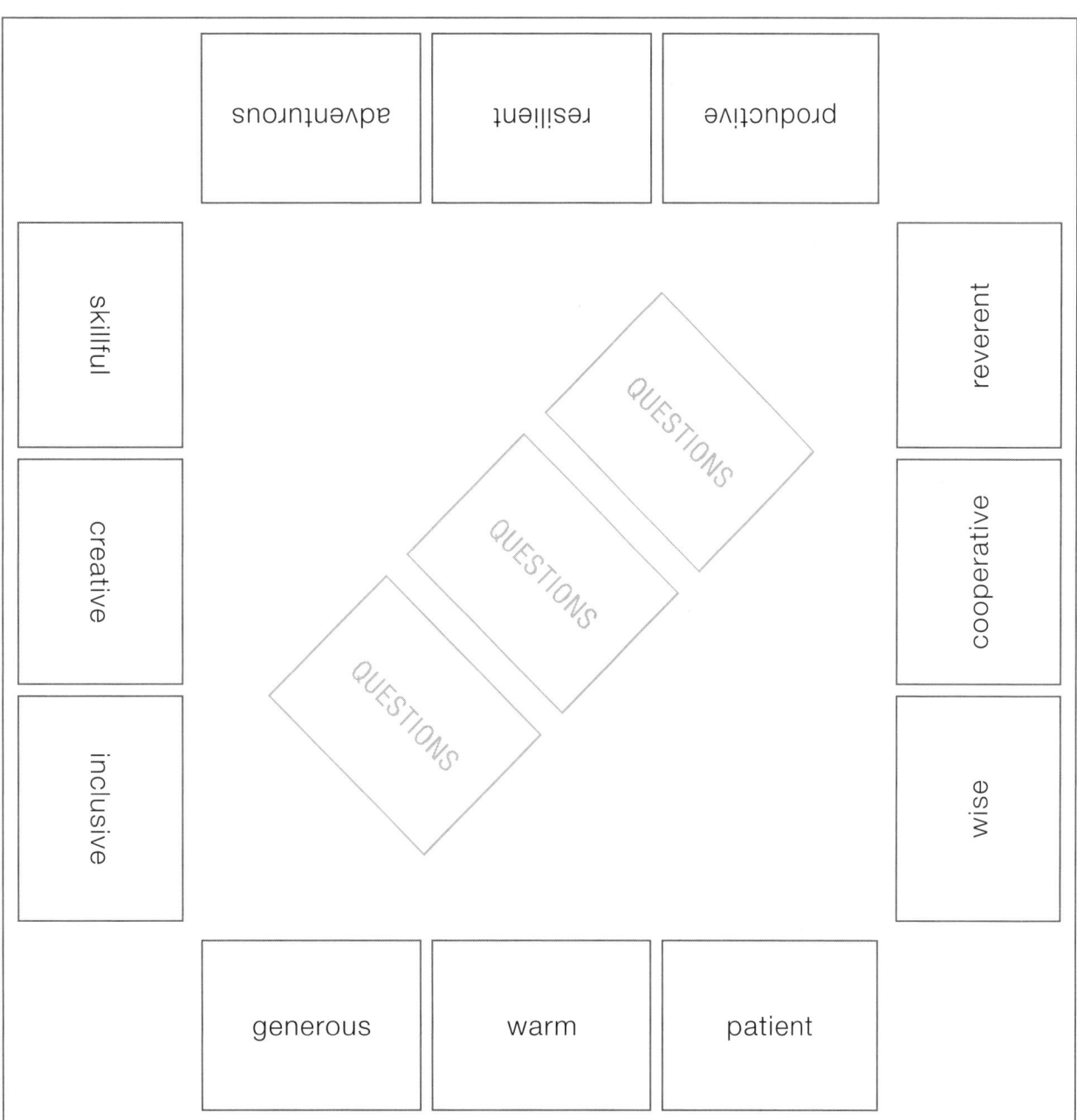

Figure 1.2: Values and Questions Card Game setup.

*Visit **go.SolutionTree.com/SEL** for a free reproducible version of this figure.*

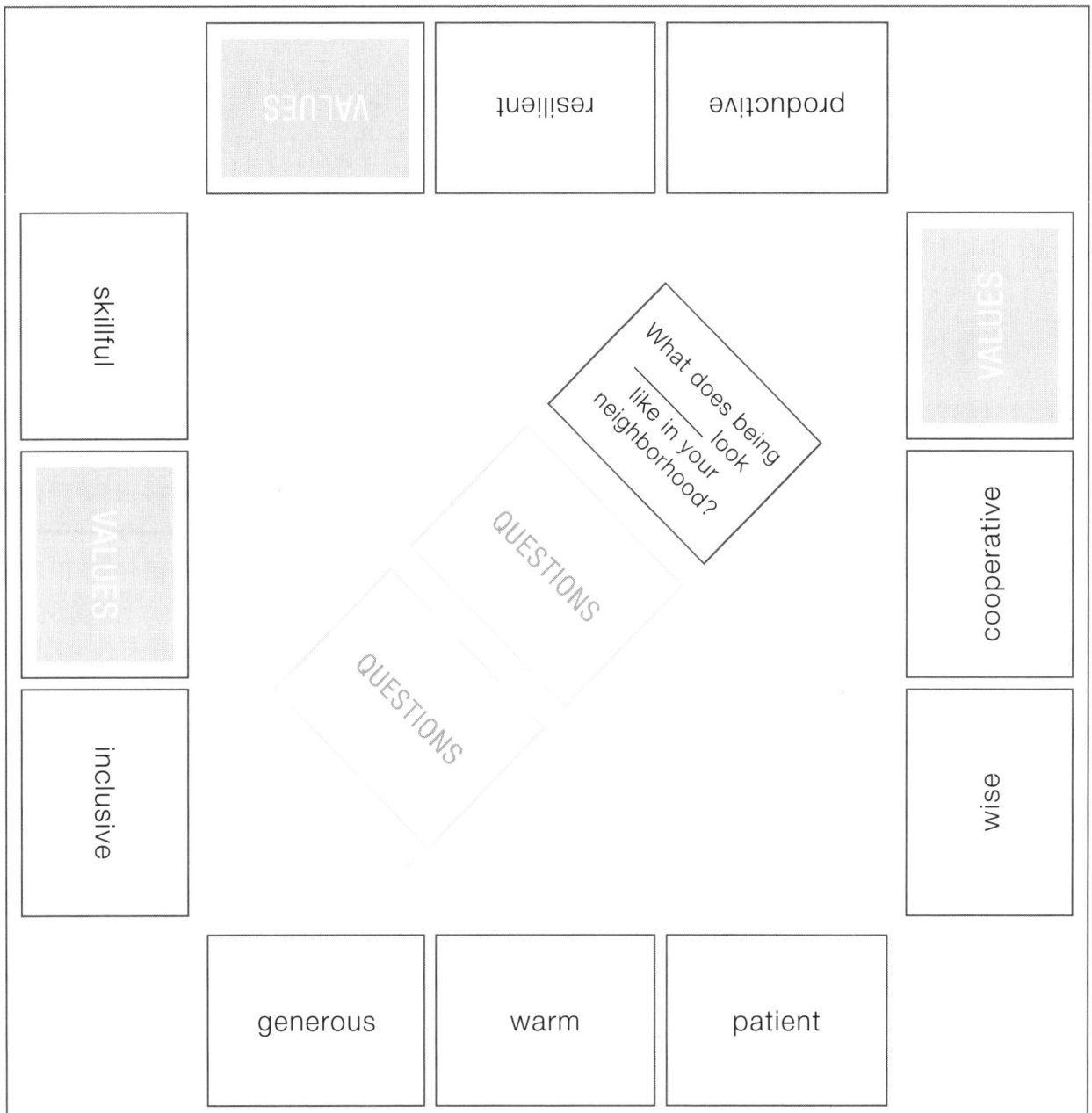

Figure 1.3: Values and Questions Card Game during the first round.

*Visit **go.SolutionTree.com/SEL** for a free reproducible version of this figure.*

Extending the Work

You might let any further discussion simply emerge, or you might ask questions such as the following to evoke further reflection and values-consistent action.

- "During the game, what did you notice yourself feeling or thinking?"
- "How satisfied are you with your own responses?"

- "How do you feel about yourself as a result of how well you listened during the game?"
- "If you were to play this game again, what would you do similarly and differently?"
- "Did you say or hear anything during the game that's staying with you now?"

In addition to playing this game with your students, we also recommend playing multiple times. Because each of the ninety Questions cards contains a blank that students can fill in with any of the sixty values, the cards can produce 5,400 possible questions to which students can respond. Students might think about the same question differently depending on what's happening in their lives and in the world, and they might respond differently depending on who is in their group. Talking about our values makes us vulnerable, so students might say very little at first but open up as they play the game more often.

Adjusting the Activity

The sixty Values cards have the same values that are on the "Examples of Values" handout (page 192). Students can respond to the resulting questions in many ways: individual reflections, partner conversations, group discussions, and games. See the "More Ways to Use the Values and Questions Cards" handout (page 206), or visit **go.SolutionTree.com/SEL** for more game ideas.

Addressing Challenges

You might find that students' responses—or your own—are short or superficial, especially if it's their first time playing the game or if students aren't used to talking about their values. You can encourage students to say more by asking follow-up questions, validating their experiences, or sharing an experience of your own that their response brings to mind. If you play the game multiple times and have other conversations about values (using any of the activities in this book), students might say more and go deeper.

If a student says they have no idea how to respond to a question, resist the urge to offer a suggestion. Instead, validate the student's uncertainty and encourage exploration by saying something like, "It's an unusual question, so it makes sense that you wouldn't have an answer. What does the question make you think about, even if it's not really an answer?" By starting with what they *do* understand or can relate to, the student might work their way toward answering the question. But the point isn't necessarily to *answer* the question but rather to *use* the question as an opportunity to reflect on how the value shows up in their life.

If a question feels inappropriate or irrelevant to a student's circumstances, tell that student to make up a different version of the question that they *can* respond to. For example, one of the questions asks, "What book are you reading right now? How could reading this book help you be _____?" But what if the student is not currently reading anything? Instead of not answering the question, the student could talk about a book she is planning to read or the last book she finished, or she could talk about how *not* reading affects her.

Finally, if you have any reservations about including a certain card when using the decks with your students, just remove it.

Your Own Exploration

As teachers, we can think about values as qualities of action in two distinct ways. First, we can think about the values we want to bring to our *own* actions and interactions. Make a list of ways you could complete the sentence, *As part of my work at school, I _____*. Set a timer for two minutes and make as long a list as you can in that time. Now look at the list of values on the "Examples of Values" handout (page 192), and choose a value you think is especially important to bring to your work as a teacher. Turn each item on your list into a question: "How can I be [*the value you chose*] when I _____?" Read these questions out loud to yourself so you can hear what they sound like. If a particular question makes you feel surprised, excited, or uncomfortable—or if you notice any change in yourself as you hear your own question—take note of it. That internal response is a sign that something important might be at stake. You don't necessarily have to be able to answer that question or make any changes to your practice, but it might prompt you to have conversations with your colleagues, your mentors, your students, and yourself. You can also repeat this exercise with any other value that feels important to you.

In addition to considering the values we want to bring to our *own* actions, we can also think about the values we want our *students* to enact. This book is about empowering students to discover and develop their own values, not to instill particular values in them. Still, as a teacher, it might be important to you to create lessons, assignments, discussion structures, and classroom routines that evoke particular qualities of action.

Make a list of ways you could complete the sentence, *As part of their work in my class, my students _____*. Set a timer for two minutes and make as long of a list as you can in that time. Now look at the "Examples of Values" handout (page 192), and choose a value you think is especially important for your students to bring to their work in your class. Turn each item on your list into a question: *What can I do that will make my students more likely to be [the value you chose] when they _____?* Again, read your own questions out loud, and notice any emotional changes or physical sensations you experience when you hear them. You can repeat this exercise with other values and use the questions that feel especially vital to prompt conversations and guide your professional learning.

From Exploration to Motivation

This chapter was about empowering students to discover how values show up in their lives. The activities were purely exploratory; they asked students to consider qualities of action that might be meaningful to them and imagine ways to make those qualities manifest—but not to assess their past actions or plan future actions based on their values. The next chapter does this. It's about empowering students to associate their actions with their values, so when they do the things they already do anyway, those actions will feel more meaningful.

Domains of Life

Your **social life** includes your relationships with your friends and with peers who aren't your friends.	Your **academic life** includes any aspects of your studies, in school or elsewhere.
Your **artistic life** includes any activity that involves creating something beautiful or appealing.	Your **athletic life** includes any activity that develops your body's skills and strengths.
Your **family life** includes your relationships with various relatives and with your family as a whole.	Your **civic life** includes anything you do to fulfill your responsibilities as a member of a community.
Your **spiritual life** includes anything you do to practice a religion or connect to a higher power.	Your **physical life** is how you take care of your body's most basic needs.

Chapter 2

• • • • •

MOTIVATION
EMPOWER STUDENTS TO ASSOCIATE THEIR ACTIONS WITH THEIR VALUES

In honor of Barack Obama's first presidential inauguration, poet Elizabeth Alexander (2009) wrote a poem called "Praise Song for the Day." It's about how every day, "all about us is noise" until we recognize the ancestors who have died to get us here and we take action, "walking forward into that light" one step at a time.

For students, so often, all about them is noise. For so many of them, each day consists of tasks they do because someone tells them they should or must—*fill out this Venn diagram, solve these equations, circle all the direct objects*—or tasks they do unthinkingly, as if they're passengers and not pilots in their own lives. At school, students complete tasks motivated by other people's demands or by habit.

A regular school day might not be infused with the same reverence that Elizabeth Alexander (2009) felt when she wrote her poem and inspired when she read it, but *any* day can become an opportunity for, as she puts it, "walking forward into that light." When we associate our actions with our values, we approach them even if they're unpleasant (Hebert, Flynn, Wilson, & Kellum, 2021), persist even if they're difficult (Murthy, Villatte, & McHugh, 2019), and stay committed to long-term goals even if we aren't enjoying ourselves in the short term (Gagnon, Dionne, & Pychyl, 2016). But most importantly, the same-old-same-old things we already do (whether because we have to do them or because we hardly think about them) become acts of—as Elizabeth Alexander (2009) calls it—*love*, and who are we to suggest a better word for what can motivate our daily actions?

This chapter's activities help students make their values, and not just their momentary preferences or someone else's demands, the reason they do what they do. Students were going to read the chapter, analyze the document, solve the equations, write up the lab report, or look at their devices anyway, but instead of doing these things only because they feel like it or are told to, they're taking these actions in the service of what matters to them.

Fun and Important Graphing

Living in accordance with our values is deeply satisfying in the long term, but not everything important is fun in the short term, and some values-consistent actions can be difficult and even painful (Hayes et al., 2012). For this activity, students classify things they're planning to do as *fun and important*, *fun but otherwise pointless*, *important but painful*, and *both painful and pointless* (adapted from Porosoff & Weinstein, 2020a). Then, they reflect on how they can approach those tasks in accordance with their values.

> **Suggested duration:** 15 minutes
>
> **When to use:** Anytime after the school year is fully underway
>
> **Materials:** Copies of the "Fun and Important Graph" handout (figure 2.1), writing supplies

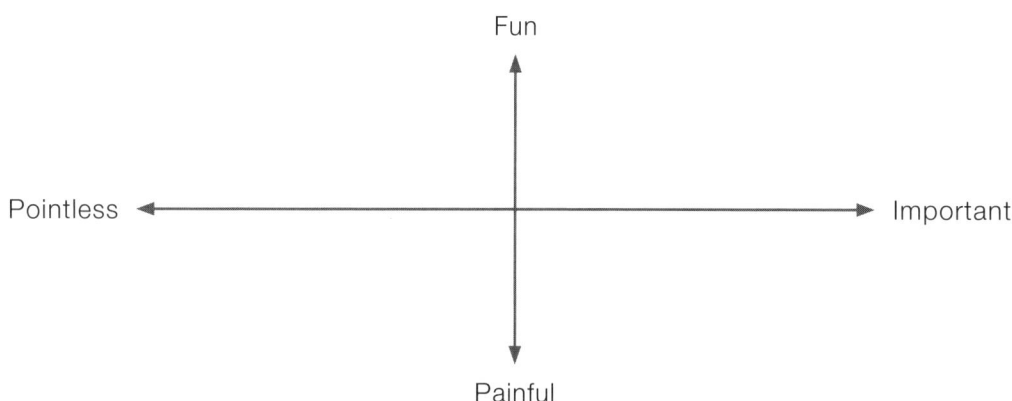

Figure 2.1: Fun and important graph.

*Visit **go.SolutionTree.com/SEL** for a free reproducible version of this figure.*

Leading the Activity

The following steps will help you effectively lead the activity.

1. Provide copies of the "Fun and Important Graph" handout (figure 2.1), or ask students to draw a vertical and horizontal axis, labeling the vertical axis *Fun* and *Painful* at each end, respectively, and the horizontal axis *Pointless* and *Important* at each end. You may wish to draw the graph on the board.

2. Ask students to consider the upcoming week: school assignments, social events, athletic practices or competitions, music or theater rehearsals, visits with family or friends, doctor appointments, and anything else they're doing. Ask the following questions, giving students time to write their answers in the relevant graph quadrants.

   - What's coming up that you think will be both fun and important?
   - What will be fun, but otherwise pointless?
   - What do you have to do that you think will be important but painful in some way, such as physically or emotionally?
   - What's coming up that you think will be both painful and pointless?

3. Give the following writing prompts one at a time, so students can spend a few minutes writing each response before they hear the next prompt. As you give each prompt, you may wish to write it on the board in the corresponding sections of the graph.

   - Choose something you wrote in your upper-right quadrant (fun and important). How will you protect the time you spend doing this activity?
   - Choose something you wrote in your lower-right quadrant (important but painful). When you imagine yourself at the end of the week, why will you be glad you did this task?
   - Choose something you wrote in your upper-left quadrant (fun but otherwise pointless). How can you make sure you fully enjoy this experience and that you don't use it to avoid important but painful tasks?
   - Choose something you wrote in your lower-left quadrant (pointless and painful). If you must do this anyway, how might you use it as an opportunity to practice a skill you find important, or to build an important relationship?

4. Invite students to share any part of their responses. Sharing could occur with a partner, in a small group, or as a whole class.

Extending the Work

This activity helps students make more intentional, values-based choices in how they approach their various responsibilities and pastimes. You could ask students to hold on to their papers or collect them just for safekeeping, and the following week, hand the papers back and ask how they actually did approach the tasks they wrote about. Were their experiences as fun or painful as they expected? Were they able to savor the fun experiences and complete the painful tasks? How do they feel about themselves as a result of doing the important tasks? Was anyone able to use an otherwise painful and pointless task as an opportunity to do something important?

Those last two questions are especially important in helping students discover how actions can be unpleasant yet worthwhile. After completing a task we expected to be painful, we might feel surprised

("Hey, that wasn't as bad as I thought it would be") or relieved ("Ugh, that was terrible, but at least it's over"). Either way, we're focusing only on how pleasant or unpleasant the task was, as opposed to how fully we brought our values to it. We sometimes can control the unpleasantness to some extent; we can take aspirin to feel better after a COVID vaccination and study for a test to minimize anxiety, but these attempts at pain control don't always work as well or as consistently as we want them to. That is, we can take the aspirin but still have a headache, and we can study for the test and still feel anxious. Or perhaps this vaccination and this test aren't so bad, but the next ones will be. However, we always have control over how we approach tasks we expect to be painful, so even when they're as bad as—or worse than—we expected, we can still feel satisfied we did them and not just glad we've gotten through them.

Adjusting the Activity

Instead of writing upcoming tasks that will be fun and important, fun but otherwise pointless, important but painful, and both painful and pointless, students could draw them. Drawing might help students visualize their upcoming experiences more clearly, which will help them choose how they want to relate to each one.

Alternatively, instead of simply listing tasks in each quadrant, students could plot and label points on the graph based on how important and fun (or pointless and painful) the tasks are. For example, seeing my cousins and performing my spoken-word poem might both go in the fun and important quadrant, but seeing my cousins might seem more fun, yet less important, than performing my spoken-word poem. Plotting points gives students practice using the coordinate plane while also helping them notice that evaluations like *fun* and *important* are relative, not absolute.

Addressing Challenges

Some teachers worry that this activity will open a Pandora's box of complaints. What if a student says your class is painful and pointless? What if *all* your students say your class is painful and pointless? What if they say your colleague's class is painful and pointless? What if they all start laughing and egging each other on?

If you do this activity, be prepared for students to express their frustrations. That's part of the point; when they notice that a class, assignment, or chore seems painful or pointless, they can choose new ways to approach that experience. Focus on naming and validating their emotions ("It sounds like you're frustrated") and helping them choose values-consistent actions. If your class feels painful or pointless (or both), this activity is an opportunity to discuss what you *and* they might try, or at least to become aware of problems you can discuss in the future. Even a response like, "I really hear you, and I want to think before I respond," shows you're listening, and you care. If the problem is someone else's class, encourage your students to set up a time to talk to that teacher, or refer them to the appropriate adult who can help.

All of that said, if a student says something hurtful, say how it makes you feel. They need to know you're a person who feels things, just like they do, and that your classroom is not a place where they can make mean or aggressive comments. Naming your own emotions helps them learn to name theirs, and telling them you're hurt by something they've said gives them an opportunity to empathize and apologize.

Values on My To-Do List

Even when students cannot choose the tasks they're assigned, they can choose how they think about and complete those tasks. This activity helps students gain agency by prioritizing tasks they have to do according to their own values. This activity is adapted from *The PD Curator* (Porosoff, 2021) and is used here with permission.

> **Suggested duration:** 20 minutes
>
> **When to use:** At a stressful time of year, such as just prior to exam week or a vacation, when students have a lot to do
>
> **Materials:** Copies of the "Things I Need to Do This Week" handout (page 44), writing supplies

Leading the Activity

The following steps will help you effectively lead the activity.

1. Provide copies of the "Things I Need to Do This Week" handout (page 44), or ask students to make their own.

2. In the chart's first column, ask students to list the things they need to do during the upcoming week. These can be school assignments, chores at home, family duties, social or artistic engagements, athletic or community responsibilities, self-care tasks, a job, or anything else they need to do in their lives.

3. In the second column, ask students to rate each task on a scale of 1 to 10 based on how excited they are to complete it (with 10 being most excited).

4. In the third column, ask students to rate each task on a scale of 1 to 10 based on how confident they are that they will complete the task successfully (with 10 being most confident).

5. In the fourth and final column, ask students to rate each task on a scale of 1 to 10 based on how important this task is in contributing to a meaningful life (with 10 being most important, based on their own definition of what makes their lives meaningful).

6. Lead a discussion using the following prompts.

    - "Look for items on your list that have higher *importance* ratings than *excitement* ratings. Why will a future version of you be glad you took these actions?"

    - "Look for items that have higher *importance* ratings than *confidence* ratings. What concerns do you have? What kinds of support will you need to accomplish these tasks to your satisfaction? Who can provide that support? Even if you don't accomplish these tasks to your satisfaction, why might they still be worthwhile?"

    - "Just because something is on your to-do list doesn't always mean you have to do it. Is there anything on your list that you can let go?"

Extending the Work

Looking at an old to-do list can be interesting, because either we did the tasks and feel satisfied (or at least relieved) that we did them, or we didn't do the tasks but managed to survive anyway. You could collect students' to-do lists for safekeeping, and then after a month or so has gone by, hand them back out. Ask students how they feel about looking at an old to-do list. Which tasks did they accomplish? Were there any tasks they simply didn't do? How do they feel about those tasks now? If they could go back in time, are there any tasks they might do differently or put more or less effort into? Since they can't go back in time, how can they approach the tasks they have to do this week?

Adjusting the Activity

If listing an entire week's worth of tasks sounds overwhelming, students could list things they need to do that day. Alternatively, you could ask them to list three things they're doing that week—one they're looking forward to, one they're dreading, and one they don't especially look forward to *or* dread—and then add any other to-do items that stand out. Framing the activity this way helps students think of tasks with a range of excitement ratings without feeling like they need to think of everything they're doing that week.

Addressing Challenges

Some students, particularly those who struggle with memory, planning, and organization skills, might not know what tasks they need to complete. Before doing this activity, you could reach out to other teachers, any learning specialists who work with your students, and families to see if there are any important assignments or deadlines coming up. That way, you can remind students of items to add to their to-do lists.

 # Four Self Responding

Projects are excellent opportunities for students to discover the values they want to bring to their work. During this activity, students consider how they might be curious, grateful, responsible, and compassionate when working on a major assignment or performance. Then, they make values-conscious plans for how they'll do their work.

> **Suggested duration:** 15 minutes
>
> **When to use:** When students have a project, test, game, show, or other major assignment or performance coming up
>
> **Materials:** Copies of the "Four Self Responses" handout (page 45), writing supplies

Leading the Activity

The following steps will help you effectively lead the activity.

1. Provide copies of the "Four Self Responses" handout (page 45; see figure 2.2, page 38, for an example), or have students make their own charts with four boxes and an oval in the middle.

2. Ask students to consider the project, test, game, show, or other major assignment or performance that's coming up. Give the following prompts, and allow time for students to write their responses.

   - Imagine your most curious self—the version of you that wonders about and is fascinated by everything. What questions would your most curious self ask about this task? Write them in box one.

   - Imagine your most grateful self—the version of you that deeply appreciates life and sees opportunities in everything. What would your most grateful self say about this task? Write this in box two.

   - Imagine your most responsible self—the version of you that carefully considers the consequences of every action and does what needs to be done. What would your most responsible self say about this task? Write this in box three.

   - Imagine your most compassionate self—the version of you that genuinely wants to be warm, thoughtful, and helpful toward yourself and others. What would your most compassionate self say about this task? Write this in box four.

3. Ask students to softly read what their selves said, and really listen to what those selves are saying.

4. Say, "Now that you've listened to your curious, grateful, responsible, and compassionate selves, how do you want to approach this task? Write that approach in the center oval."

1 What topics do I need to know? How much time should I spend studying? What's the best way to study? Would flash cards help me? Should I study with Ari and Walker or will we just distract each other and stress each other out? Why do I have to take a state test? Who makes these tests? Are they actual scientists?

2 Even though I think state tests are dumb and I'd so much rather do a project, I'm grateful that I have a chance to review the stuff I learned and study the stuff I didn't learn. I want to be a mechanical engineer, and if I'm going to invent things that use biomimicry, I need to understand biology really well. I'm also grateful that Ms. Wooten is giving us so much time to review in class so I don't have to do it all for homework. I'm grateful to her for helping me understand stuff that's confusing.

I'm going to plan out my study time so I review every day. I'm going to give my family advance warning before I start studying so they know to be quiet and I don't have to yell at them. I'm going to see if Ari and Walker can meet ONCE to study, and I'm going to try to stay on topic and ask them to call me out if I'm not. I'm going to make memes for my friends and Ms. Wooten because they're probably stressed and it's good to laugh when you're stressed.

4 All my friends are taking this test too, and they might be more stressed about it than I am. I want to be a good friend and not bother them if they're trying to study. Ms. Wooten works really hard to teach us. She also went on medical leave earlier this year, so she might not feel that well. I don't think she's making us take this test anyway, so I don't want to complain to her too much. My classmates might have a hard time studying, so I want to make sure I'm not taking up too much of Ms. Wooten's time so she can pay attention to the kids who need help. When I get stressed out, I yell at my family to be quiet, and they probably find that annoying.

3 Again, even though I hate tests, especially state tests, I want to do well. I want to be able to take chemistry because I'm more interested in that than bio, but if I fail bio, I'll have to take it again. I am going to use the study methods Ms. Torres taught me so I know the material really well. I'm not going to put off studying and have to cram the day before. I'm going to do a little bit each day.

Figure 2.2: Four self responses.

5. Invite students to share any part of their responses. Sharing could occur with a partner, in a small group, or as a whole class.

6. Ask students how it felt to think about the task from the perspectives of their various selves.

Extending the Work

After students have completed the assignment or performance, you could repeat this activity. What are their curious, grateful, responsible, and compassionate selves telling them *now*? If they really listen to those selves, how might they approach similar assignments or performances in the future?

You can also repeat this activity before any assignment or performance, so students get used to hearing these different selves—which of course are not separate selves at all but *them* finding new ways to connect the tasks they have to do anyway to values they can choose to live by.

Adjusting the Activity

Curiosity, gratitude, responsibility, and compassion work well for this activity because students are sometimes rigid, apathetic, forgetful, and competitive to their own detriment when completing major assignments. We're not passing judgment against students for behaving in these ways. Students usually don't have much choice in the tasks they perform at school. This activity helps students choose how they approach doing those tasks, even if they didn't choose the tasks themselves.

That said, you can choose any four qualities of action to use during this activity. What would a student's most *trustworthy* self say about an essay assignment, a group research project, or a school play? What would their *creative* self say? How about their *playful* self, their *generous* self, or their *humble* self? The "Examples of Values" handout (page 192) has many more examples of values you can choose from, or students can choose their own.

Addressing Challenges

Some students might insist they don't have a curious, grateful, responsible, or compassionate self. They might say things like, "I'm not at all curious about 18th century literature," "Why would I be grateful for a math test," or "I don't have a compassionate bone in my body." (You might find yourself agreeing with statements like these!)

If students get stuck trying to imagine these versions of themselves, try asking them to take another perspective. Was there ever a time when they *were* especially curious? Are there people in the world who actually *would* be grateful for the opportunity to learn mathematics and see how much they learned? Can they imagine a compassionate friend or ancestor—what would *that* person say? The idea of a compassionate self—or any other self—is really just a different perspective from which students can view their own lives. From that perspective, they become aware of more possibilities for how they can choose to live.

 ## Values on My Device

Students often hear that they should limit the time they spend on screens, and they encounter rules about where and when they can use their devices, but they don't always learn how to assess and regulate their own use based on what's important to them. During this activity, students consider how using a smartphone, tablet, or other electronic device can both support and interfere with values-consistent living.

> **Suggested duration:** 30 minutes
>
> **When to use:** Anytime your students are considering impacts of technology on their own lives or in society—such as in a history course when studying the invention of the printing press, in an English class when reading science fiction, or in a civics class when discussing gun safety laws
>
> **Materials:** A list of values such as the "Examples of Values" handout (page 192), copies of the "Enacting My Values When I Use Devices" handout (page 46), writing supplies

Leading the Activity

The following steps will help you effectively lead the activity.

1. Provide students with a list of values such as the "Examples of Values" handout (page 192). Give them time to silently read over the list and notice which values they feel more drawn to and less drawn to.

2. Ask students to choose three values that feel especially important in their lives right now.

3. Provide the "Enacting My Values When I Use Devices" handout (page 46), and ask students to copy the three values they've just chosen into the first column's three rows.

4. Ask your students to think about the ways their devices—smartphones, tablets, laptops, gaming devices, and any other screen-based technologies—help them enact each value, and write their responses in the second column. Encourage the students to be specific by asking the following questions.

    - "Which apps or features help you enact the values you chose, and when do they help?"
    - "How do they provide new ways for you to enact your values—or make it easier for you to do things you might do anyway?"

5. Ask your students to think about how their devices sometimes get in the way of their enacting the values they chose, and write their responses in the third column. Again, encourage the students to be specific about which apps or features get in the way, when, and how.

6. Have students take turns sharing and discussing their lists with a partner. Pairs might look for interesting similarities and differences in their responses, ask each other questions, or just say what they notice.

7. Invite the group to share what came up in their discussions.

8. Ask students to write commitment statements, beginning with the words *I will* and stating a specific action they will take so their device can better support them in living by their values—or at least interfere less. Students can write their commitment statements at the bottom of their graphic organizers.

Extending the Work

Some students might fully intend to keep their commitments but use their devices so automatically that they forget. To help them remember, ask students to draw a small, simple icon to represent a value they might have trouble enacting. Stick figures, geometric symbols, arrows, and other simple representations are best. Invite your students to share their icons and the values they represent. Some icons might not make sense to anyone else in the room, but it only needs to make sense to the person who drew it.

Then, give each student a dot sticker (with the backing attached) and a black marker so they can draw their icons on their stickers. Ask them—if they want to—to stick the sticker on their phone, tablet, or other device where they might want to remind themselves to use it in a way that moves them toward and not away from their value.

Adjusting the Activity

Instead of having students think individually about how their devices support and interfere with living by the three values they chose, you could make this a collaborative brainstorm. Ask students to choose just one value (not three). After checking for duplicates, ask students to write the values on pieces of chart paper that they tape up around the room. Hand out markers, and have students circulate around the room, adding their ideas for how devices make it easier and harder to live by the values they identified. Then, ask them to move to one of the pieces of chart paper, and in the resulting groups, they can discuss which points resonate most for them.

Addressing Challenges

Many students frequently hear that they spend too much time on screens. Your school might have screen-free zones, screen-free weeks, or screen-free pledges. At home, students might have rules about when they are and aren't allowed to access their devices. These rules can be very helpful, especially for students who can't or won't monitor their own technology use. But consequently, some students internalize the message that adults just want to get them off their screens—or to legislate when it's good and when it's bad to use them.

This activity isn't about telling students when, where, or how to use their devices; it's about clarifying the values they want to live by, noticing when a device supports or interferes with living by those values, and choosing to use their devices in values-conscious ways. Nevertheless, any mention of technology use at school might evoke groans, eye rolls, and defensiveness before you even get the discussion going. That's why we highly recommend doing this activity alongside your students and being open and honest about how your devices help and hinder *you* as you strive to live by your values. That helps your students see that you're not creating rules for them to follow. You're empowering them—and yourself—to choose meaningful lives.

Your Own Motivation

Just as students have many tasks assigned to them, so do teachers. With all the papers to grade, reports to write, lessons to plan, emails to send, meetings to attend, hand sanitizer to restock, markers to coax back to life, and so many other tedious aspects of the job, we can easily lose sight of the values that led us to start teaching in the first place and that we want to bring to our actions now. Books like this one can sound like they're just adding more *stuff* to an endless to-do list. And now we're going to ask you to do one more thing.

Look back over the four activities in this chapter and imagine yourself leading your students through them. Give each activity the following.

- An excitement rating: How excited would you be to lead it?
- A confidence rating: How confident are you that you'd be able to lead the activity successfully?
- An importance rating: How important is it to you for your students to do this activity so they can associate their actions with their values?

Now ask yourself these questions.

- If an activity has a higher *importance* rating than its *excitement* rating, why will my future self be glad I did this activity with my students?
- If an activity has a higher *importance* rating than its *confidence* rating, what concerns do I have? What kinds of support might I need? Which of my colleagues could provide that support? Even if this activity doesn't go the way I hope it does, why might it still be worthwhile?
- When I look at the list of values on the "Examples of Values" handout (page 192), which ones feel especially important to bring as I lead these activities?
- Regardless of whether I end up doing any of this chapter's activities, why is it important to me for my students to associate their actions with their values?

When we associate our actions with our values, the things we already do—whether because we have to or because we hardly think about them at all—become acts of love.

From Motivation to Participation

This chapter was about empowering students to associate their actions with their values, so when they do the things they would have done anyway, it's with a greater sense of purpose and vitality. The next chapter is about how students can find or create their own opportunities to take values-consistent action, and thus become more active participants in building meaningful lives for themselves.

Things I Need to Do This Week

Things I Need to Do This Week	Excitement Rating	Confidence Rating	Importance Rating

Four Self Responses

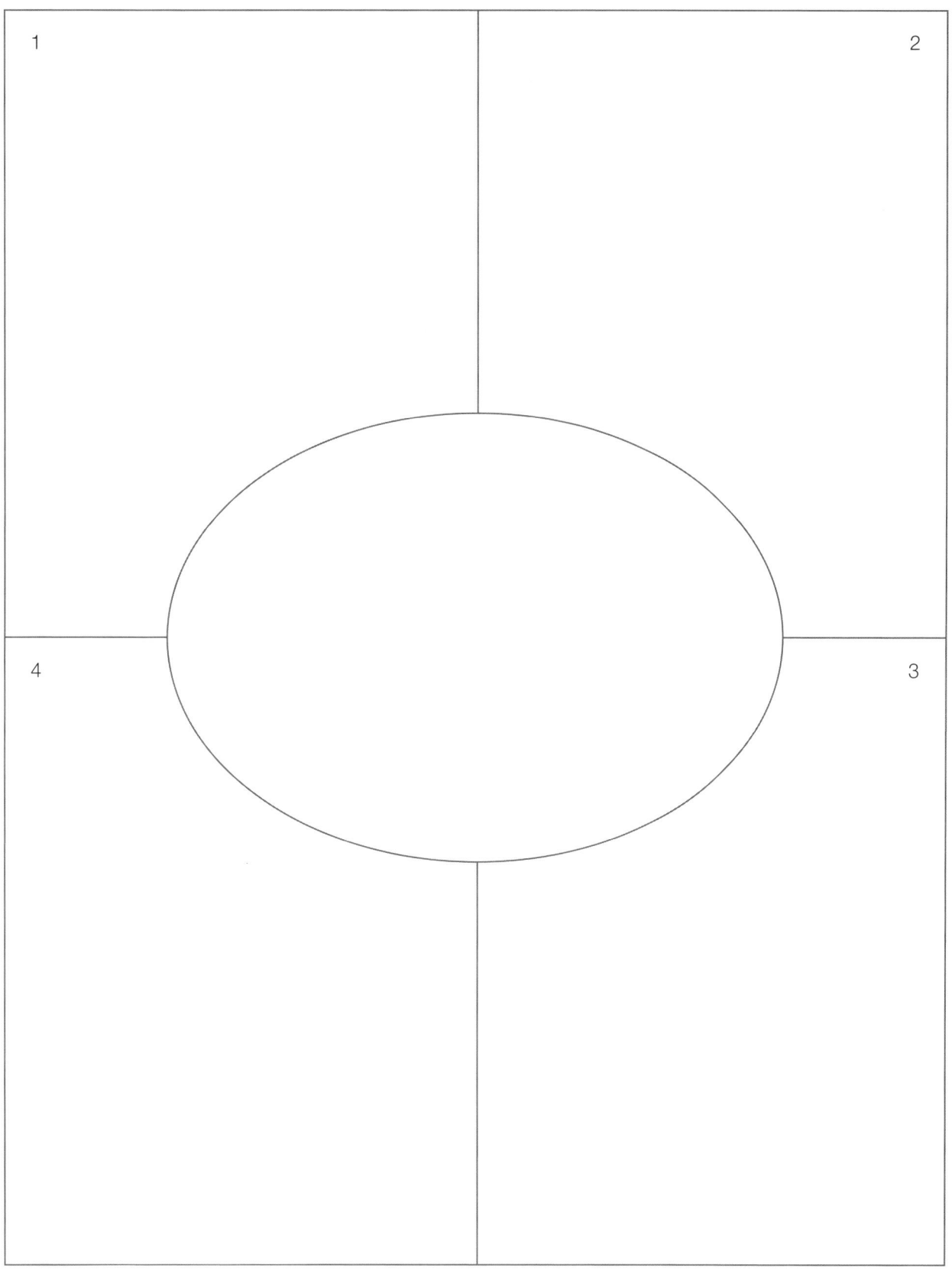

Enacting My Values When I Use Devices

What qualities of action matter to me?	How do my devices help me be _____?	How do my devices get in the way of my being _____?
1.		
2.		
3.		

Chapter 3

• • • • •

PARTICIPATION
EMPOWER STUDENTS TO CREATE THEIR OWN WAYS TO ENACT THEIR VALUES

All day long, students get messages about how to spend their time. Their families might tell them to spend more time on schoolwork, household chores, a sport, or a musical instrument. Their friends might compete for their attention. As they get older, students might get jobs, start dating, and take on more family responsibilities, all of which occupy their time. Meanwhile, they usually have more classes with more teachers, many of whom send the message that *this* subject is the most important. Too often, students come to our classes, wait for instructions, and follow them so they can get through the period with as little pain as possible—and sometimes with little effort, joy, or agency either.

In Jeanette Winterson's (1999) short story "The World and Other Places," which can be found in an anthology of the same name, the narrator describes how, as a child, he built model airplanes and would narrate imaginary trips to his family because they had no money for real ones. Later in life, he joins the Air Force and at last gets to travel for real:

> Bombay, Cairo, Paris, New York. I've been to those places now . . . the curious thing is that no matter how different they are, the people are all preoccupied with the same things, that is, the same thing; how to live. We have to eat, we want to make money, but in every pause the question returns: How shall I live? (Winterson, 1999, p. 95)

Is this a question that preoccupies students? Among all the questions students answer during the course of a school day, or a school year, or their school career, how often are they explicitly invited to ask themselves, "How shall I live?" How often do students explicitly think about their lives as *theirs*?

According to psychologists Matthieu Villatte, Jennifer Villatte, and Steven Hayes (2016), building meaningful lives includes linking our actions to our own values (as opposed to someone else's values) and

48 | EMPOWER MOVES FOR SOCIAL-EMOTIONAL LEARNING

broadening our repertoire of values-consistent actions. The more ways we have of serving our own values, the more we can access the vitality and fulfillment inherent in living a meaningful life.

This chapter's activities are about how students can create their own values-consistent ways to engage with the world. They make their own plans for the week or the semester, in or beyond school, based on their values. The activities involve honestly assessing their experiences, in terms of not simply what felt good in the moment or what someone else wanted them to achieve, but what is genuinely meaningful and fulfilling for the student. Each activity then turns from assessing the past to planning for the future based on the student's own values. Rather than waiting for a teacher or someone else with authority to tell them what to do, the student becomes a more active participant in their own life and community, and chooses to do things that matter to them.

Emotions and Values Audit

Our language is full of expressions—such as *Cheer up* and *Calm down*—that tell us to control or change how we feel. Even when we say, "It's OK to be sad," or "You have every right to be angry," we imply that these emotions are allowed but not ideal. We even call some emotions *positive* and others *negative*. This activity helps students understand all emotions as positive because the emotions are part of their humanity and reveal their values. Students identify experiences during the previous week that made them feel various emotions. After discovering how those emotions reveal what matters to them, they make values-consistent plans for the upcoming week.

> **Suggested duration:** 45 minutes
>
> **When to use:** At the end of any week (or semester, or event; see the variations)
>
> **Materials:** Copies of the "About Emotions" handout (figure 3.1), the "Noticing My Emotions" handout (page 65; see figure 3.2, page 50, for an example), and the "Emotions Reveal What Matters to Us" handout (figure 3.3, page 52), writing supplies

Leading the Activity

The following steps will help you effectively lead the activity.

1. Provide copies of the "About Emotions" handout (figure 3.1). Use it to lead a discussion about emotions with your students. Make sure they understand that there are basic emotions we're all capable of feeling; we can feel multiple emotions at once, at various levels of intensity; and we can move quickly from one emotion or level of intensity to another—and that all of this is normal, healthy, and expected.

2. Provide copies of the "Noticing My Emotions" handout (page 65; see figure 3.2, page 50, for a example), or ask students to make their own charts with three columns and nine rows.

We're capable of feeling many different emotions.
Robert Plutchik's (1980) Psychoevolutionary Theory of Emotions

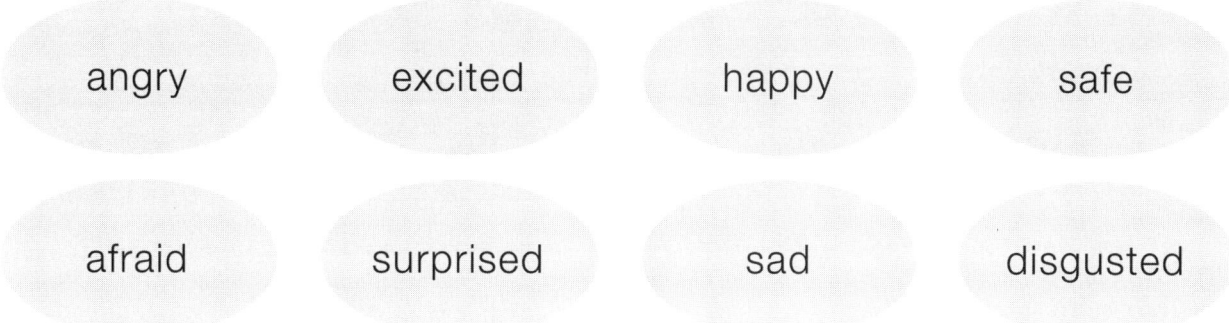

We can feel multiple emotions at once. Sometimes we have words for these combinations, and sometimes there is no word for a particular combination of emotions—but we can still feel it!

We can feel emotions at various levels of intensity. Just as colors can range in intensity from pale pastels to deep jewel tones, so can emotions.

furious **angry** annoyed	vigilant **excited** interested	ecstatic **happy** content	confident **safe** OK
terrified **afraid** worried	shocked **surprised** distracted	devastated **sad** pensive	horrified **disgusted** bored

Feeling any of these emotions, moving quickly from one emotion to another or from one level of intensity to another, or feeling multiple emotions at once is *normal*, *healthy*, and *expected*.

Source: Adapted from Plutchik, 1980.

Figure 3.1: About emotions.

*Visit **go.SolutionTree.com/SEL** for a free reproducible version of this figure.*

I felt . . .	when . . .	because I care about . . .
angry	Ms. Hall misgendered me AGAIN.	being respected other kids being respected trans rights justice
excited	I found out we're visiting my cousins, who I never see.	my cousins having relationships with my family, especially when they're my age
happy	My whole family and all my friends liked my essay about Holden Caulfield being nonbinary.	my writing/schoolwork my family and friends being appreciated for who I really am
safe	I tested negative for COVID-19.	my life my family
afraid	I thought I had COVID-19.	my life my family
surprised	My English teacher didn't think my argument about Holden being nonbinary was supported by the text, even though I used TONS of textual evidence.	nonbinary representation writing about stuff I actually know about
sad	Asher didn't respond to any of my messages.	Asher our friendship
disgusted	Kids didn't wear their masks properly, especially in math class because Ms. Gallo is pregnant.	Ms. Gallo her baby my own health my family, especially my grandparents everyone staying healthy people taking care of each other

Figure 3.2: Noticing my emotions.

3. Point out that the first column is labeled *I felt . . .* and then lists the eight basic emotions: (1) angry, (2) excited, (3) happy, (4) safe, (5) afraid, (6) surprised, (7) sad, and (8) disgusted. If students are making their own charts, they should write in the emotion words themselves.

4. In the second column, which is labeled *when . . .*, ask students to write moments during the past week when they felt each emotion. Tell your students to fill out their charts as if they're completing a series of sentences: "I felt angry when _____," "I felt excited when _____," and so on. It's not, "I felt excited *about* _____," "I felt afraid *of* _____," or "I felt happy *that* _____." They're writing that they felt these emotions *when* something happened. This will help them tell each other the stories of specific moments, as opposed to venting about general patterns, and notice what was at stake in those specific moments.

5. Invite students to share their stories. If the group is large, you could ask for a few volunteers to share, or students could share with partners or in small groups, but then you might create parameters for how group members respond to one another. You could instruct students to listen in silence and then thank their peer for sharing. How you structure sharing will depend on the class's history of working in small groups, following discussion norms, and caring for one another.

6. Tell your students that there's one more thing about emotions that you haven't shared yet, and then provide copies of the "Emotions Reveal What Matters to Us" handout (figure 3.3, page 52). Explain that emotions tell us something important is at stake.

7. Have students label the third column of their charts *because I care about . . .*, and ask, "What can your emotions reveal about what matters to you?" (If *because I care about* had already been on the handout, students might have skipped past emotions that reveal vulnerabilities, or written that they felt a certain way at a certain moment to prove they care about something they think they should care about.) Give them time to identify what was at stake for them when they felt each emotion. They might write that they care about a person or group, a place, or something abstract such as justice or safety.

8. Invite students to share one or more complete sentences from their chart: "I felt _____ when _____ because I care about _____." They can go around the room and share one at a time, or they can all write their sentences on the board.

9. Ask a final discussion question: "Based on what's important to you, what plans do you want to make for next week?" Sharing and writing down these action plans helps students enlist one another's support and hold themselves accountable to their values.

Extending the Work

What you teach about emotions might depend on what you teach in general. For example, a life science teacher might share a video about the physiology and evolution of emotions, or a language teacher

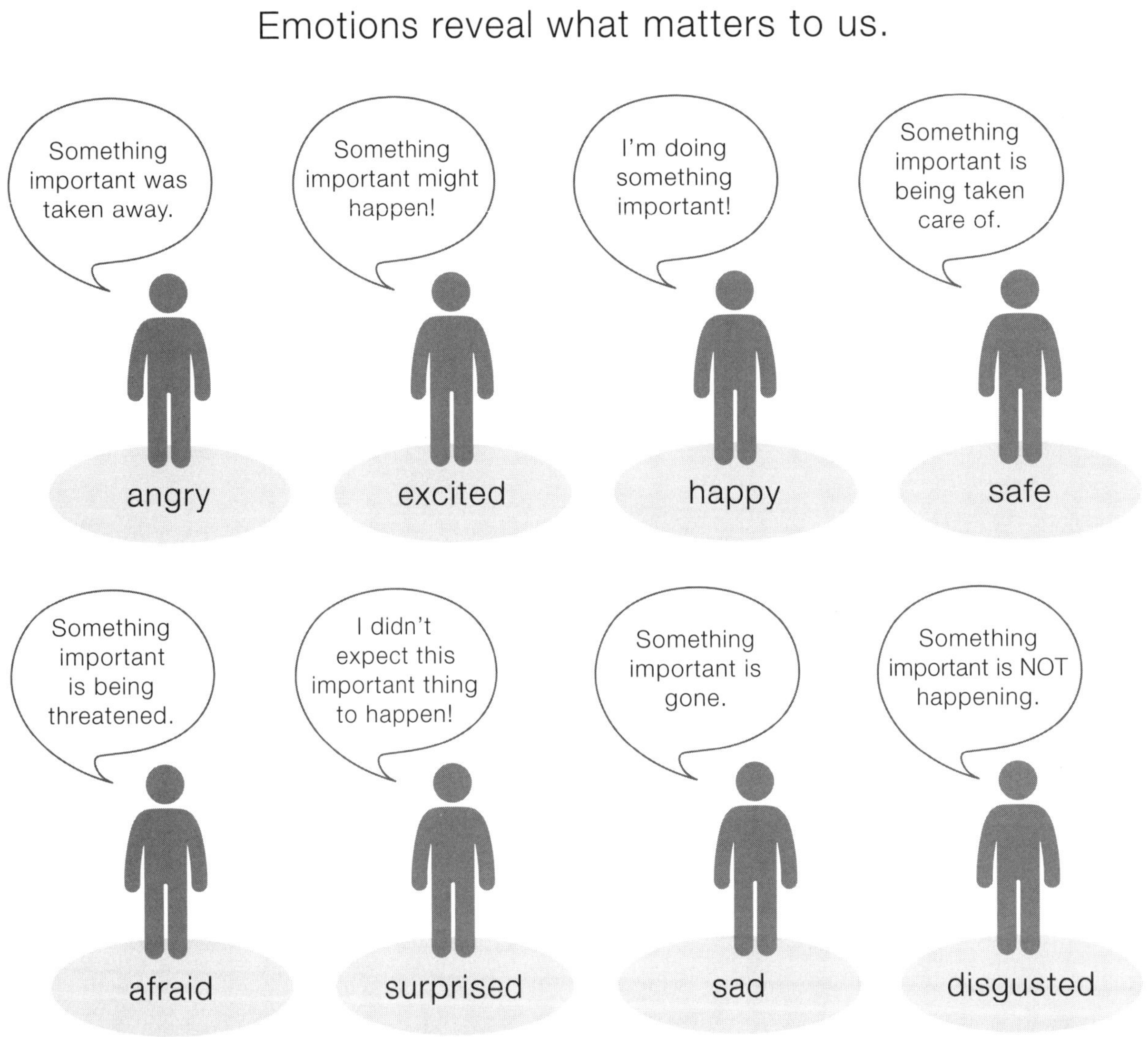

Emotions reveal what matters to us.

angry	Something important was taken away.
excited	Something important might happen!
happy	I'm doing something important!
safe	Something important is being taken care of.
afraid	Something important is being threatened.
surprised	I didn't expect this important thing to happen!
sad	Something important is gone.
disgusted	Something important is NOT happening.

Figure 3.3: Emotions reveal what matters to us.

*Visit **go.SolutionTree.com/SEL** for a free reproducible version of this figure.*

might teach words for emotions in the target language. Many languages have emotion words that don't exist in English. For example, the German word *Sehnsucht* is sometimes translated as *nostalgia* or *longing*, but it refers more specifically to a feeling of discontent with the present because of something in the past that almost happened but never did (Magill, 2019). *Gemütlichkeit* is a feeling of coziness, warmth, and peace that comes from being accepted by a group of friends (The Local, 2018).

After students fill out the second column (step 4), you can give them time to check in with themselves before they share with one another. The following questions could stimulate discussion, or they could be silent reflection.

- "Which emotions are part of a familiar pattern—you typically feel that way when you have an experience like that? Which emotions were unexpected, either because you don't usually have that kind of experience or because you don't usually feel that way when you do?"

- "Which emotions have you told someone about, and which have you kept to yourself? Even if you told someone about the event or experience, did you tell them how you felt about it?"
- "Are there any emotions you didn't recognize when you felt them?"

After students complete the activity, you could have them work in pairs to look for any interesting similarities and differences between their responses. Even if they wrote about very different experiences, had different emotional responses to the event, or care about different things, they both *have* emotions and values, and talking about them can build students' relationships with one another. Talking about emotions and values also helps students learn to open up, however tentatively, about what genuinely matters to them. Building relationships through awareness of one's own and the other person's emotions and values, and through safe self-disclosure to a responsive partner, is integral to wellbeing (Kanter, Kuczynski, Manbeck, Corey, & Wallace, 2020).

Finally, and perhaps most importantly, you could use this activity as a regular check-in. Many teachers use emotion-noticing as part of a weekly check-in. This activity reminds students that it's normal, healthy, and expected if they feel all of their emotions, every single week. Instead of trying to change, control, manage, or regulate their emotions, they can focus on *noticing* their emotions and *choosing* their actions.

Adjusting the Activity

We have written many activities and protocols in our various books, and the Emotions and Values Audit is probably the most versatile. You can use it to have students review any period of time, single event, or academic unit in terms of the emotions they felt while experiencing it.

For example, you can use the Emotions and Values Audit to frame family conferences. Ask students to think about times during the semester when they felt each emotion, and then ask what those emotions reveal about what matters to them. Perhaps Xinhua felt sad about doing poorly on a science test she spent a lot of time studying for or angry at a friend who didn't do his share of the work on a history project. These emotions might reveal she cares about studying *effectively*, acting *responsibly*, and dividing labor *fairly*. Based on what matters to students, how do they want to approach the next term? How can their families and teachers help them pursue what matters to them? Xinhua might discuss how she could study for tests more effectively, hold herself responsible without overburdening herself, and ask for help in how to have a conversation with a work partner who isn't doing his share. This conversation might get students to a similar place as a traditional goal-setting exercise, but instead of basing those goals on someone else's expectations, students derive their goals from their values.

You can use this protocol to frame discussions about current events. Often, when news outlets cover a controversial or traumatic event, students come to school already knowing (or thinking they know) about it, and teachers aren't sure how to lead a safe conversation. Ask students to recall moments when they felt each emotion as they witnessed, heard about, discussed, or even just thought about the event or its aftermath. Invite students to share their feelings, and then ask what their emotions can tell them about what matters to them. If that's what matters to them, what are some steps they can take? What questions can they ask? What research can they do? How can they act for justice in accordance with their values?

You can even use this protocol to help students review academic content, which is its purpose in our book *Two-for-One Teaching* (Porosoff & Weinstein, 2020a). Imagine high school students who have just completed a unit on the geometry of circles. They need to review their notes anyway to solidify their understanding and prepare for the unit test. As they look through their notes, they can recall moments during the unit when they felt each emotion. After noticing what their emotions tell them about what matters to them, the teacher could ask, "Based on what matters to you, how might you study for the upcoming test? How might you approach our next unit?"

Or imagine that students in a middle school English class have just finished reading a book and have been practicing the skill of annotation. Their teacher wants them to review their annotations so they reinforce the skill and choose a topic for their upcoming essay. As they look through their annotations, students can identify moments when they felt each emotion while reading the book. After the students discover what their emotions tell them about what matters to them, the teacher could ask, "Based on what matters to you, what might your essay be about?"

Using this protocol to review any aspect of students' lives helps them practice noticing, naming, honoring, and learning from their own emotions. With an understanding of how their past emotions reveal their present-moment values, students can choose future actions consistent with those values.

Addressing Challenges

Some students might struggle to remember specific times when they felt a particular emotion. They might say things like, "I'm pretty much always angry," or "I don't think there's actually been a time when I felt completely safe ever since the pandemic started." Resist the urge to push back or make suggestions like, "No one is *always* angry," or "It seemed like you felt safe when you were sharing that story about your sister." Comments like these reflect what psychologists William Miller and Stephen Rollnick (2013) call the *righting reflex*, a helper's well-intentioned desire to correct someone and direct them toward a healthier path. While the righting reflex comes from a selfless and loving place, corrective comments can feel invalidating, imply that you somehow understand the student's internal experiences better than they do, and get them to defend their claim (Miller & Rollnick, 2013).

If students get stuck trying to remember a time when they felt a particular emotion, tell them to look at the more and less intense versions of those emotions. For example, if a student felt a low-simmering anger all the time, maybe there was a time when she felt especially furious. If a student never felt completely safe, maybe there was a time when he felt sort of OK. If they still think they didn't feel a particular emotion at any point during the week, they should just leave that row blank.

Sometimes the "something important" will not be obvious. Let's say a student felt sad when one of his friends had to take a medical leave of absence. That student was most likely sad because he cares about his friend and will miss seeing her every day, but he might *also* be sad because he cares about everyone with illnesses getting the support they need or about all students staying connected to the school community, or about equitable access to health care. As students are filling out the third column, you might offer this or another example and let the students know they can write more than one thing in a box.

When it's time to share, some students might need examples of what a complete sentence from the chart might sound like. You can offer examples such as, "I felt happy when Mr. Silva told me my essay was creative because I care about expressing my ideas," or "I felt sad when Gina went on medical leave because I care about her, our relationship, and everyone feeling connected to their friends." Even better: make your own chart and share your own examples. Sharing statements like these can make students feel vulnerable because they're proclaiming what matters to them. If you participate in this activity, you'll show your students that when you ask them to be vulnerable, you're willing to be vulnerable too.

Enjoyment and Satisfaction

Students reflect on what they did while working on a project and distinguish between enjoying a task in the moment and being satisfied with its outcome. They then consider what they might choose to do the next time they have a similar assignment.

> **Suggested duration:** 20 minutes
>
> **When to use:** After a project
>
> **Materials:** Copies of the "Choice Reflection" handout (page 66), writing supplies

Leading the Activity

The following steps will help you effectively lead the activity.

1. Provide copies of the "Choice Reflection" handout (page 66; see figure 3.4, page 56, for an example), or ask students to make a four-column chart with a wide first column, a narrow second column, a wide third column, and a narrow fourth column.

2. Ask students to label column one *What I Did* and list everything they did to complete the project, including tasks that weren't explicitly part of the assignment. For example, a science research paper might not have required students to come up with titles for their papers, but some students might have done so anyway.

3. Ask students to label column two *Enjoyment* and rate how much they enjoyed each task they listed, on a scale of 1–10, with 10 being most enjoyable.

What I Did	Enjoyment	What I Accomplished	Satisfaction
Read Moby-Dick (Melville, 1851/1999)	7	Read a book I always wanted to know about, can now understand references to it and appreciate effects of resentment	10
Read The Wall by John Hersey (1977)	8	Learned about Jewish history—the Warsaw Ghetto Uprising (although I wonder whether it was the best source for that information)	6
Read The Naked and the Dead by Norman Mailer (1948)	6	Learned about racial and political tensions in a small U.S. Army platoon (although it was probably stereotyped)	7
Wrote down quotations on note cards	3	Thought about how the things I read related to my topic or didn't	6
Sorted through the quotations and picked which ones to include in the paper	4	Learned the books really well, organized my thinking, eliminated things I didn't need	6
Wrote an outline	1	Fulfilled that part of the assignment but it didn't help	1
Wrote a rough draft	1	Integrated the quotations and linked them together into a coherent paper	5
Revised	1	Incorporated feedback and wrote more clearly and coherently about the books and their relationship to my overall theme	4

Figure 3.4: Choice reflection.

4. Ask students to label column three *What I Accomplished* and write the outcome of each task—what they accomplished in their learning, work, or relationships as a result of doing whatever they did.

5. Ask students to label column four *Satisfaction* and rate how satisfied they are with each outcome, on a scale of 1–10, with 10 being most satisfied.

6. Give the following writing prompts one at a time, so students can spend a few minutes writing each response before you give the next prompt.
    - "Find something with a higher satisfaction score than its enjoyment score. What made this task worthwhile?"
    - "Find something with a higher enjoyment score than its satisfaction score. What choices might you make so future projects are more satisfying?"
    - "Find something with high scores for both enjoyment and satisfaction. Where might you find more opportunities to do that kind of task?"
    - "Find something with low scores for both enjoyment and satisfaction. If you must do similar tasks in the future, what might you do to make them more satisfying?"
7. Invite students to share anything they noticed while making the chart or responding to the questions. When students discover that they're dissatisfied with the outcomes of their choices, they might make more effective choices in the future. Even if they keep making ineffective choices, they're learning how to evaluate their choices for themselves, based on their own experiences.

Extending the Work

All the reflection questions ask students to consider their actions in the future. You could ask students to save what they wrote (or collect it just for safekeeping) so they can revisit their responses the next time a similar project is assigned. Based on how much they enjoyed themselves and how satisfied they ultimately felt last time, what choices will they make this time?

If you ask students to do the Enjoyment and Satisfaction activity after *every* project, the various reflections, taken together, could form the basis of a conference with families. Over time, have students been making their schoolwork more enjoyable? Have the outcomes of that work become more satisfying? What kinds of tasks do students find most enjoyable, and how can their families and teachers support them in seeking out more opportunities to do those kinds of tasks? What kinds of outcomes do the students find most satisfying, and how can their families and teachers help them achieve those outcomes?

Adjusting the Activity

This activity is designed to help students reflect on choices they made while working on a project. Even if students didn't choose the type of work product they created, they might have chosen their topic or subtopic, the strategies they used to complete the work, how much time and effort they allocated to each task, whom they worked with or asked for feedback, and so on. If there's one part of the project that involves a lot of decision making, you could use this activity to help students reflect on that one part as opposed to the entire project.

You can also use this activity to have students reflect on something other than a project, such as their participation in a class discussion, their actions during a field trip, or their overall week in class. In any of these cases, students are noticing that they're always making choices, those choices have an impact, and they might make similar or different choices next time—based on not only how they felt in the moment but also how satisfied they feel with the outcome. According to psychologists Louise McHugh, Ian Stewart, and Priscilla Almada (2019), being able to describe our internal experiences at a given moment is essential for maintaining a healthy sense of self. For example, Jonathan saying, "I didn't enjoy looking through dozens of note cards for quotations to put into my term paper," contextualizes his unpleasant feelings (perhaps boredom and frustration) in a specific situation (writing a term paper). That's very different from general statements such as, "I hate writing term papers," or "I hate writing," which can easily become self-labels ("I am a person who hates writing").

Self-labels "can be extremely constricting in terms of the way we see ourselves and the decisions we make" (McHugh et al., 2019, p. 131). Saying, "I hate writing," might rigidly guide Jonathan's behavior, even in situations where it doesn't apply—such as writing poems, letters, eulogies, or this book. However, if he says, "I didn't enjoy looking through dozens of note cards for quotations to put into my term paper," he isn't defining himself or creating any rules. If a different teacher asks Jonathan to sort through quotations, he might dread the task, but he won't see a conflict between doing it and being who he is. Moreover, if he's learned to distinguish enjoyment in the moment from satisfaction with the outcome, he might look for ways to connect that next task to his values so it's more satisfying.

Addressing Challenges

Some students might struggle to remember what they did throughout the project. You can help them by writing a list of things you asked them to do, but tell them not to simply copy it, but rather to use it to stimulate their memory. Let's say a history teacher asked his students to make outlines for their essays. Instead of simply writing *made an outline*, his students should think critically about whether they outlined and to what extent. Maybe one student used a graphic organizer, and another wrote the first half without outlining but then outlined the second half. Students should list the things they actually did, not what they were told to do.

Some students might say, loudly, that there was *nothing* they enjoyed or narrate giving low enjoyment ratings to every part of the project. "Choosing a topic? Two! Making the outline? One. Writing the intro? A big three! Writing the body paragraphs? One." A student who does this is probably feeling frustrated that they don't feel engaged or energized by their work, or they're seeking attention from their peers (or both). You could reassure the student that this activity will help you discover what makes work enjoyable and satisfying for your students, which you'll take into account when you create assignments—but that inevitably, some parts of an assignment will be more fun than others. Even if this student didn't find this assignment fun, were any of its outcomes important? What can the student do next time to make their work more satisfying, even if it isn't fun?

Assessing My Classes

Students rate one of their favorite classes based on how they experience their relationships with others, the content, the process, and themselves in the learning environment. Then, they consider how they might make other classes more fulfilling.

> **Suggested duration:** 20 minutes
>
> **When to use:** In the middle of each term
>
> **Materials:** Copies of the "Class Assessment" handout (page 67), writing supplies

Leading the Activity

The following steps will help you effectively lead the activity.

1. Explain to students that, in school, they are often assessed; they're told how well they're doing, according to whatever standards the teacher is using to define "doing well." They will now have an opportunity to assess one of their classes. Note that this is an assessment of how they experience the learning environment and is *not* an evaluation of the teacher.

2. Provide copies of the "Class Assessment" handout (page 67). Review the directions at the top, and give students time to rate one of their favorite classes.

3. Ask students to please not share their ratings—that could easily lead to an unhelpful debate or even less helpful complaint session about a particular class—but invite them to share *how it felt* to rate their class in these ways or anything they thought about or noticed as they filled out the form.

4. Explain that students usually do not choose and cannot change who their classmates and teachers are, what they learn about in class, or what their lessons and assignments entail—but they can choose how they *approach* their classes. Lead a discussion, asking one or more of the following questions.

   - "What are *you* bringing to your relationships in the class you rated? What would happen if you took that same approach to relationships in *other* classes?"

   - "How are *you* engaging with the content in the class you rated? What would happen if you took that same approach to content in *other* classes?"

   - "How are *you* engaging in the learning process in the class you rated? What would happen if you took that same approach to the learning process in *other* classes?"

   - "How are *you* choosing who you are in the class you rated? What would happen if you brought that version of yourself to *other* classes?"

5. Ask students to think of something they can try so they might have a more fulfilling experience in another class. At the bottom of the page, have them write commitment statements beginning with the words *I will*.

6. Invite students to share their commitment statements.

Extending the Work

After a few days or weeks have passed, you can ask students if they kept their commitments. For those who did, how did it feel? What might they try next? For those who didn't, what got in the way? Will they try again, or will they try something different? For everyone, how do they feel about themselves as a result of considering new ways to approach their classes?

You can also use this activity as an opportunity for students to express their gratitude to the teachers of their favorite classes. Have students write thank-you notes to their teachers that say why the class is such a positive experience for them, whether that's because of their relationships, the content, the process, who they are in that class, or some combination. You might spend a little time asking students to think of specific details to include in their notes. For example, if Lauren says she feels seen, heard, and respected in Ms. Silber's class, what, specifically, does Ms. Silber do that makes her feel that way? Or if Jonathan says he likes the version of himself that he is in Coach Quilty's class, what does Coach Quilty do to bring out that self? Although this will add time to the activity (which is itself an extension of the original activity), asking students to identify these specific details will not only make the teacher feel more appreciated; it will also teach the students how to express gratitude and help them notice features of learning experiences they find fulfilling so they can seek out more learning experiences that have those same features.

Adjusting the Activity

This activity intentionally begins with a positive experience (a favorite class) so the student can distinguish between what they get out of that class and what they put into it—and then make a values-based choice about how they might put similar efforts into a different class. You could, alternatively, ask students to rate their least favorite class as a way to acknowledge the frustration, disappointment, and anxiety they might feel. Having an opportunity to express those feelings can be very healing, but be prepared for bitter and cynical statements like, "She's just a terrible teacher," or "There is literally nothing I can do to make that class better—I just need to survive it." Some students might be able to think of small ways they can approach their least favorite classes differently and make the experience more fulfilling, but you'll need to leave room for the possibility that some students won't think it's worth the effort. Have you ever been in a situation that you just had to endure so you could move on? Sometimes the best we can do for our students is to validate how they feel, honor their decision that something is *not* worth their energy, and let them know we're someone who will protect them—and help them protect themselves by teaching them how to associate their actions with their values.

Addressing Challenges

Some students might say they don't like *any* of their classes; they're all *meh* at best. If that happens, resist the urge to say something like, "I'm sure they're not *all* terrible," or to remind them of something positive they said about one of their classes. Such statements are likely to evoke resistance (Miller & Rollnick, 2013); the student will just dig in and attempt to prove how awful all their classes are. Instead, ask the student to think about their classes last year, or the year before, or the year before that. Tell them to go back as far as they need to until they can think of a class they considered a positive learning experience. If they say they've never had a positive learning experience in school, ask if they can think of a positive learning experience they had outside school, whether it was in an organized activity, such as a team sport, religious group, or music lesson, or an informal learning experience at home. Depending on the learning experience they choose, some of the questions on the form might feel less relevant, but ultimately they'll be able to consider how *they* approached that learning experience and how they might bring some of those qualities of action to school—which is the activity's main purpose.

Value of the Week

Students choose a value of the week that the whole class will try enacting. They collaboratively generate ideas for how they might enact that value, commit to taking one of those actions over the course of the week, and write those actions in their planners so they don't forget. Although not every student will ultimately endorse every value, they all have an opportunity to explore and experiment with different values together. Thus, students not only discover new ways to enact their values as individuals, but they also have the sorts of mutually supportive conversations that contribute to collective well-being (Allison, Waters, & Kern, 2021).

> **Suggested duration:** 10–15 minutes, plus 5–10 minutes for the follow-up discussion a few days later
>
> **When to use:** At the beginning of any week
>
> **Materials:** Either a list of values such as the "Examples of Values" handout (page 192) or the Values card deck (page 193), students' existing planners or calendars

Leading the Activity

The following steps will help you effectively lead the activity.

1. Early in the week, ask one student to choose a value of the week that the whole group will try enacting. They can either select a value from the list on the "Examples of Values" handout (page 192) or pick a random Values card (page 193) from the deck.

2. Lead students in brainstorming ways they can enact that value at some point over the course of the week. Write their suggestions on the board or appoint a student to scribe. Ask them to suggest behaviors that have the following characteristics.

    - *Specific:* Help us imagine exactly what we could do to enact this value.
    - *Concrete:* Help us imagine a physical action, not a state of being. If we can picture exactly what this action looks like in the world, we'll be able to see it when we're doing it and know we've successfully done it.
    - *Positive:* Tell us what we could *do* as opposed to what we could *not* do.
    - *Diverse:* Give us a wide variety of choices for how we can enact this value. For example, think about how we might enact this value in different classes, in after-school athletic and artistic activities, at home, with our friends, in our communities, and in how we take care of ourselves.

3. Ask students to choose one specific way they will enact the value of the week in the coming days. They can write their actions in their planners, on a particular day and at a particular time. If they use digital planners, ask them to set alerts so they don't forget.

4. Ask students to notice any thoughts and feelings that came up as they set a date and time for their actions and wrote it in their planners. Invite them to share.

5. A few days later, ask students to share whether they did the thing they planned to do. For those who did, how did it go? How do they feel about themselves as a result of doing it? For those who didn't, what got in the way?

6. Invite students to choose new ways to enact the value of the week and again to write their actions in their planners. Those who completed their actions might do the same thing again or try something new. Those who didn't complete their actions might pick a new day and time for it, or they might choose a different action that will work better for them.

Extending the Work

Although this can be a stand-alone activity, it's best to have a value of the week for several consecutive weeks—if not an entire semester or year—so students can build momentum. If they don't do the actions they chose on a particular week, they'll have many more opportunities to try new behaviors and discover whether the value of the week might be a value they want to live by every week.

Adjusting the Activity

Instead of writing students' action ideas on the board, you could ask students to write them on sticky notes that they stick to the board. Although this version is a bit more chaotic than leading a discussion yourself, more students will be able to participate, and they'll generate a longer list of possible actions more quickly. After a few minutes of brainstorming, students can sort the action ideas into categories and remove any duplicate suggestions. This extra step adds a bit of time to the activity but also encourages students to think critically about the actions, which might help them choose one that they're more likely to try.

Addressing Challenges

If you won't be able to repeat this activity enough times for every student to choose a value of the week (or if you aren't sure), have the student who selects the value of the week randomly draw a card from the Values deck (page 193). That way, students who don't get a chance to select a value won't feel like they've missed out. The process of discussing and choosing ways to enact the value is more important than which value it is.

Students might struggle to come up with specific, concrete, positive, diverse action ideas. You can offer a few suggestions yourself, but try to contribute sparingly—just enough to get them thinking of their own actions. This shouldn't be another occasion when the teacher tells students what to do; it's an opportunity for students to come up with their own ways to enact their values—or at least to discover how it feels to take action consistent with a particular value that they might or might not adopt more fully.

Your Own Participation

Any of this chapter's activities would be good to do alongside your students, not only because you'd be able to model generating ideas for values-consistent action and then committing to those actions, but also because teachers, like their students, have busy schedules. Many of us fall into understandable patterns of doing everyday tasks and ceding to everyday demands without thinking much about them. If our actions aren't in the service of our values, then they just seem like yet more tasks to add to an already overwhelming to-do list. All of this chapter's activities could help you make values-conscious choices about how you spend your time in your professional and personal life.

But if you're only going to do one activity from this chapter—and really, from this book—we suggest the Emotions and Values Audit (page 48) as a way for you and your colleagues to have an opportunity to share your stories, bear witness to one another's emotional experiences, and be affirmed in your own.

Sometime, when you meet with a group of your colleagues, ask the group to reflect on the many emotions they felt during a particular event or time period. Next, take some time to share your stories—not just what happened, but how you felt. If your group is large, break into smaller groups so each person has a chance to talk about their experiences and hear their colleagues' words of support. The mere act of acknowledging our own emotional experiences in an empathetic group is tremendously empowering (van Kleef & Fischer, 2016), but the activity isn't finished.

When you (and your colleagues) felt each emotion, what was the *something important* at stake? The *something* might be a person or group, such as a particular student or the members of a particular community. It might be a place, such as your classroom or ancestral homeland. The *something* might be a process, such as writing an essay or voting. Or it might be an abstract quality, such as love or liberation.

Tug on any emotion, and you'll pull up your values. Emotions are the leaves and blossoms that promise a deep and wide network of values under the surface.

If you and your colleagues look over what you said you cared about, those people, places, processes, and ideas probably still matter to you right at that moment. How do you want to approach those people, places, and processes? If you said you cared about certain qualities, such as belonging or creativity, how can you build an environment that promotes those qualities?

As members of a community, we need opportunities to connect—not just with our own values but with each other, as a community, and with the shared values that *make* us a community. When you and your colleagues tell your stories and hear each other's, you can more fully experience your own emotions, discover the values underneath, and connect with what you care about—as individuals and as a group. Buoyed by a sense of common purpose, you can turn to choosing how you want to enact your values as a community. You're not just doing the "right" actions or using the "best" practices; you're choosing, together, to be the best versions of yourselves.

From Participation to Openness

This chapter's activities help students assess past experiences based on their values and more actively choose the actions they want to take in the future so they can live their values more fully. The next chapter is about how students can build community by opening up about their values, particularly when they see those values in one another.

Noticing My Emotions

I felt . . .	when . . .	
angry		
excited		
happy		
safe		
afraid		
surprised		
sad		
disgusted		

Choice Reflection

Satisfaction					
What I Accomplished					
Enjoyment					
What I Did					

Class Assessment

Think about your experiences in one of your favorite classes. Decide how true the following statements are, and rate them accordingly.

		Rarely			Sometimes				Often		
Relationships	I feel seen, heard, and respected by the people in the room.	1	2	3	4	5	6	7	8	9	10
	If I need support, I can get it from someone in the room.	1	2	3	4	5	6	7	8	9	10
	We talk through conflicts and find good solutions.	1	2	3	4	5	6	7	8	9	10
Content	I'm learning about topics that matter to me personally.	1	2	3	4	5	6	7	8	9	10
	I'm learning about topics that matter in the world.	1	2	3	4	5	6	7	8	9	10
	My communities are richly and accurately represented.	1	2	3	4	5	6	7	8	9	10
Process	We learn in ways that tap into my strengths.	1	2	3	4	5	6	7	8	9	10
	We learn in ways that challenge me to develop new skills.	1	2	3	4	5	6	7	8	9	10
	We meaningfully contribute to each other's learning.	1	2	3	4	5	6	7	8	9	10
Yourself	I can put something of myself into the work I do.	1	2	3	4	5	6	7	8	9	10
	I'm learning about myself through the work I'm doing.	1	2	3	4	5	6	7	8	9	10
	I like the version of myself that I am in this class.	1	2	3	4	5	6	7	8	9	10

EMPOWER Moves for Social-Emotional Learning © 2023 Solution Tree Press
SolutionTree.com • Visit **go.SolutionTree.com/SEL** to download this free reproducible.

Chapter 4

• • • • •

OPENNESS
EMPOWER STUDENTS TO SHARE HOW OTHER PEOPLE MOVE THEM TOWARD THEIR VALUES

In *Braiding Sweetgrass*, botanist Robin Wall Kimmerer (2013) describes the difference between transaction and connection. She imagines buying a pair of socks from a store, and although she'd feel grateful for the wool and labor, the exchange of money for goods fulfills all obligations: "I don't write a thank you note to JCPenney," she says (Kimmerer, 2013, p. 26). But, if the same socks were knitted by her grandmother, the gift would create responsibilities—to write a thank-you note, take care of the socks, wear them, and make a gift for her grandmother in return.

Even in schools that cultivate community, students often learn to communicate in transactional ways. Just look at academic standards from kindergarten all the way up through twelfth grade, and you'll see the same three purposes for writing: (1) making an argument, (2) conveying information, and (3) narrating a series of events (National Governors Association Center for Best Practices & Council of Chief State School Officers, 2010). How could all those years of learning to prove themselves right, advance their own views, and hear their own voices *not* have an impact?

It's no wonder so many people struggle to express a message of connection. An invitation. (*Do I sound desperate?*) A condolence card. (*What do I say to someone I barely know about someone I barely knew?*) A thank-you email. (*Am I saying enough? Am I saying too much? Do I sign off with "thanks again" when I've already used the word "thanks" three times?*) Maybe you know people who are good at communicating in these ways; how many of them learned these skills at school?

This chapter's activities help students share honestly and authentically about how other people help them move toward their own values. These small acts of appreciation foster a sense of community, responsibility, and mutual care. Students learn some of the skills they'll need to be able to say to someone, "You're making a meaningful contribution in my life. You've given me a gift. You matter."

Leading With Values

Students identify classmates who inspire them by enacting certain values and who support them in bringing those values to their own actions. The activity is not about publicly recognizing peers with leadership qualities; rather, it helps all students look beyond themselves, appreciate one another in new ways, and see leadership as a form of values-consistent action.

> **Suggested duration:** 20 minutes
>
> **When to use:** Several months into school, once students have been working together for long enough that they'll be able to recognize one another's positive contributions
>
> **Materials:** A list of values such as the "Examples of Values" handout (page 192), copies of the "Values Leaders" handout (page 84), writing supplies

Leading the Activity

The following steps will help you effectively lead the activity.

1. Provide students with a list of values such as the "Examples of Values" handout (page 192). Give them time to silently read over the list and notice which values they feel more drawn to and less drawn to.

2. Ask students to choose five values that feel especially important in their lives right now.

3. Provide copies of the "Values Leaders" handout (page 84), and ask students to copy the five values they've just chosen into the first column.

4. Ask students to identify classmates who bring these qualities to their actions. For example, a student might look around the room for classmates who are *curious, generous, imaginative, inclusive,* and *serious* (if those were her listed values).

5. Ask students to identify classmates who help them bring these qualities to their *own* actions. For example, a student might look around the room for classmates who help her be more *curious, generous, imaginative, inclusive,* and *serious* (if those were her listed values).

6. Give students time to write explanations in the space provided or on a separate page. They might write specific examples of how their classmates enact the various values or clarify how they're interpreting a particular value. For example, a science student might think her classmate

comes up with *imaginative* drawings and that a different classmate helps her be *imaginative* when she's trying to solve a problem.

7. Invite students to share who displays the various qualities they wrote and who helps them enact those qualities. If they hesitate to publicly recognize one another by name, ask how it felt to recognize their peers privately, for themselves. The point of sharing isn't really to give public recognition; it's for the student doing the sharing to express appreciation in another way.

Extending the Work

This activity is called *Leading With Values* because leadership can mean inspiring people through one's own positive actions and supporting people who strive to be their best selves. What someone considers a *positive* action or a *best* self depends on their values. This activity could prompt further discussion about leadership. What qualities or actions do students usually associate with leaders? Which leaders have they studied in their various classes? Who has a formal leadership position at the school or in the community? How might this activity offer a different way to define leadership? How do students want to lead with their values? That is, how do they want to inspire others to enact certain values, and how do they want to support others who are striving to act on their own values?

You could also collect students' charts—if you tell them in advance that you will so students know their writing will not be completely private. Then, you can use the charts to discover strengths that students don't display in your classroom or that you simply hadn't noticed. For example, although many of Lauren's teachers saw her as *perceptive* and *creative*, few saw her as *playful* because she was quiet in class—but one of her friends might have recognized that playfulness. Jonathan's teachers saw him as *inquisitive* and *curious* based on his consistent participation in class, but few would have noticed his enthusiasm for sharing his discoveries with peers. If you read the charts, look for names that surprise you. Maybe these students have strengths they could bring more fully to your class.

Adjusting the Activity

When students share, instead of having them announce to the whole class what they wrote in their charts, you could have them write notes of appreciation that you collect and distribute. As wonderful as it is to get recognition in front of their peers, some students might feel uncomfortable—especially if they have a complicated history with the person who's recognizing them, if they're often recognized for a particular quality that they don't think is central to who they are, or if they've experienced trauma and as a result feel suspicious of praise (van der Kolk, 2014). This activity's purpose isn't so much for students on a classmate's list to receive public recognition as it is for students to make the lists and openly appreciate their classmates' contributions.

Addressing Challenges

Any time you do an activity in this book, you run the risk of students not taking it seriously. If students don't take this particular activity seriously, they might say things that hurt each other. A student might say something like, "Lauren helps me be a more active soccer player because she literally never goes near the ball." Or they might fill out their chart sarcastically, such as by saying, "Lauren inspires me by being such an active soccer player," when everyone knows how slow, clumsy, and passive Lauren is on the field.

Students might also reveal information about a classmate's life that the person wanted to keep confidential. Imagine that a classmate says Jonathan is resourceful because his mother has cancer and he sometimes has to fend for himself. Even if the classmate were trying to express admiration, Jonathan might not want his whole class knowing about his mother's illness. He also might want to be identified in terms of what he puts into the world, not what he endures from it. Depending on the group, you might want to establish certain ground rules before doing this activity, such as that students should only share about actions they've witnessed in the classroom, or have students privately ask the peers they plan to share about for consent before actually sharing.

The Acknowledgments Section

Help seeking is a key skill for academic achievement, and stronger students are more likely to seek help—yet many students avoid asking for help for fear of appearing weak (Karabenick & Newman, 2006; Ryan, Hicks, & Midgley, 1997). During this activity, students learn to see help as integral to excellence and express appreciation for the people who have helped them succeed in ways that matter to them. The activity thus frames help seeking as positive, not only because it supports achievement, but also because it acknowledges relationships.

> **Suggested duration:** 25 minutes
>
> **When to use:** As students are finishing up a project, test, game, show, or other major assignment or performance
>
> **Materials:** Copies of the "Types of Help" handout (figure 4.1), writing supplies, acknowledgment sections from several books

Leading the Activity

The following steps will help you effectively lead the activity.

1. Ask students to share examples of types of help that benefit people when they're learning or making something. This prompt frames help as positive so that during step 3, when students consider who helped *them* with a project, they're less likely to feel defensive about getting help.

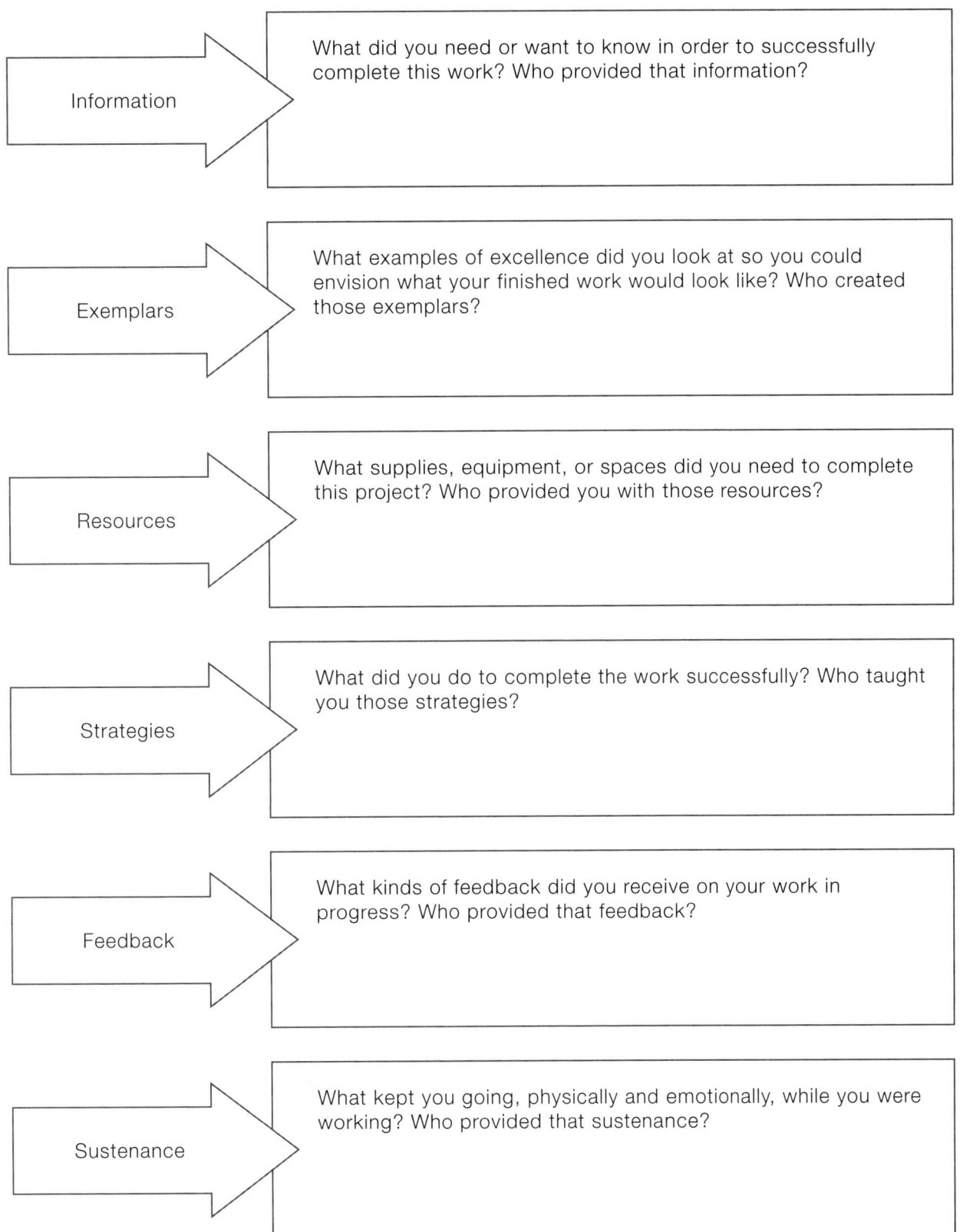

Figure 4.1: Types of help.

Visit **go.SolutionTree.com/SEL** *for a free reproducible version of this figure.*

2. Provide copies of the "Types of Help" handout (figure 4.1, page 73), and ask students what stands out or surprises them. Briefly review how each type of help benefits people who are learning or making something.

3. Ask students to list people who helped them as they worked on the project or assignment they've just completed. You might guide your students through the graphic organizer, one part at a time so students can share examples of helpers as they go along, or you could wait until after most students have filled out most of their organizers before inviting students to share.

4. Read the acknowledgments from a few familiar books, and ask volunteers to share what they notice. Your students will get a sense of what acknowledgments can sound like and how much detail they can include. They'll also hear how the authors of books they know sought help, which reinforces the message that help seeking is a sign of strength, not weakness.

5. Using their graphic organizer to guide them, have students write a set of acknowledgments that describe who helped them as they worked on their projects and how those people helped. They can include this acknowledgments section somewhere in their finished product or read it out loud after a performance.

Extending the Work

After your students turn in their acknowledgments, you might ask them to share how it felt to write them. Ask questions such as these.

- "How did it feel to acknowledge these different types of help?"
- "How does it feel to acknowledge help seeking itself as a sign of strength, not weakness?"
- "How do you feel about yourself as a result of having written appreciatively about those who helped you?"
- "As you acknowledged help you *did* get, did you notice any types of help you *didn't* seek out or people who could have helped you but who you didn't ask?"
- "What kinds of help will you ask for next time? Who will you ask?"
- "What kinds of help are most meaningful to you? What does that tell you about your values?"

You don't have to ask all of these questions, but asking a few will help students see help seeking as part of meaningful learning, working, and living.

If students write acknowledgments after *every* project, they're more likely to see help seeking as a normal, expected part of working on something important. Over time, you can see whether students acknowledge the same people and get the same kinds of help or whether they begin to expand their support networks as well as their help-seeking repertoires. Seeking more kinds of help from a larger and more diverse network suggests that students are willing to ask for help because it's important even if it's uncomfortable, and are building the sorts of relationships in which they can be vulnerable enough to ask for help. These outcomes, in turn, suggest that students view help as positive and might continue to seek help in the future, with schoolwork and other aspects of their lives.

Adjusting the Activity

You can use this activity at the end of a unit or term, so students can acknowledge those who contributed to their learning. It's also a good activity to do as students approach graduation: who helped them successfully complete elementary, middle, or high school, or whatever stage of education they're about to finish? Used this way, the acknowledgments will sound more like a graduation party speech—which you can encourage your students to make, in person or virtually, with or without the party.

Addressing Challenges

Too often in school, help seeking is framed as a sign of weakness. We set up office hours to provide extra help, as if reteaching material and giving feedback are extras and not integral to everyone's learning. Students who get outside help—whether from a parent, peer, tutor, or website—don't always admit it. They feel like it's cheating and fear their teacher will tell them not to use outside help, or they feel ashamed that they can't do the work in the first place. Some teachers try to get students around these feelings of fear and shame by creating guidelines about what kinds of help are allowed and how to inform the teacher of the help they've received. The teacher might encourage students to ask for help, but all the guidelines can nevertheless make help seem like it's bad or wrong.

Help seeking is a strength. Most authors write acknowledgments, thanking people whose contributions improved the book. Movie end credits often thank communities that provided filming locations and resources. When star athletes get interviewed, they almost always recognize their coaches, teammates, and families. Biographies of great artists, politicians, and business leaders usually describe a network of mentors, collaborators, assistants, allies, advocates, heroes, and friends whose support was integral to the person's success.

That said, some students might struggle to see help seeking as positive—especially in schools with a very competitive and individualistic culture. The best way to address any discomfort with help is to notice and name it—and then connect help seeking to the student's values. What thoughts and feelings come up when students ask for help? Do those thoughts and feelings make it more or less likely that they'll accomplish a goal that matters to them? Is it possible to *have* those thoughts and feelings, and *still* ask for help?

While listing sources of help, students might ask *does it count if* questions, such as, "Does it count if the person just loaned me a pencil?" or "Does it count if the person who inspired me to write my song is dead?" Instead of saying yes or no, ask your student to consider how the help mattered to them. What was important about it? Did it make a difference in their learning? Their work? Their attitude? Maybe the pencil doesn't seem important because they would've found some other way to sketch their diagram, or maybe it does seem important because it made them feel cared for and confident as they worked.

Students might notice that the same people come up on multiple lists of helpers or that they have go-to people for certain kinds of help. A parent might have provided resources, strategies, *and* sustenance. Two friends might always provide feedback to each other. You, as the teacher, might be on every list! (Imagine a world where all students name their teachers as people who emotionally sustain them!) Tell your students that they can appreciate their reliable supporters *and* think beyond them. Who *else* is a potential source of help?

Satisfying Our Needs Together

Inspired by a classic picture book, students discuss what it means to fully satisfy their needs and how they can support one another in doing so. They learn to see increased needs as signs that they're growing, distinguish between healthy and unhealthy ways they meet their individual needs, and build interdependence in meeting their collective needs.

> **Suggested duration:** 20 minutes
>
> **When to use:** Before a high-stress time of year
>
> **Materials:** A copy of Eric Carle's (1969) *The Very Hungry Caterpillar*, blank sheets of paper, writing supplies

Leading the Activity

The following steps will help you effectively lead the activity.

1. Explain to students that they're going to use writing to explore the idea of being metaphorically hungry for something in life. Ask students if they can think of examples of things someone might be *hungry* for.

2. Read *The Very Hungry Caterpillar* (Carle, 1969) aloud to students. Ask them to notice any thoughts or emotions that come up as they listen to the story.

3. Turn back to the fruit pages, where the caterpillar keeps looking for more and more food. Give the first writing prompt and allow time for students to write their responses: "Sometimes, like the little caterpillar, we're hungry for more and more and more because we're growing. What's a part of your life where you're growing and need more than you used to?"

4. Turn to the page where the caterpillar eats cake, cheese, salami, and lots of other unhealthy foods—and then gets a stomachache. Give the second writing prompt and allow time for students to write their responses: "Sometimes, we attempt to satisfy our needs in ways that feel good in the moment but end up not being good for us. Has that ever happened to you? What did you need? What did you do to try to satisfy that need? What was the consequence?"

5. Turn to the next page, where the caterpillar eats a leaf and feels better. Give the third writing prompt and allow time for students to write their responses: "When the caterpillar has a stomachache from overeating, the cure is more eating. Was there ever a time when you gave yourself the wrong thing but then felt better when you gave yourself the right thing?"

6. Turn to the ending, where the caterpillar transforms into a butterfly. Give the fourth writing prompt and allow time for students to write their responses: "The caterpillar finds the food he needs on his own. How could you and your classmates work together to find what you need or even provide for each other's needs?"

7. Invite students to share any part of their responses. Sharing could occur with a partner, in a small group, or as a whole class. If you notice any positive themes that emerge while sharing, such as a focus on interdependence or healthy boundaries, name it as something that seems important to the group.

Extending the Work

This activity asks students to explore how their needs grow and change, how they satisfy their needs in healthy and unhealthy ways, and how they can work collaboratively to meet their needs. You can ask them to write commitment statements, beginning with the words *I will* and stating a specific action they will take to satisfy their needs in a healthy, collaborative way. Invite students to write their statements on the board or in a shared document, so everyone can see them. Then, ask students to look for commitments they can make along with that classmate or help that classmate keep.

After a few days or weeks, ask students if they've kept their commitments. For those who did, how did it feel, and what happens now? For those who didn't, what got in the way, and what might they try now? For everyone, how can the class continue to work together as a community to make sure everyone's needs are met?

Adjusting the Activity

This activity uses children's literature to prompt a conversation about satisfying needs. You can use other picture books to foster conversations about students' lives. You might already know of good books to use, but you could also ask your students about significant books in their lives. You might offer some of the following prompts to help them remember books that had various kinds of significance for them.

- "What book taught you about an important topic?"
- "What book taught you about an important relationship?"
- "What book could you really relate to?"
- "What book helped you take someone else's perspective?"
- "What book did someone you care about share with you?"

- "What book helped you see what you could do in a similar situation?"
- "What book helped you imagine a situation you wish you could be in?"
- "What book got you to think differently about the world?"
- "What book got you to think differently about yourself?"

Many websites, such as We Need Diverse Books (https://diversebooks.org) and Project LIT Community (@ProjectLitComm on Twitter or Instagram), offer lists of diverse, personally and culturally affirming literature for children and young adults.

Addressing Challenges

You might worry about how middle and high school students will respond to a picture book. Some might joke about it: "Story time!" These jokes sometimes disguise a deep need to be read to—which is so often an act of love. You can also explain to your students that although very young children can understand the story, you're using it as a metaphor to discuss struggles that occur throughout life.

A bigger concern is the fact that this activity uses hunger for food as a metaphor. Metaphors make a less familiar concept more accessible by linking it to something more familiar. In this case, students access the concept of taking values-consistent action to satisfy various needs through the metaphor of eating to satisfy physical hunger. Food and eating are often useful metaphors because everyone must eat to survive and therefore can understand the metaphor. However, for students who are dealing with food insecurity, hunger is not a metaphor; it's a very real and traumatic part of their lives. If you have students dealing with food insecurity, or if you might, you can do the activity without reading the book and adjust the prompts so they don't reference the book or use the hunger metaphor.

Bringing Our Full Selves to Our Friendships

According to a meta-analysis of 135 studies, close friendships across sociocultural groups significantly reduce prejudice and improve intergroup attitudes (Davies, Tropp, Aron, Pettigrew, & Wright, 2011). During this purely exploratory activity, students examine their friend groups, discuss the value of having friends who have similar *and* different identifiers from theirs, and decide how they can bring their full selves to all their friendships. They learn to be open and curious, not judgmental, about their own identities and their friends' identities, and to see both affinity and diversity as positive aspects of a group.

> **Suggested duration:** 30 minutes
>
> **When to use:** Anytime
>
> **Materials:** Copies of the "People I'm Close To" handout (page 85), writing supplies

Leading the Activity

The following steps will help you effectively lead the activity.

1. Give each student a copy of the "People I'm Close To" handout (page 85).

2. In column one, ask students to write the names of four friends, or anyone they feel especially close to, at school or beyond. Explain that they can write anyone's name based on their own definition of *close* and that their papers will remain entirely private. In fact, ask them to please *not* share who they wrote, even after the activity concludes, so no one feels left out.

3. Ask students to label column two *Race*. They can write an S next to each person they think would identify racially in the same way they do, and a D next to each person they think would identify differently in terms of race. Explain that they might not know how the people on their lists self-identify, and we don't get to choose another person's identity, but that this activity is about how we *perceive* the people we feel close to.

4. Ask students to label column three *Gender*. They can write an S next to each person they think would identify in the same way they do in terms of gender, and a D next to each person they think would identify differently. Emphasize that the S or D is based on how they perceive the other person, and we can't assume how someone identifies based on how they present.

5. Ask students to label column four *Age*. They can write an S next to each friend they consider to be their age—which for students usually means being born the same year—and a D next to each friend they consider to be a different age. Remind students to keep their lists private and not ask anyone their age or any other identifier.

6. Ask students to label column five *Religion*. They can write an S next to each person they think practices the same religion they do and a D next to each person they think practices a different religion.

7. Lead a discussion to help students think about their charts, asking the following questions.
   - "In which ways are your friends most diverse? Least diverse? Why might this be?"
   - "Why is it valuable to have friends who share your identities? Why, for example, would you want to have friends who have the same racial or gender identity as yours?"
   - "Why is it valuable to have friends who do not share your identities? Why, for example, might you want to have a friend who's a few years older or who practices a different religion?"
   - "Do you talk about race, age, gender, and religion with your friends? Do you talk about identity with your family?"
   - "What other identifiers exist beyond race, age, gender, and religion? How are all of these part of our full selves?"
   - "What does it mean to bring our full selves to our friendships?"
   - "What can happen when we bring our full selves to our friendships?"

Extending the Work

After students have explored their own relationships, you could have them explore patterns in the class. Each student will need a black marker and four dot stickers in each of four colors. Dot stickers often come in sheets of twenty-four that include red, green, yellow, and blue stickers, so we'll use those colors as our examples here. Every two sticker sheets will be enough for every three students. You'll also need four pieces of chart paper.

Assign a color to each identifier; for example, red for race, green for gender, yellow for age, and blue for religion. Tell students to use the black marker to label their dots with Ss or Ds, according to the color code. For example, a student whose Race column has three Ss and one D would write Ss on three of her red dot stickers and a D on one red dot sticker.

While the students write on their dots, put up four sheets of chart paper, each labeled with the appropriate identifier: *Red-Race*, *Green-Gender*, *Yellow-Age*, and *Blue-Religion*. Draw a line down the middle of each sheet and label the halves *Same* and *Different*. Then, ask students to stick their dots on the appropriate halves of each paper. Figure 4.2 shows what a *Gender* poster might look like for a class of twenty-six students.

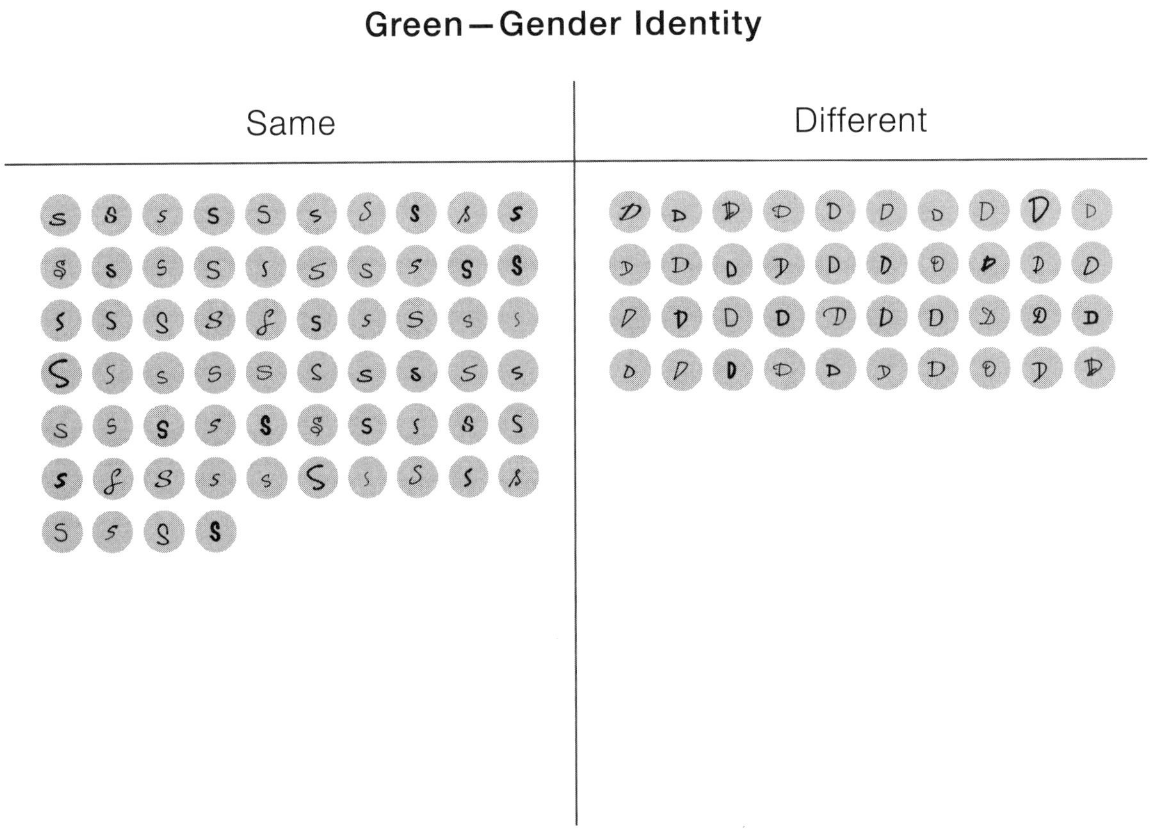

Green—Gender Identity

Figure 4.2: Sample poster showing students' friendships based on gender.

You can then lead them in reflecting further, asking questions such as the following.

- "Which D side got the fullest? Why do you think that is?"
- "Which S side got the fullest? Why do you think that is?"
- "Do you see anything that surprises you?"
- "What questions can we ask instead of making assumptions about a friend's identity?"
- "How can we express curiosity about a friend's identity without turning them into a spokesperson for their group?"
- "Does anything change when you and a friend share multiple identifiers, as opposed to sharing some but not others?"
- "Does anyone have further thoughts on how you can bring your full self to your relationships—not regard*less* of your identity, but fully regard*ing* who you are?"

Adjusting the Activity

You can pick other identifiers for students to explore, such as socioeconomic class, ethnicity, immigration status, first language, or sexuality. Keep in mind: *students are not asked to share how they identify*—although many do self-identify during the discussion. Rather, they're only sharing whether they identify in the same way or in a different way than they think their four closest friends do, and those data are aggregated with their classmates.

If asking your students to explore their friendships seems too risky, you could do this activity with book characters, historical figures, artists, or scientists. Instead of exploring how they identify as compared to their friends, students could explore how they identify as compared to the main characters in the last four books they read, or four people they studied in a recent unit. Discussion questions can be similar: Why is it valuable to read about characters who share our identities *and* characters whose identities are different from ours?

Addressing Challenges

Some students might become anxious when asked to write the names of four people they feel close to. Reassure them that yes, they can write the name of a cousin, a sibling, or someone they see virtually but have never met in person. Others might worry about hurting the feelings of someone they don't list, but the only way that can happen is if they *say* who they listed—which is why everyone keeps their lists private. Some students might become anxious, wondering whether anyone listed *them*. If so, that's a good opportunity to have a one-to-one conversation with that student about how they can become closer to others.

Sometimes during the discussion, students will express frustration about not being in control of who they have opportunities to befriend. For example, a student might observe that all his closest friends are boys because he spends a lot of time playing sports, and sports teams are segregated along the traditional gender binary. Or students might say that as kids, they have little choice in where they go and how much time they can spend socializing, and that affects who they spend time with and can become close to. In situations like these, validate how the student feels, and ask if they want to think about how they can develop close and authentic friendships in the time and space they do have.

Some students might become defensive if they notice a lot of Ss on their charts. They might say that categories like gender and religion "don't matter" or that they "don't see" race. Comments like these indicate a need to do more extensive identity work with your students, but in the moment, you can say that these might not feel important to *that* student, but social identifiers have a big impact on how people relate to one another, the world, and themselves. Claiming to "not see" race can make someone feel like we don't see *them*, which adversely affects their sense of belonging and maintains racial biases (Byrd, 2017; Leslie, Bono, Kim, & Beaver, 2020; Reynolds, 2019). How important is it to this student that his friends feel seen? Is it worth feeling some discomfort when confronting his own attitudes about race?

Other students might congratulate themselves for having diverse groups of friends, or they might lament the fact that their friends are too similar to them—but this activity isn't about judging ourselves based on how diverse our friends are. People who share identifiers can often provide safety and support for one another. Talking to people like ourselves can help us understand our own experiences more fully, appreciate the diversity *in* our identity groups, and confront internalized oppression. No one wants to be the "diversity friend"—the person whose friendship just makes people with historically dominant identifiers feel good about themselves. If you hear students judging themselves, ask about the friendships they do have. How do they want to approach their friends, not regard*less* of their identities, but fully regard*ing* who they are?

Your Own Openness

Sharing about how other people support, push, and inspire us often isn't any easier for teachers than it is for students. We're expected to be good at our jobs *already* and be able to work *independently*. And telling another person that they've affected us in an important way can leave us vulnerable. What if they don't see their impact as important? What if they don't see it at all? What if they feel pressured to respond but don't know what to say? What if they don't feel about us the way we feel about them? What if they just think it's weird when people open up about what matters to them, especially at school, where people expect to learn or work together but not to share their thoughts and feelings about their relationships?

Psychologists Gareth Holman, Jonathan Kanter, Mavis Tsai, and Robert Kohlenberg (2017) define *courage* as "being able to, despite vulnerability, express oneself appropriately, meaningfully, fully, and effectively in social situations" (p. 72). What they call a *social situation* isn't just hanging out with friends; it's any interpersonal interaction, including students' interactions with their classmates and our interactions with our colleagues.

You can practice the courage it will take your students to openly express appreciation for one another by expressing appreciation for your colleagues. What are some of the values you most want to bring to your work as an educator? (Look at the list of values on the "Examples of Values" handout, page 192, if it helps.) Which of your colleagues brings these qualities to their actions? Which of your colleagues helps you bring these qualities to your actions? What if you were to tell these colleagues exactly how they inspire and support you?

Or think about a big task you recently completed—writing reports, planning a new unit, reorganizing your classroom library, meeting with *that parent*, or something similar. Who provided you with helpful information? Who gave you exemplars you could use to model your own work after? Who gave you resources you needed? Who shared strategies that helped you succeed? Who gave you feedback on your work in progress? Who gave you the physical or emotional sustenance you needed to get through the task? What would it be like to acknowledge these people? How would you go about that?

As you consider telling the people in your life about the contributions they're making, notice any doubt or discomfort that comes up. How will you respond to those thoughts and feelings? Is it possible to *have* those thoughts and feelings and *also* express your appreciation, needs, and values?

Imagine what school might be like for students and for you if we treated it not as a transactional economy but as a community connected by the gifts we give one another.

From Openness to Willingness

This chapter was about opening up to the people whose actions shape the ways we live by our values. Other people can be important sources of influence, yet sometimes our biggest obstacles to values-consistent living are in ourselves. The next chapter is about how students can cultivate the willingness to act on their values when it's hard.

Values Leaders

Your name:		
Value	**Which classmates bring this quality to *their* actions?**	**Which classmates help you bring this quality to *your* actions?**

Please use this space to explain any of your responses.

People I'm Close To

People I'm Close To				
1.				
2.				
3.				
4.				

Chapter 5

WILLINGNESS
EMPOWER STUDENTS TO SERVE THEIR VALUES WHEN IT'S ESPECIALLY HARD

When our older child, Kalino (whose pronouns are ey/em), was in second grade, ey came home one night with the assignment to write a paragraph about any topic that interested em, as long as it had five sentences and began with a topic sentence. Despite having many interests, Kalino was completely stuck trying to figure out what to write about. As parents, the two of us tried suggesting different topics—birds, the moon, cooking, building—but ey rejected them all, saying ey just didn't know what to say. Then we realized, ey could write about how hard it was to write a paragraph! This was the paragraph Kalino ended up writing.

> It is hard to write a paragraph. Because it is hard to think of something to write. Because you have to think about what you want to write. I wish my mom could write this paragraph. It was really annoying to write this paragraph.

We were so proud that Kalino had written about eir struggle and fulfilled the assignment. (We know dependent clauses aren't technically complete sentences, but Kalino hadn't learned about that yet.) But at school the next day, Kalino's teacher made em erase the last sentence because it described the assignment as *annoying*, and the teacher didn't like that. Not only did the teacher invalidate Kalino's emotions and the hard work ey'd done the night before, she also missed an opportunity to start an honest discussion with her whole class about how writing can, in fact, be annoying—and tedious, frustrating, upsetting, anxiety provoking, and aversive in so many other ways—yet worthwhile.

So much of what students experience at school can feel aversive. Fill out this Venn diagram. Solve these thirty-five equations. Circle all the direct objects. Make sure your paragraph has five sentences. Success in school often depends on sitting still, shutting up, and following directions. Students have a right to understand how their assignments relate to the overall course, their other courses, their lives beyond school, and the wider world. If their work is tedious or frustrating—as all important work sometimes is—then their effort should be dignified by the knowledge that what they're doing matters, not just because it will affect their future, but because it contributes to a meaningful life right now.

Still, knowing something matters doesn't always mean we choose to do it. If you've ever foregone a salad in favor of pizza for lunch—or if you've ever skipped the gym to binge watch your favorite reality series instead, or canceled plans at the last minute because you didn't feel like going out in the rain, or put off your colonoscopy appointment because *ugh*—you already know that we don't always act in accordance with our values. Sometimes people say things like, "If you really cared, you'd do it anyway." If only it were that simple! This chapter's activities help students notice their own barriers to values-consistent action so they can choose how to relate to those barriers.

Guests in Our Houses

According to psychologist JoAnne Dahl and colleagues (2009), people have trouble acting on their values when they get stuck in beliefs about who they are, what other people will do if they take action, what must happen before they take action, or the action's impact. Rather than trying to get rid of unhelpful thoughts or convince ourselves they're not true, we can learn to see them for what they are: thoughts. When students learn to see their thoughts as thoughts, they better understand that they can choose their actions in accordance with their values (Luciano, Salas, Martínez, Ruiz, & Blarrina, 2009). For this activity, students consider the thoughts that make it harder for them to act on their values—and then learn how to accept these thoughts without allowing them to dictate their actions.

> **Suggested duration:** 45 minutes
>
> **When to use:** Whenever students have identified actions that will be good for them in the long term but that are difficult or painful in the short term
>
> **Materials:** Copies of the "Barriers to Enacting Values" handout (figure 5.1), a list of values such as the "Examples of Values" handout (page 192), drawing supplies

Leading the Activity

The following steps will help you effectively lead the activity.

1. Ask students to think of something they know is important to do, but they've been putting off. Maybe it's something they know they'll do eventually, or maybe they think they'll somehow be able to avoid it. What's stopping them from doing it? Ask students to privately list all the reasons they aren't doing it. Tell them you're not going to ask them to share, and in fact, you're going to ask them to *not* share what's on their lists.

Beliefs about ourselves

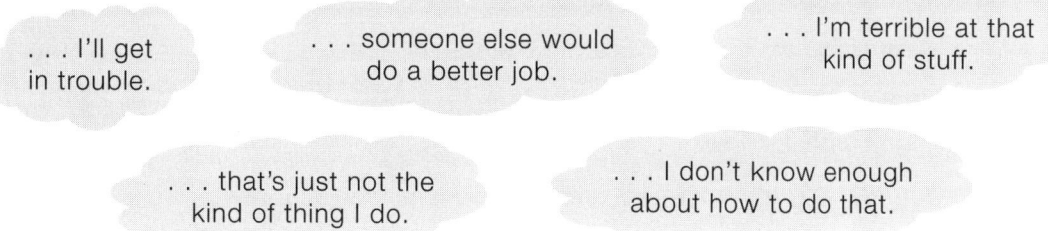

Beliefs about what other people will think, feel, say, or do

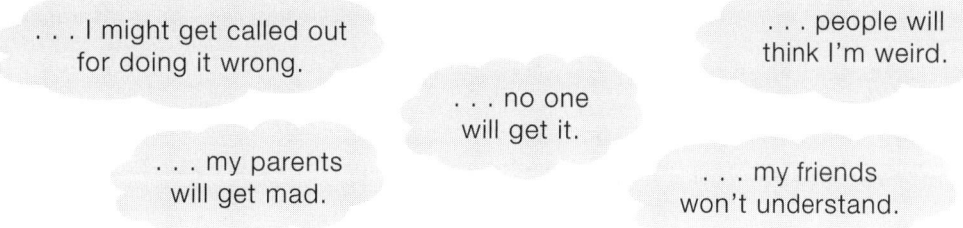

Beliefs about what must happen beforehand

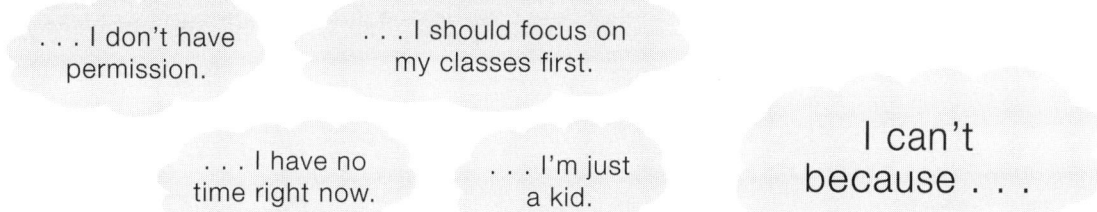

Beliefs about the impact

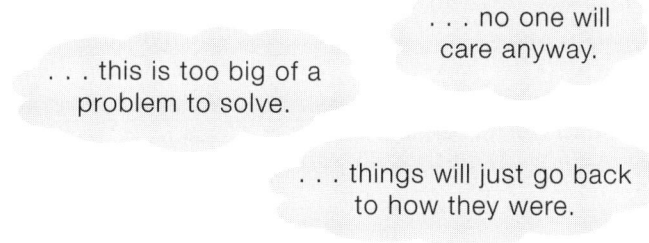

Source: Adapted from Dahl et al., 2009.

Figure 5.1: Barriers to enacting values.

*Visit **go.SolutionTree.com/SEL** for a free reproducible version of this figure.*

2. Tell students again that they should keep their lists private, but ask if anyone would like to share how it *felt* to make the list.

3. Provide a list of values, such as the "Examples of Values" handout (page 192). Ask students to use the list to help them name some of the values that the action they've been putting off would serve in the long term.

4. Let students know that it's extremely common for people to encounter barriers to living by their own values—so common that researchers who study values have identified four kinds of barriers (Dahl et al., 2009). Give students copies of the "Barriers to Enacting Values" handout (figure 5.1, page 89), and ask students to use the four kinds of barriers to help them add to their lists of reasons they haven't taken the action.

5. Ask students if they're willing to relate to the barriers they've identified in a different way. If they say yes, ask them to take out a separate sheet of paper, or use the back of the handout, and draw a house.

6. Tell students, "This house represents your life. Draw yourself in the house because it's your life."

7. Ask students to write some of the values they identified as important on the frame of the house. They could use a different color or highlight them so they stand out. Values are like the frame of the houses of our lives; they give our lives shape and meaning.

8. Ask students to imagine that the barriers they listed earlier are guests in their house. Tell them to draw these guests and to include speech bubbles to show what they're saying. For example, if a student wrote that one barrier to writing an essay is that they can't think of what to write, their houseguest might be saying, "You can't think of what to write!"

9. Invite students to consider their drawings, asking the following questions.
   - "How was that?"
   - "What (if anything) felt different as you made your drawing, as compared to when you made your list of barriers?" This question helps students notice how conceptualizing their thoughts as guests, and actually drawing those guests, might help them relate differently to those thoughts—a process called *cognitive defusion* (Hayes et al., 2012).
   - "How can you interact with these guests? What choices do you have?"

10. Tell students that when they're getting ready to take the action, they might hear some of their houseguests shouting at them (that is, experience thoughts that make it difficult for them to act upon their values). In those moments, they can choose to listen to the houseguests. In real life, it's possible to kick a guest out, but these "houseguests" are thoughts, and it's hard to kick a thought out of our own heads. Or students can let the guests stay as long as they like while they take the action anyway.

Extending the Work

This activity was inspired by a poem called "The Guest House" by Rumi (2004), translated by Coleman Barks. Barks is an American poet who wrote his own interpretations of poems by Rumi, a 13th century Persian poet, scholar, and devout Sufi Muslim (Rumi, 2004). "The Guest House" is one of those interpretations. You could find the poem and, as part of the activity, ask if a student would be willing to read it out loud for the group. We suggest doing this between steps 4 and 5.

Many thoughts suggest a response, and we respond so quickly that we don't notice that the thought is independent from the response. When we see our thoughts as thoughts, we have more choices in how we respond—including learning something important about our lives (Hayes et al., 2012). "The Guest House" (Rumi, 2004) refers to thoughts not only as guests but also as guides. Whether you use the poem or not, you can ask your students to imagine that one of the thoughts they listed is a guide—not because they should follow or obey it, but because there's something they might learn from the thought itself. For example, the thought, *I can't tell my teacher I didn't do my homework because she'll get mad*, suggests a response: the student should not, in fact, tell his teacher he didn't do the homework, and instead he should lie or skip class. However, if the student notices the thought as a *thought*, he doesn't have to obey it; he can have it and tell his teacher he didn't do the homework. He can also get curious about what that thought reveals about him, his teacher, their relationship, classroom power dynamics, and his understanding of homework's purpose.

Ask students to write about what one of their thoughts might teach them—about themselves, other people, their community, or the world—and then invite them to share.

Adjusting the Activity

This activity helps students overcome their own unhelpful thoughts. You can use it to encourage upstander behavior as part of any prevention programming (for example, against racism, bias, bullying, harassment, relational aggression, or drug use). Students can discuss thoughts that might stop them from speaking up when someone is self-harming or harming another person. How will they relate to these thoughts? Will the thoughts stop them from interrupting the harm? What values do they want to bring to their actions in moments when they witness harmful behavior?

Addressing Challenges

When looking at the various barriers to values-consistent action, some students might find certain examples confusing. Explain that some examples might not apply to their specific situation, but the broad category more likely will. For example, if Oren is putting off writing an essay, it's unlikely that it's because he thinks his parents will be mad if he writes it. A student who's putting off coming out as transgender might have that worry, but Oren might just be worried that his teacher won't like his writing. As different as these situations are, both involve students putting off values-consistent actions because they're worried about what someone else might think.

Some students might notice that the barriers on the handout are all internal but that they have external barriers, such as a lack of time or money. If a student brings that up, validate the fact that we don't always have access to the time, space, resources, and support we need to do the things that matter to us—and that's an injustice.

However, sometimes we can find creative workarounds. For example, if Oren is putting off his essay because he needs more time to think of a good idea, but has no time because of his after-school job, is there someone who would be willing and even excited to pick up one of his shifts so he has the time he needs to write? Is there someone who would love to help Oren talk through the topic and clarify his thinking? Is Oren's entire problem a lack of time, or is part of his problem that he's worried his coworkers and friends will think he's a burden if he asks for help? Sometimes, the barriers we see as external are, to some extent, internal.

That said, this activity might bring up struggles students can't resolve on their own because they're rooted in systemic inequities. Maybe what the student has been putting off is telling someone about that struggle. You might or might not be able to help, and you might or might not be able to put the student in touch with someone who can. Sometimes, all you can do is be a safe and empathic person for students to talk to.

Freak Out, Act Out, Zone Out

Students examine some of the unhelpful ways they behave in stressful situations. They distinguish their actions in the world from their psychological experiences, which frees them to consider more helpful ways they can respond to stress.

> **Suggested duration:** 30 minutes
>
> **When to use:** During any stressful time of year
>
> **Materials:** Copies of the "Three Kinds of Out" handout (page 102), copies of the "Getting Back In" handout (page 103), writing supplies, scissors, glue sticks

Leading the Activity

The following steps will help you effectively lead the activity.

1. Provide copies of the "Three Kinds of Out" handout (page 102). Ask students to recall a time when they were freaking out, a time when they were acting out, and a time when they were zoning out. Ask them to make very simple drawings of those times in the corresponding boxes on the organizer (row B). They can use speech bubbles to represent what they're saying, but they should only draw things that would be visible or audible to other people.

2. Ask students to try to recall the thoughts they were having and the emotions they were feeling during each episode and to write these thoughts and feelings in the boxes below each moment (row A).

3. Explain that our thoughts and emotions are private events: other people don't see or hear them. People see our actions and hear our words, often without knowing about the thoughts and feelings underneath. Ask students to fold their papers along the dashed line so the bottom row (row A) is no longer visible, noting this represents the idea that other people can't see or hear our thoughts and feelings—only our actions.

4. Ask students to look at their drawings and consider the fact that these are the actions other people see and hear. Ask them to write or draw, in the top row (row C), how other people respond to the actions they've drawn. Figure 5.2 (page 94) is an example.

5. Lead a brief discussion, asking the following questions.
    - "How did it feel to make these drawings?"
    - "How did it feel to identify the thoughts and emotions underneath the actions?"
    - "How did it feel to consider how other people respond to those same actions?"
    - "Do the thoughts and feelings you wrote down *cause* the actions you drew? That is, is it possible to have those thoughts and feelings *and* act differently?"

6. Ask students to cut their papers along the dotted line to represent the fact that their thoughts and feelings don't have to cause them to act in certain ways. While they're cutting their papers, provide the "Getting Back In" handout (page 103).

7. Ask students to glue row A onto the "Getting Back In" handout, where indicated. Ask them, "What do you want other people to say or do when you're having these thoughts and feelings? Write or draw those responses in the top row, C2." Figure 5.3 (page 95) is an example.

8. Ask students to make very simple drawings that show what they might say or do to get other people to respond in the ways they've just identified. These drawings go in the middle row (row B2), as shown in figure 5.3 (page 95).

9. Lead a discussion, asking the following questions.
    - "How did it feel to name the ways you want other people to respond when you're having difficult thoughts and emotions?"
    - "Freaking out, acting out, and zoning out all involve taking ourselves *out* of our own psychological experiences. When we develop the willingness to be *in* those experiences, we make possible new ways to live. When you look at the actions in both sets of drawings, which ones are easier? Which ones would build the relationships you want to have? Which ones represent the person you want to be?"
    - "What can you do when you notice yourself starting to freak out, act out, or zone out?"

	"freaking out"	"acting out"	"zoning out"
C	Sometimes try to calm me down Sometimes get mad/annoyed Tell me what to do/what not to do	My parents get mad at me for yelling and making a mess	Thinks I don't hear him and talks louder Gets annoyed/mad if I still don't answer Thinks I'm ignoring him and don't care—feels bad
B	 *(drawing: person with phone, "freaking out")*	 *(drawing: person at closet with clothes, "acting out")*	 *(drawing: person on couch with phone while someone talks, "zoning out")*
A	Why isn't she texting me back? Is she mad at me? Does she hate me? What did I do? Should I text her again? Worried Annoyed A little angry	Literally none of my clothes fit. I look terrible. It's my mom's fault. Why can't I have nicer clothes? What's Zoe Feldman gonna say about my outfit? Anxious Mad Embarrassed	Not really thinking anything . . . Sort of calm but numb Sort of annoyed

Figure 5.2: Example of "Three Kinds of Out" after step 4.

Extending the Work

This activity helps students consider how they behave when they're upset, how those behaviors impact them and others in ways that might go against their values, and what they might choose to do instead. As a follow-up, provide a list of values such as the "Examples of Values" handout (page 192), and ask students to notice the ones they most want to live by. When they have the thoughts and feel the emotions they wrote on their strips, which of those values are hardest to live by? When they behave in the ways represented in their second set of drawings (row B2), how are they enacting some of their values?

You can also normalize the fact that *everyone* freaks out, acts out, and zones out sometimes. Ask students to look again at their first set of drawings and think about the fact that everyone in the room drew themselves freaking out, acting out, and zoning out. How does it feel to notice that? How can they respond when they notice someone else starting to freak out, act out, or zone out?

C2	Just listen Help me calm down and think more clearly MAYBE help me figure out if the other person has a reason not to text me back or what I might have done wrong	Ask if I'm OK Listen to what I'm upset about Maybe buy me new clothes?	Ask if it's OK to interrupt and respect me if I say no Understand that if I need space, it doesn't mean I don't like them Not let me stay checked out for TOO long
B2	"Hey... I'm really upset about something right now. Do you have a minute?"	"Mom, can we discuss my clothes? I'm really upset."	"Thanks. I just need some alone time, but can we hang out later?"
A	Why isn't she texting me back? Is she mad at me? Does she hate me? What did I do? Should I text her again? Worried Annoyed A little angry	Literally none of my clothes fit. I look terrible. It's my mom's fault. Why can't I have nicer clothes? What's Zoe Feldman gonna say about my outfit? Anxious Mad Embarrassed	Not really thinking anything... Sort of calm but numb Sort of annoyed

Figure 5.3: Example of "Getting Back In" after step 8.

Adjusting the Activity

This activity uses drawing to help students visualize their own behaviors and distinguish between behaviors other people can see and hear, and private events such as thoughts and emotions. However, if drawing would be a barrier for your students, you can have them write.

Addressing Challenges

Some students might have trouble remembering times when they were freaking out, acting out, or zoning out. As a teacher—and as a human—you have almost certainly seen such behaviors before, and giving several examples usually helps students think of their own. However, if you give examples of students freaking out, acting out, and zoning out, a student in the room might feel like you're talking about them. Instead, you could give examples of times when *you* have freaked out, acted out, and zoned out. You could even talk a little bit about how freaking out, acting out, and zoning out have looked different for you at different points in your life. Your own willingness to be authentic and vulnerable will set a tone for your students so they can be authentic and vulnerable too.

Frustration Coloring Book

Playing with words and turning psychological experiences into physical objects are both processes commonly used to help people disrupt an unhelpful thought's influence on their actions (Assaz, Roche, Kanter, & Oshiro, 2018). For this activity, students change the way they relate to a frustrating assignment by turning words they associate with it into a coloring page that they can choose how they fill in.

> **Suggested duration:** 20 minutes
>
> **When to use:** While students are working on a high-stress assignment or task
>
> **Materials:** Sheets of unlined paper, black permanent markers, coloring supplies

Leading the Activity

The following steps will help you effectively lead the activity.

1. Ask students to think of an assignment they have to complete that seems unnecessarily difficult, confusing, or complicated. Perhaps it has a lot of steps, must be completed according to very specific rules, or must meet seemingly unattainable standards.

2. Ask students to make a list of the assignment's components, details, or rules they find especially frustrating.

3. Invite students to share how it felt to make them, without saying what's on their lists. This gives students an opportunity to notice their emotions without the activity turning into a complaint session about specific assignments.

4. Have students use the black permanent markers to write one or more words or phrases from their lists in large bubble letters, taking up as much of their papers as possible.

5. Explain to students that they might not be able to choose the assignment or the rules they have to follow to complete it, but they can choose how they approach it. To represent that, they are going to color in the pages they've just created in any way they like.

6. Lead a brief discussion, asking the following questions.

    - "How did it feel to make this?"
    - "What were some of the choices you made when you were coloring?"

- "Notice that the word is still there on the page, just as the frustrating assignment it represents still has to get done. But just as you added color, there might be something you can add into the experience of doing the work to make it better. Can anyone think of ways to do that?"
- "Who did the coloring? Even if this is an annoying or frustrating assignment you never would have designed, you're the one doing it. How can you make it your own?"

Extending the Work

The playfulness of making a coloring page helps students relate differently to frustrating assignments, but that doesn't make the assignment itself any easier. You can lead a discussion about how they might dignify the struggle of completing the assignment by bringing their own values to it. Provide a list of values such as the "Examples of Values" handout (page 192), and ask students to identify qualities they want to bring to their works. Lead a discussion about what that might look like. What actions might they try? How can they support one another?

Adjusting the Activity

Instead of writing bubble letters by hand, students could type their words in an outline font or using word art, then print their coloring pages. If they're working on the same frustrating assignment—perhaps writing the same essay, preparing for the same test, or filling out the same application form—they could choose a few words or phrases as a class, print them for everyone, color them independently, and compare how they colored the words. Their different ways of coloring the same words could represent how, even though they're faced with the same assignment that has the same rules for everyone, each of them can bring their own values to it.

Addressing Challenges

Some students might resist the idea of personalizing an assignment they have to complete according to someone else's rules and standards. They might say things like, "There is literally nothing I can do to make this fun," or "I just have to get it done." In cases like these, validate the fact that the task probably *won't* be fun. But is there any way to make the struggle worthwhile? Even if they can't choose whether they do this annoying task, can they choose how they approach it?

Discovery Drawings

Students create realistic, hyperbolic, metaphorical, and abstract illustrations of their struggles. Drawing the same struggle in several ways helps them notice more aspects of their experience. They also can relate to their own experiences in three different ways: as (1) subjects (because their experiences are depicted), (2) artists (because they depicted the experiences), and (3) viewers (because they can observe the drawings, observe themselves making the drawings, and observe themselves observing). These three ways of relating to the drawings mirror our three senses of self: (1) our constructed understandings of who we are, (2) our ongoing process of knowing who we are, and (3) our ever-present observing perspective (Hayes et al., 2012; McHugh et al., 2019). Being able to step back from our struggles frees us to choose how we want to live (Hayes et al., 2012; McHugh et al., 2019).

> **Suggested duration:** 30 minutes
>
> **When to use:** Anytime
>
> **Materials:** Copies of the "Four Illustrations" handout (page 104), writing and drawing supplies

Leading the Activity

The following steps will help you effectively lead the activity.

1. Ask students to think of something they're currently struggling with. It could be an academic, athletic, artistic, social, emotional, or physical struggle or any other struggle in their lives.

2. Provide copies of the "Four Illustrations" handout (page 104). Figure 5.4 is an example.

Figure 5.4: Example filled-out "Four Illustrations."

3. In the center oval, ask students to write a phrase or sentence describing the struggle.

4. In the upper-left box, ask students to make a realistic drawing of the struggle. *Realistic* doesn't mean they can't draw stick figures; it means they draw what was physically there, in as much detail as they can remember and render, and not draw anything that wasn't physically there, such as a shattered heart or steam coming out of someone's ears. They can draw speech bubbles because that's the only way to depict words people said, and those words were physically there.

5. In the upper-right box, ask students to draw the same struggle, but they make their drawings *hyperbolic*. That is, they can amplify elements of the situation itself to convey its impact. Sometimes, people who struggle are told that the thing they're trying to do isn't that hard, that they're misinterpreting other people's reactions, or that they're exaggerating what it's like. Hyperbole helps us reclaim our right to convey the event's internal impact. Students might think about the size of different elements relative to each other or draw things that weren't physically present but that were psychologically present for them.

6. In the lower-left box, ask students to draw a metaphorical representation of the struggle. This time, they don't draw what was actually there—they think of something else to represent it. For example, different people might be represented by different animals, or different parts of a task might be represented by different landforms or weather.

7. In the lower-right box, ask students to draw an abstract representation of this struggle. This time, they don't draw any recognizable objects or people; they use lines, shapes, shading, and (if possible) color to somehow represent the struggle. Tell the students not to worry if their abstract representations wouldn't make sense to anyone else.

8. Lead a discussion and ask the following questions.

    - "What do you notice as you look at your drawings?" There are no right or best answers to this question. It's important that they engage in noticing, not that they notice something in particular.

    - "How, if at all, is the feeling of looking at the drawings different from how you felt as you made them?"

    - "Did you choose the struggle? Did you choose how it made you feel? Can you choose how you see it? Can you choose what you do next?" These questions help students notice that even when they can't choose what happens to them, they often can choose what they do, and they can always choose how they frame their experiences.

    - "Based on what you see in your drawings, what choices do you want to make in how you respond to your struggle?"

Extending the Work

Sharing struggles can be a powerful way to build authentic and trusting relationships (Kanter et al., 2020). However, struggles are very personal, and students might not feel safe enough to share their drawings with the group. Use your judgment to decide whether to invite students to share their drawings, and make that sharing completely voluntary. You might invite them to share just with you or with a partner rather than with the whole group. You can give them the option of talking about their drawings (such as in a circle share) or letting the drawings speak for themselves (such as in a gallery walk). You can also suggest that students share and discuss their drawings with family members or other adults who can support them with their struggles.

If your students do share, you can ask questions about that experience. How was it to show your drawings to someone else or to hear about their drawings? What (if anything) do your various struggles have in common? How might you support one another in facing your individual struggles, or how might you face collective struggles together?

Adjusting the Activity

You can use this activity after a painful news event to help students get closer to their feelings about it. In the oval, they write a phrase or sentence summarizing the event. Then, they create realistic, hyperbolic, metaphorical, and abstract drawings of what happened. Because they're depicting something that happened in the news and not in their own lives, they might feel safer sharing their drawings, and then they can notice patterns in how they and their classmates responded to it. From there, you can lead a discussion about how students can take action. How might they learn more about what happened and the factors that contributed to it? What values-consistent actions might they take in their community?

Addressing Challenges

Some students might become anxious about the idea of drawing, especially realistic drawing, and say they "can't draw." Reassure them that their drawings can be very simple. They can make stick figures, basic shapes, lines, swirls, zigzags, and so on. The point is not for the student to create beautiful artwork but rather to bring their ideas of what the struggle looks and feels like into the physical world by drawing it in different ways. Once they have these physical pictures, they can look *at* them instead of *from* them. That shift in perspective enables them to distance themselves from the struggle so they can notice more options and then choose what they want to do.

Your Own Willingness

You might have noticed that all the activities in this chapter involve drawing. Drawing helps us bring images from our minds into the physical world, where we can relate to them differently. Although we might not want to spend time observing and rendering our own uncomfortable psychological experiences, doing so gives us agency (Hayes et al., 2012). We can step back from labels and get closer to the event itself, and we can focus on how we experienced the event—our own memories, thoughts, emotions, associations, and priorities. From there, we can choose what we want to do.

As a teacher, you undoubtedly have your share of frustrating, annoying, intimidating, and otherwise challenging tasks. Choose one of these tasks, and make your own realistic, hyperbolic, metaphorical, and abstract illustrations of it. No really—try it! What do you notice as you look at your drawings? You might have chosen to become a teacher, but did you choose to make this task part of that work? Do you choose how it makes you feel? Can you choose how you approach it?

What might change in your work if you acknowledge the full range of thoughts and feelings you have about it? What might change in your relationships with your students? In your relationship with yourself?

From Willingness to Empathy

This chapter was about noticing various ways we struggle to enact our values and developing the willingness to fully engage with those struggles. The next chapter will turn to how students can understand and connect with peers who are struggling.

Three Kinds of Out

C			
B			
	"freaking out"	"acting out"	"zoning out"
A			

Getting Back In

C2		
B2		

Glue row A here.

EMPOWER Moves for Social-Emotional Learning © 2023 Solution Tree Press
SolutionTree.com • Visit **go.SolutionTree.com/SEL** to download this free reproducible.

Four Illustrations

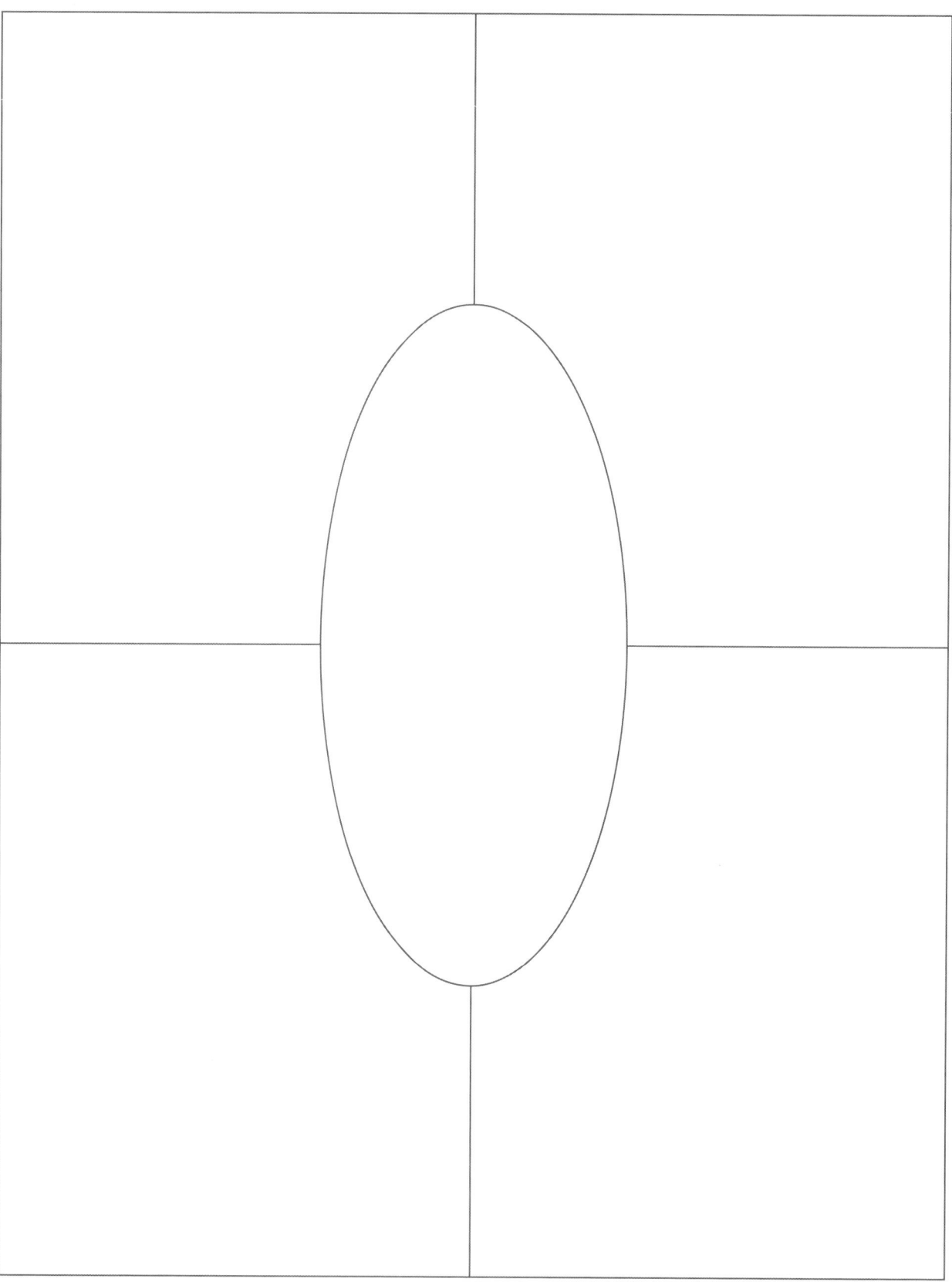

Chapter 6

• • • • •

EMPATHY
EMPOWER STUDENTS TO UNDERSTAND AND CARE ABOUT ONE ANOTHER'S VALUES

Lauren was raised by Jewish parents whose friends were all Jewish, and she went to a Jewish day school where her friends were all Jewish—until she transferred to a public middle school, which was then called *junior high*. Until that point, she was only vaguely aware that other religions existed. She knew about Christianity because that accounted for church bells and the beautiful lights she'd make her mom drive by every December, but Lauren didn't know about Christian beliefs until the eighth grade.

One day, her eighth-grade history teacher said something about *love thy neighbor*, which didn't violate any rules or laws because he wasn't proselytizing, just idly quoting. Like many students in many classes, Lauren wanted to impress hers, and she squealed, "*V'ahavta l'reacha kamocha*," as if his having uttered the English translation meant he'd know the Hebrew.

It would be an embarrassingly long while before Lauren learned that many cultures have expressions of common humanity. Mayan philosophy includes *In lak'ech hala ken*: "I am another you; you are another me." *Namaste* translates from Sanskrit as, "I bow to you," but in India, just means, "Hello," lacking solemnity, but rooted in the idea that each person deserves to be respected and welcomed. These various expressions have different meanings in their cultural contexts, yet they tell us the idea of common humanity is . . . well . . . common.

The activities in this chapter are about how students can build a sense of common humanity by listening more deeply to each other, recognizing their peers' strengths and struggles, showing up to another person's experiences, and finding shared values—or at least noticing that other people *have* their own values, and valuing that.

 Storytelling Circles

The ability to respond to a vulnerable disclosure with understanding and validation is essential for building close relationships (Maitland, Kanter, Manbeck, & Kuczynski, 2017). During this activity, a peer describes a personal struggle. Then, students respond with their observations, questions, and interpretations—but no judgment of any kind—so their peer feels heard, affirmed, and supported.

> **Suggested duration:** 30 minutes
>
> **When to use:** Anytime, in a group that has established some trust
>
> **Materials:** A list of values such as the "Examples of Values" handout (page 192), writing supplies

Leading the Activity

The following steps will help you effectively lead the activity.

1. Ask one student to volunteer to tell a story about a personal struggle. Have everyone else sit in a circle with that person.

2. While listening to the story, have other students in the group write down details that stand out for any reason and questions about anything that makes them curious.

3. Be sure the storyteller is silent while each listener responds with something that stood out to them. They shouldn't say why it stood out, and they don't even have to know why.

4. At this point, the storyteller can choose to hear questions or move on. If they choose to hear questions, each listener asks a question while the storyteller records the questions. After hearing all the questions, the storyteller can choose to respond to certain questions or use them as the basis for private reflection.

5. Ask listeners to take a few minutes to reflect on what seems important to the storyteller. If this person is struggling, it means they're trying to accomplish something important. What actions, relationships, or qualities seem to matter to the storyteller? Listeners may wish to consult a list of values such as the "Examples of Values" handout (page 192) to help them notice qualities the storyteller wants to bring to their actions.

6. Ask each listener to say what seems important to the storyteller. After hearing from everyone, the storyteller can choose whether and how to respond.

7. Ask listeners to share how it felt to offer their observations, questions, and interpretations.

8. Give the storyteller an opportunity to share how it felt to tell the story and to hear group members' observations, questions, and interpretations.

Extending the Work

You could immediately have another student tell a story. However, it might make more sense to wait until another day to repeat this activity, so the first student doesn't feel like their struggle is overshadowed by someone else's. After your students have practiced this protocol a few times, you could use it regularly as a way for students to open up to and empathize with one another.

Adjusting the Activity

Telling stories of personal struggles makes us vulnerable. Students might not feel ready to share their stories, even if they'll ultimately receive nonjudgmental, supportive, loving responses from their peers. We recommend starting with relatively low-stakes struggles, but if even that seems like more than your students are ready for, you can have the group practice nonjudgmental responses using a published story. StoryCorps (https://storycorps.org) and The Moth (https://themoth.org) are websites with extensive archives of recorded stories. Choose a story in which someone describes a personal struggle your students will be able to relate to, and have everyone use the nonjudgmental responding prompts to imagine what they'd say to the storyteller.

You might choose to do this activity as a fishbowl. The storyteller and several students form an inner circle, while the rest of the group forms an outer circle. During the activity, only the students in the inner circle share observations, questions, and interpretations. Afterward, you can invite students in the outer circle to share what they noticed. Using the fishbowl format allows you to select students you think will be perceptive, compassionate listeners so they can model nonjudgmental responses for other students in the group.

Addressing Challenges

Listeners are supposed to offer no judgment of any kind. However, questions can be criticisms or suggestions in disguise (which is why the storyteller has an opportunity to decide whether to hear the group's questions at all). Imagine, for example, that a student tells a story about how she became anxious during a test, and her mind went blank. A classmate might ask, "Why don't you just study more?" Although this is phrased as a question, it contains an implicit criticism that she should have studied more for the test and an implicit suggestion to study more in the future. It also trivializes her emotional experience; it makes the problem her study skills rather than her feelings during the test. Asking, "How did you study for the test?" or "Do you tend to feel less anxious when you study?" invites the storyteller to consider how their actions might have helped or hindered them without necessarily suggesting what they should or shouldn't have done.

It's difficult to make rules about the kinds of questions students can ask. For example, telling students not to ask *why* questions means they wouldn't be allowed to ask, "Why didn't you study?" (which feels judgmental), but they also wouldn't be allowed to ask, "Why do you think you felt so much more anxious for this test than you felt in the past?" (which invites potentially helpful comparison between various experiences).

Instead of making rules about which questions are and aren't allowed, you can discuss different ways to frame a question. Another option is to have students write questions on index cards so you can assess whether they're judgments in disguise. None of this guarantees that no one will ask an implicitly judgmental question. If you hear one, you can name it as such. At the end of the activity, when the listeners and storyteller have a chance to share how they felt, they might bring up how hard it is to ask nonjudgmental questions, and then you have an opportunity to discuss other ways the question could have been framed. Like any skill, nonjudgmental responding takes practice.

Finally, asking students to think of a struggle might bring up serious issues such as poverty, substance abuse, racism, transphobia, and other forms of oppression and violence. Even if a student doesn't share that story, they might think of it when a classmate tells their story, or just the prompt to "think of a struggle" might bring up those thoughts. If you hear a story that suggests a student is in danger, be prepared to follow up according to your school's policies and state's laws. If a student's reaction to a peer's story makes you suspect they need more support, inform the counselor or a school leader. In the moment, you can offer students a break using a coping strategy: go for a walk, get a drink of water, or do some deep, slow breathing (Linehan, 2015; Najavits, 2002).

Common Values and Complementary Strengths

Students who enter into a working relationship examine their own values and strengths. Then, they discover how their values align with their partner's and how their different strengths can benefit the work they're about to do together.

> **Suggested duration:** 30 minutes
>
> **When to use:** Whenever students enter into a collaboration, such as becoming coauthors of an essay, lab partners in science class, castmates in a school play, or members of a peer leadership training cohort
>
> **Materials:** Copies of the "Examples of Values" handout (page 192), copies of the "Values and Strengths" handout (page 119), writing supplies

Leading the Activity

The following steps will help you effectively lead the activity.

1. Provide copies of the "Examples of Values" handout (page 192). Ask students to circle values they consider most important in their lives. To prevent them from circling too many or too few, ask them to circle exactly twenty values.

2. Ask students to think about the fact that each of these qualities can also be a strength—but just because something is a value doesn't mean it's also a strength. For example, someone might think it's important to be compassionate but also struggle to be compassionate. That person might be very perceptive yet not think perceptiveness is especially important. With that in mind, students read the qualities of action again and put dots next to the ones they consider to be strengths, regardless of whether they are also values.

3. Provide copies of the "Values and Strengths" handout (page 119). In the appropriate sections of the Venn diagram, ask students to write the values that are also strengths (which are circled and dotted), values that are not strengths (which are circled but not dotted), and strengths that are not values (which are dotted but not circled).

4. Have partners look at their papers together and have a discussion, guided by the following questions. Visit **go.SolutionTree.com/SEL** for a free reproducible version of these questions.

   - "What values do my partner and I have in common? How will our common values benefit us when we work together?"

   - "What's one of my values that's also a strength? How do I hope to bring this quality to the work we're about to do together?"

   - "What's one of my values that is not a strength? How is the work we're about to do an opportunity to grow in that area?"

   - "What's one of my partner's strengths that isn't a strength for me? How can we use our collective strengths to do great work together?"

5. Invite students to share anything that came up in their discussions or how it felt to do this activity.

Extending the Work

This activity works best at the beginning of a collaborative project. While students are working on the project, they could periodically revisit their values and strengths to assess their collaboration. Do they feel like they're bringing their values to the work? To the partnership itself? Do they feel like they're using their greatest strengths? Are they making space for their partner to use theirs? Figure 6.1 (page 110) has a rubric students can use to help them assess the extent to which they're bringing their values and strengths to their work on a collaborative project.

Adjusting the Activity

Instead of having students circle their values and dot their strengths, they can do a card sort. You'll need one deck of Values cards (page 193) for each pair of students to use. Partner A selects the twenty qualities they consider to be most important to them. Partner A ends up with another pile of forty qualities they consider less important. Then, that partner sorts each pile again, based on whether the qualities are strengths. This person should now have four piles: (1) values that are also strengths, (2) values that

Actions	Yes	Sometimes or to Some Extent	No
I bring my greatest values to creating this piece of work.			
I bring my greatest values to my relationship with my partner.			
I use my greatest strengths in creating this piece of work.			
I make space for my partner to use their greatest strengths.			
I make space for my partner to bring their greatest values to this work.			
The values my partner and I share help us work through challenges.			
The strengths my partner and I don't share help us do excellent work together.			

Figure 6.1: Values and strengths self-assessment.

*Visit **go.SolutionTree.com/SEL** for a free reproducible version of this figure.*

are not strengths, (3) strengths that are not values, and (4) qualities of action that are neither values nor strengths. Partner A fills in their "Values and Strengths" handout (page 119) accordingly and passes the cards to partner B, who can now do their own card sort.

Instead of doing this activity when forming partnerships, students could do it after finishing a partner project as a way to assess their actions and set goals for next time. You'd need to change the language in the reflection questions from future tense ("How *will* our common values benefit us when we *work* together?") to past tense ("How *did* our common values benefit us when we *worked* together?"). Also, partners might not have brought their values and strengths to their partnership, so ask them to reflect on what might have gotten in the way and what they'd like to try the next time they work with a partner.

Addressing Challenges

If two students haven't worked well together in the past, or if they have any kind of animosity toward one another, they might have trouble noticing and naming one another's strengths. We think that's a reason they *should* do this activity together so they can heal their relationship in the process of discovering common values and complementary strengths, but they might need more individualized support. If you notice two students arguing or simply refusing to see each other's perspectives, have them complete the individual parts of the activity (steps 1–3) and then facilitate the discussion between them.

# From Conflict to Connection

Students learn to move through conflict by becoming more aware of their own internal experiences, imagining the other person's perspective, and seeking common values that can guide them toward a satisfying resolution.

> **Suggested duration:** 30 minutes
>
> **When to use:** Anytime
>
> **Materials:** Copies of the "Compassionate Responding" handout (page 120), writing supplies

Leading the Activity

The following steps will help you effectively lead the activity.

1. Ask students to think of a sustained conflict they have with someone. The conflict should be something minor enough that the outcome won't be life altering but major enough that they care what the outcome is. The person could be a parent or caregiver, friend, classmate, teacher, or anyone else. It could be a conflict that results in constant arguing or nagging, or it could be a silent conflict.

2. Ask students to write about the conflict. Tell them this will be completely private writing; you will not collect it or ask students to share what they wrote.

3. Provide copies of the "Compassionate Responding" handout (page 120), and explain that its questions will help students think about their own experiences as well as the other person's. You can ask more elaborate versions of the questions, such as the following, to help students notice more details.

   - "*What happened?* You've already written about the conflict, but can you summarize in a few sentences what occurred? Focus on things an outside observer would be able to see and hear."

   - "*What are you experiencing?* What do you want or need? What emotions have you felt throughout this conflict? In your life beyond this conflict, what are you struggling with that might have an impact here?"

   - "*What might the other person be experiencing?* You don't actually know, but what emotions might this person be feeling? What does it seem like they need? In their life beyond this conflict, what might they be struggling with that could have an impact here?"

   - "*What's important to you?* Emotions reveal that something important is at stake. If we feel worried or scared, it means something important *might* be taken away. If we feel annoyed or angry, it means something important *was* taken away. If we feel sad, it means something important is gone. If we feel disgusted or bored, it means that something important that should be happening isn't. If we feel disappointed, it means we expected someone to do something important, and they didn't. What can your emotions during this conflict tell you about what matters to you?"

- "*What's important to them?* You don't know how they're feeling, but if you had to guess at their emotions during this conflict, what could those emotions tell you about what matters in their life?"

- "*What do you and this person have in common?* Can you find any similar needs, struggles, emotions, or concerns? Do you and this person both have needs? Do you both have emotions? Do you both have things that are important in your lives, even if they aren't the same things?"

4. Lead a discussion, using some or all of the following questions.

- "How was that? What did you notice?"

- "When you imagine interacting with this person a month or two from now, what do you want those interactions to be like? Interacting doesn't necessarily mean being friends or talking to each other; it could just mean being in the same class or seeing each other in the hallway."

- "Imagine yourself a year or two from now. When that future you looks back on this conflict, what do you want to be able to say you did in response to it?"

- "Based on the things you and this person might have in common, how can you move forward?"

- "You imagined what the other person *might* be experiencing and then inferred what *might* be important to them, but you don't actually know. How can you ask them? If they won't tell you, how can you move forward?"

Extending the Work

Some students might want help resolving the conflict. They might want someone to facilitate a conversation with the person, or they might just want to talk further about their own experiences and values. Ask students to fold their papers in half for privacy, and pass around a stapler or tape dispenser so students can keep the papers shut. Then, tell them to write their names on their papers; if they want help talking to the person or continuing to reflect, they should write that on the outside. You won't open the papers; you'll just read their notes and respond accordingly.

After a few weeks, hand back the papers and have students open them. Did they end up resolving the conflict, or is it still going on? What are they experiencing now? What's important to them now? How do they feel about themselves as a result of how they've handled the conflict so far? If they have similar conflicts in the future, with that person or someone else, what will they do?

Adjusting the Activity

Students who have a history of being ignored or silenced might shut down when they see the "Compassionate Responding" handout. They might not be ready to think about the other person's perspective until after they've fully articulated their own. Instead of handing out the organizer, you could just ask the questions. That way, the student can take time to notice and fully describe their own experiences before moving on to the other person's.

Addressing Challenges

Exploring conflict will almost certainly bring up uncomfortable feelings. Students might feel angry, disappointed, confused, disgusted, or frustrated with the other person, the situation, or themselves. You might feel the urge to comfort students, but keep in mind that this activity's very purpose is to give students a chance to notice, name, and stay inside their emotions so they can discover what matters to them and how they might move forward. If students share that they're uncomfortable, thank them for expressing that discomfort. If they want to stop doing the activity, you can say something like, "You always have that option. Why might it be important to *you* to let yourself feel your emotions?"

Similarly, some students might be unwilling or unable to take the other person's perspective, especially if the student doesn't have an otherwise positive relationship with that person or if the other person was disrespectful or cruel. The student might say things like, "The only thing that's important to her is herself," or "His experience is that he's a total (fill in the blank with the expletive of your choice)"—or they might simply refuse to write about the other person's experiences and concerns at all.

In cases like these, you can explain that imagining someone else's perspective doesn't mean justifying or excusing their actions. Rather, they're making themselves aware of what the other person might be experiencing and what might be at stake for them. With that awareness comes a choice: how do they want to move through this conflict?

You can also try reflecting back what the student feels or values: "It sounds like it's important to *you* to be considerate of others" or "We're not doing name-calling, and at the same time, you have every right to be angry." Interrupt harmful statements, but resist the urge to redirect the student to the other person's perspective. They'll do that if and when they're ready. If nothing else, students who avoid taking other perspectives during this activity will see their classmates doing it and eventually might do it too—even if you don't get to see it.

Finally, even though the activity explicitly asks students to think of a low-stakes conflict, some might think of damaging experiences such as bullying, abuse, neglect, microaggressions, or violence. Even if a student doesn't write about such an experience for the activity, just thinking about it might be very distressing. As you would whenever students become upset or overwhelmed, encourage them to take breaks, breathe, or move their bodies. Keep the counselor informed of any students who seem to become withdrawn, confused, irritable, aggressive, or dysregulated, as these might be signs that they need more support.

Building an Apology

We all have moments when we do something that goes against our values and hurts another person. Holding ourselves accountable for our actions and seeking the other person's forgiveness begins the process of healing the harm, repairing the relationship, and rebuilding a positive sense of self. Professor Roy Lewicki and his colleagues (2016) identified six parts of an effective apology. During this activity, students examine those six parts and then write an apology to someone who was harmed as a result of their actions.

> **Suggested duration:** 30 minutes
>
> **When to use:** Anytime, in a group that has established some trust
>
> **Materials:** Copies of the "Six Parts of an Apology" handout (page 121), writing supplies

Leading the Activity

The following steps will help you effectively lead the activity.

1. Ask students to think of a time when they made a mistake or did something wrong, and someone was harmed as a result. The harm could be intentional or unintentional, and it could be emotional, social, academic, financial, physical, or any other type of harm. The person could be a parent or caregiver, friend, classmate, teacher, or anyone else.

2. Ask students to write about the incident. Tell students this will be completely private writing; you will not collect it or ask students to share what they wrote. They're writing so they can recall the incident more fully and notice any feelings that come up.

3. Ask students to notice how they feel, emotionally and physically. Discomfort isn't bad; it's a sign that they might be out of alignment with their values. They now have an opportunity to move toward their values.

4. Explain that researchers have found that effective apologies contain six parts. Provide copies of the "Six Parts of an Apology" handout (page 121), and explain that its prompts will help them build an apology that they might end up giving to the person, or at least they'll imagine what an effective apology would sound like so they can make more effective apologies in the future. As students respond to the prompts, you can ask more elaborate versions of the prompts, such as the following, to help them notice more details.

    - "*Name what you did and say you're sorry.* Try to be specific so the person understands that you know exactly what you did."

    - "*Explain why you did it without making it seem like it was OK.* There's a difference between explaining and making excuses. You're not excusing what you did, but there must have been a reason. Was it a lack of knowledge or understanding? Were you trying to look good or sound smart? Was it a way to avoid or escape something you didn't want to have happen to you? It can help the person rebuild trust in you if they understand where you were coming from."

- "*Accept responsibility for your actions and the harm they caused.* This can be a very simple statement like, 'I know I messed up,' but if you can, be specific so the person knows you understand the harm your actions caused."

- "*Express how you feel about your actions and what you've learned from them.* When people do things that harm someone, they often feel embarrassed or regretful about their actions, and they often feel disappointed in themselves. Be specific about how you feel and what you learned. Your learning might include realizing what's important to you in your actions and relationships."

- "*Suggest what you can do to repair the damage your actions caused.* The damage might be to someone's sense of safety or belonging, their relationships, their academic standing, or something else that isn't so easy to fix. Think about what you can do to help make the person whole—as opposed to what you can do to make yourself feel better. You might also invite the person to make their own suggestions about how you can repair the damage to them or to your relationship."

- "*Ask for forgiveness.* This, too, can be a simple statement like, 'I hope you'll forgive me.'"

5. Lead a discussion and pose some or all of the following questions.

    - "You don't have to deliver this apology, but how do you imagine it would feel if you did?"
    - "How would you make sure your apology was really about the other person and not just about making yourself feel better?"
    - "If you felt uncomfortable or awkward, why would those feelings be worthwhile?"
    - "Would you apologize in writing or in a conversation? What are the benefits and drawbacks of each way?"
    - "Even if the person doesn't forgive you, what might make apologizing to them worthwhile?"
    - "How do you feel about yourself as a result of learning more effective ways to apologize?"

Extending the Work

Writing an apology might help the student empathize with the person they harmed, but healing that harm means they have to actually deliver the apology, make repairs, and behave differently in the future. After a few days or weeks have passed, ask students if any of them apologized to someone. Maybe they sent their written apology, or maybe they apologized in a conversation. Maybe it was too late to deliver the apology they wrote during the activity, but they apologized for something else they did. If they apologized for anything at any point since doing the activity, how did it go? Did their apology include all six parts?

If not, which parts did it include? How did the other person respond? How does the student feel about themselves as a result of having apologized? What will they do to address the harm? What will they do to rebuild trust in the relationship? How will they ensure they don't do the same kind of harm in the future?

Beyond the structure of an apology, the context also matters (Tomlinson, Dineen, & Lewicki, 2004; Xiaobao & Jinhan, 2017). For example, does the apologizer seem sincere? What information does their tone, posture, and facial expression convey? Is the harm isolated or part of a pattern? What was the relationship between the two people before the harm occurred? Did they meet recently or know each other for a long time? Were they close friends or casual acquaintances? You might discuss some of these contextual factors with students and ask for examples or provide examples yourself. The more students understand about factors that shape trust, the better equipped they'll be to understand another person's perspective if they violate that trust.

Adjusting the Activity

This activity asks students to think about a time when their actions led to harm, but it doesn't distinguish between what professor Roy Lewicki and his colleagues (2016) call *competence-based* and *integrity-based* violations. That is, the student might have made a mistake based on a lack of knowledge or skill (the former), or they might have done something they knew was wrong (the latter). For example, imagine that Jonathan eats more than his half of the sushi he's sharing with Lauren. It matters whether he mistakenly thought Lauren had already eaten her fill or whether he was sneaking extra pieces of soft-shell crab roll and hoping she was too focused on *Project Runway* to notice.

You could explore the distinction between competence-based and integrity-based trust violations with students and then have them choose a violation depending on which type they most want to explore. Although any violations will be hard to discuss, students might find it easier to admit messing up because they misjudged themselves or their situation, as opposed to admitting they intentionally did something they knew was wrong. However, students might find it tremendously helpful to revisit a time when they did something they knew was wrong, consider the other person's perspective, craft a thoughtful apology (even if it's too late to deliver it), and commit to doing the right thing in the future.

Addressing Challenges

All the activities in this book invoke vulnerability, but this one especially does. That's why we suggest doing this activity after the group has established trust, but they still might feel embarrassed, guilty, or ashamed as they think about a harm they caused and imagine the pain and suffering another person went through because of something they did. Students might respond to these thoughts and emotions with all kinds of avoidance moves, including denial ("I honestly can't think of anything I've done that hurt someone"), justification ("What if it was his fault too?"), assuagement ("He truly did not care"), or refusing to do the activity. Resist any urges to push back, because the more you do, the more defensive students are likely to become (Miller & Rollnick, 2013). Instead, validate the student's experience and ask a question that redirects them toward their own actions, such as by saying, "Even if he didn't care, do you care that you did it?" or, "It's pretty common for there to be wrongdoing on both sides. Even if it was his fault, and even if he doesn't recognize his part in the problem, are you able to recognize yours?"

Your participation will also make a difference. Although they're keeping their mistakes and wrongdoings private, if you share one of yours, your students will see that it's possible to admit a misdeed and apologize. You can also share any emotions you're feeling, the values those emotions reveal, and how you're choosing to realign with those values. Even if they continue to resist, your students will see that emotions are messages that something important is at stake. At that point, they have a choice in how they proceed.

Your Own Empathy

Maybe you're lucky enough to work in a school that's highly collaborative—but collaborative doesn't necessarily mean compassionate. Having common planning time doesn't mean seeking common values. Sharing our practices doesn't mean sharing the struggles it took to develop them. Collaboration can lead to teaching that represents the best of everyone's work, but it can also lead to conflict. We might resolve that conflict by compromising, agreeing to disagree, or quietly deciding to avoid mentioning certain topics in the future without ever discovering the experiences that shaped our different perspectives in the first place.

A good relationship at work sometimes just means relying on someone to cover your class in an emergency and nod when you complain about the attendance policy. Sometimes that's enough, but maybe you're looking for more. Maybe you want to understand your colleagues' stories, strengths, and struggles more fully—and to develop a relationship of deeper personal and professional support. Maybe when you have conflicts, you don't want to just get past the distress but work with it and in it to discover the common values underneath.

This might sound utopian, and it certainly requires administrative support and a loving (there's that word again) culture you might not have. Or maybe this kind of culture exists in pockets, and maybe you're part of that pocket, or maybe you see it but aren't a part of it because you've never been invited in.

You might not be able to solve the systemic problems at your school, but try this. Use the "Examples of Values" handout (page 192) or the Values cards (page 193) to help you identify the qualities you think are most important in your practice. Then identify the qualities you consider to be your strengths as a teacher. Notice the values that are also your strengths, the values that are not your strengths, and the strengths that are not such important values for you.

Now comes the hard part: can you ask a colleague to do the same thing? You might feel awkward, even if it's a colleague you regularly talk to and collaborate with. Can you notice that feeling—and what it might be telling you is at stake—yet have the conversation anyway? If your colleague identifies their values and strengths, can you take the next step and look for some of your common values and complementary strengths? How might those values and strengths benefit your work? How might they benefit your relationship? How might you draw on them if you and your colleague ever have a conflict? What might your professional life be like if you could really listen to your colleagues' struggles and honor the values they reveal?

From Empathy to Resilience

This chapter was about how students can listen for and truly take in their peers' struggles, strengths, experiences, and values so they can build stronger and more authentic relationships. While this chapter focuses on how students can relate to another person's experiences, the next chapter is about how students can relate to their own experiences in ways that help them recommit to the values they want to live by.

Values and Strengths

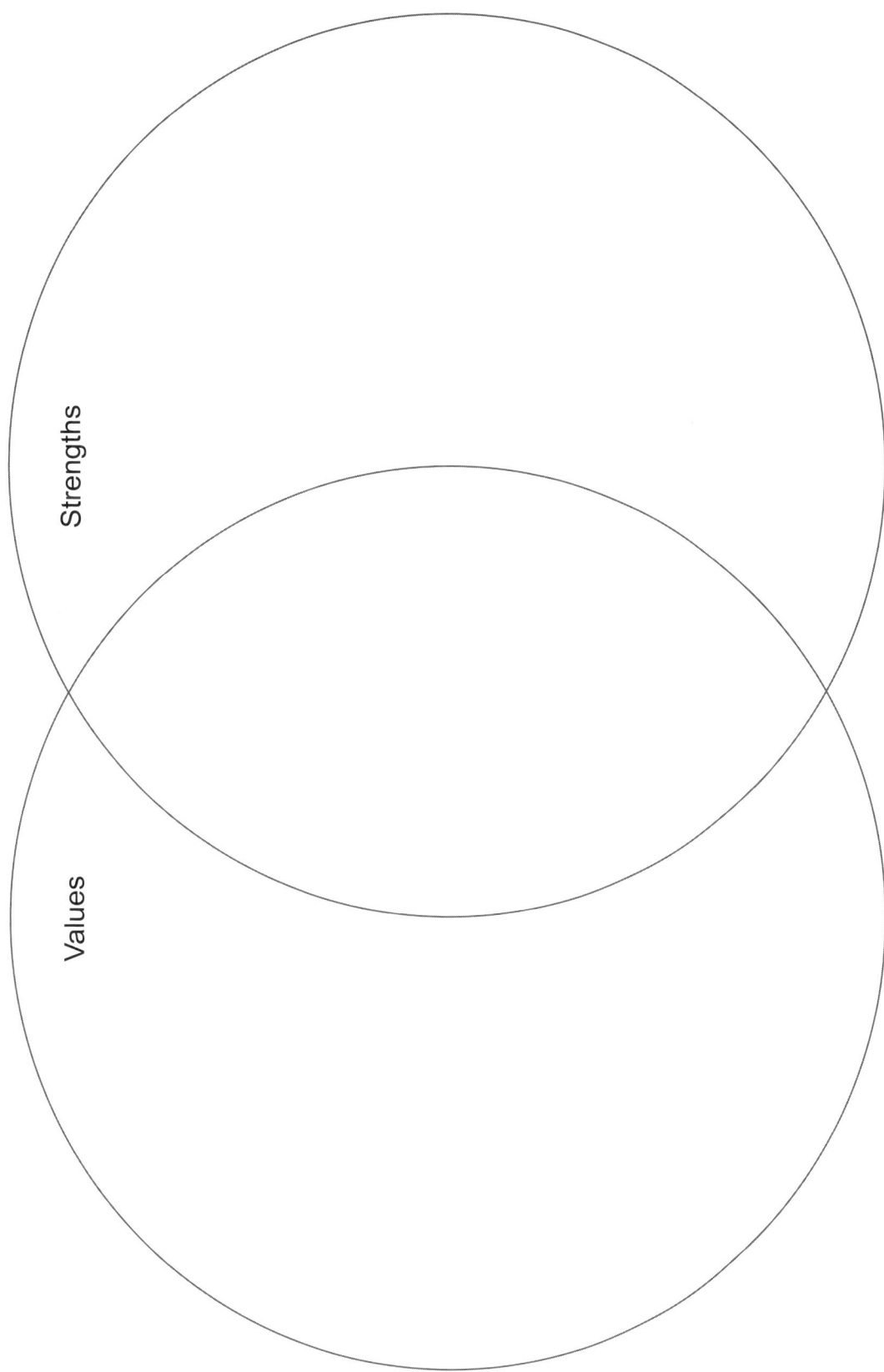

Compassionate Responding

Conflict
What happened?

What am I experiencing?	What might _____ be experiencing?
What's important to me?	What seems important to _____?

Connection
What do we have in common?

Six Parts of an Apology

1 Name what you did and say you're sorry.

2 Explain why you did it without making it seem like it was OK.

3 Accept responsibility for your actions and the harm they caused.

4 Express how you feel about your actions and what you've learned from them.

5 Suggest what you can do to repair the damage your actions caused.

6 Ask for forgiveness.

Source: Adapted from Lewicki, R. J., Polin, B., & Lount, R. B. (2016). An exploration of the structure of effective apologies. Negotiation and Conflict Management Research, 9(2), 177–196.

Chapter 7

RESILIENCE
EMPOWER STUDENTS TO TURN THEIR STRUGGLES INTO OPPORTUNITIES TO REAFFIRM THEIR VALUES

Author Neil Gaiman (2012), in a commencement speech at the University of the Arts in Philadelphia, offered brilliant advice to the graduating students—and to anyone who's suffering a setback:

> Sometimes life is hard. Things go wrong. In life and in love and in business and in friendship and in health and in all the other ways that life can go wrong. And when things get tough, this is what you should do: make good art. I'm serious. Husband runs off with a politician? Make good art. Leg crushed and then eaten by a mutated boa constrictor? Make good art. IRS on your trail? Make good art. Cat exploded? Make good art. Someone on the internet thinks what you're doing is stupid or evil or it's all been done before? Make good art. Probably things will work out somehow; eventually, time will take the sting away, and that doesn't even matter. Do what only you can do best. Make good art.

As Gaiman speaks, the video occasionally shows students, sometimes cheering, and sometimes smiling blankly or whispering to each other. Sure, *Neil Gaiman* can turn his struggles into art. He's a famous, accomplished, brilliantly imaginative writer who makes actual money for his work. How many of the students listening to him believed they could turn their greatest struggles into art—or into *something* meaningful that gave them a sense of satisfaction and vitality? How many believed their real-world responsibilities would mean they'd have to play by the rules he said they should break? How many of them had made it to their university graduation because they *had* played by the rules of school?

Gaiman begins the graduation speech by saying he never expected to be in the position of giving one because he never went to college. Instead, he "escaped from school as soon as [he] could, when the prospect of four more years of enforced learning before [he] could become the writer [he] wanted to be seemed stifling" (Gaiman, 2012). Yet school is an ideal place for students to learn who they are, what they can do, and how they want to respond when inevitably they encounter life's challenges.

This chapter's activities help students use their struggles as opportunities to recommit to their own values. These activities are *not* about teaching students—particularly Black, Brown, queer, trans, disabled, and neurodivergent students—to tolerate harmful programs and policies. We define resilience as coming back from an individual failure, not enduring a systemic one.

Feedback Comics

Evaluative feedback—whether in the form of grades or comments—can bring up difficult emotions. For this activity, students notice how evaluative feedback makes them feel, what the feedback suggests they might try next time, and how they feel about the possibility of approaching their work differently—and in a way that might be more consistent with their values. An example of this activity's form is shown in figure 7.1.

> **Suggested duration:** 15 minutes
>
> **When to use:** Any time students receive a grade or any other kind of evaluative feedback
>
> **Materials:** Copies of the "Feedback Comic Panels" handout (page 140), pencils, thin markers or colored felt-tip pens

Leading the Activity

The following steps will help you effectively lead the activity.

1. Provide copies of the "Feedback Comic Panels" handout (page 140). In panel 1, ask students to create pencil drawings to show what they did to work on the project, assignment, or test they recently received evaluative feedback on.

2. In panel 2, ask students to create pencil drawings to show how they feel about the feedback they got. Tell them to avoid writing words and instead use lines, shapes, and shading to represent their emotions.

3. In panel 3, ask students to create pencil drawings to show what the feedback suggests they might try the next time they have a similar assignment.

Figure 7.1: Example filled-out feedback comic.

- If they felt happy with the feedback, that's a sign that their actions worked for them. What do they want to keep doing? Is there room for growth or creative risks?

- If they felt upset with the feedback, that's a sign that their actions didn't work out for them. What do they want to try instead? What do they want to do more or less of? Despite their disappointment, what *is* working for them that they want to keep doing?

4. In panel 4, ask students to create pencil drawings to show how they feel about the possibility of trying something new. Again, tell them to use lines, shapes, and shading, but not words, to represent their emotions.

5. Ask students to look in their four panels for what's still in their control. Can they change what happened in the past? Can they choose their emotions? Can they choose what they do next?

6. Have students use a thin marker or felt-tip pen to emphasize anything they've drawn that's still in their control and to add any statements about what they plan to do. Using a different color makes these additions stand out against the pencil drawings. They might write affirmations like *I've got this*, add sound effects or *emanata* (sweat drops to depict anxiety, a question mark for confusion, a light bulb for an idea, and so on) to emphasize the actions they already drew, or

write a caption for their action, such as *I'll make a study outline next time*. Whatever they write or draw reinforces for them that they have the power to act on their values no matter what grades they get.

7. Lead a discussion, asking some or all of the following questions.

    - "How did it feel to make this comic?"

    - "What did you notice as you made the comic? What do you notice as you look at it now?"

    - "Why do teachers give feedback to students? How do you imagine they hope students will use it?" This is an opportunity for you to assess how well students understand functions of teacher feedback and to educate them on those functions. Usually, teachers give feedback to help students understand what to keep doing and what to work on, hoping the student will use it to improve. Sometimes, feedback also shows that we paid attention to the details of a student's work and that it had a meaningful impact on us (Porosoff & Weinstein, 2020a).

    - "How do students *actually* use their teachers' feedback?"

    - "How *could* you use your teachers' feedback?" This is an opportunity for students to notice values-consistent ways to approach similar assignments in the future. Any feelings of disappointment are worth noticing. If they're disappointed in themselves, they might try something different next time, but if they're disappointed that the teacher didn't understand or appreciate their work, they might simply accept that as out of their control and focus on how they want to move forward.

Extending the Work

You can collect the comics, and when students are working on a similar assignment, hand back the comics and ask students if they've tried any of the actions they drew in their third panels. If they have, what was it like? How do they feel about themselves as a result of trying new actions or continuing to act in ways that work for them? For those who haven't tried the actions yet, do they plan to? When will they start? What might get in the way? What will they do if they encounter those obstacles? Can the group share more strategies?

You could also repeat this activity for several similar assignments. That way, students can use their comics to track their actions' effectiveness over time. Are they using the same strategies regardless of how well they work? You can't force students to change and probably wouldn't want to, but you can keep helping them explore the costs of *not* making values-guided choices in the face of difficult emotions. If nothing else, students will get better at noticing and depicting their own emotions if they have practice, and that might be reason enough to repeat this activity.

Adjusting the Activity

If hand drawing would be an insurmountable hurdle for your students—for example, if they have dysgraphia—they could use an online drawing program. However, the more sophisticated programs take time to master, and the simpler ones can limit how students express their ideas.

Addressing Challenges

Students and teachers tend to see evaluative feedback differently. When we give a grade, fill out a rubric, or write comments, we intend to inform our students about how well they did so they can decide where and how to direct their efforts in the future—much as a thermometer simply informs us about the temperature so we can decide what to wear.

If students saw their grades as merely information that can help them make decisions, they wouldn't get so caught up in what their grades are. Some literally jump for joy when they get an A or burst into tears when they get anything besides an A. Others are less visibly emotional but still feel happy, angry, disappointed, frustrated, hurt, embarrassed, and all kinds of other emotions when they get a grade (or number, percentage, emoji, check mark, badge, or any other performance indicator).

This activity helps students honor their own emotions *and* look beyond those emotions toward what the feedback suggests they do—and discover how the possibility of continuing to work toward their goals makes them feel. The drawings allow students to bring their internal experiences into the outside world to give them shape and texture. That literally gives students a new perspective on their emotions because they can physically see them, and it gives them some agency because they're the artists. From this empowered perspective, they get to decide how they want to relate to their emotions. The comics also have multiple panels, which helps students see that their experience includes more than the grade that resulted; it's neither the end nor the beginning of their learning self.

Some students might focus so much on their artwork that they have trouble moving on, while others might draw so few details that they won't discover how well their own actions served them. For each step that involves drawing, set a time limit. One or two minutes per panel is usually enough, but regardless of how much time you give, knowing that amount of time in advance helps more artistic students rein themselves in, and those who dread art push themselves to add more detail, knowing an end is in sight.

When students draw their past and potential actions, the drawings should depict what they actually did, not exaggerations or metaphors. If you see pictures of climbing mountains, light bulbs over heads, or Rodin's *The Thinker* poses, ask the student if this is what they *actually* did or plan to do. If they say yes, they actually *will* sit chin in hand on a rock, ask how effective they think that action will be. You can't stop students from turning the activity into a joke—or using any other avoidance move—but you can keep prompting them to explore their choices.

Some students might have trouble thinking of what to do next time. The weakest students will often be the ones who have the most trouble thinking of strategies; if they knew exactly what to do, they'd do it, and then they'd be stronger students! If the feedback they received includes comments that offer specific strategies to try in the future, refer your students to them. They don't *have to* follow the suggestions, but it's a place to start. You could also lead a quick share of learning or work strategies that helped most, and you can suggest a few yourself.

Finally, students might not understand the difference between choosing our emotions and choosing actions that tend to elicit certain emotions. They'll say things like, "I can choose to be happy," but if you ask how, they'll describe actions: "I can hang out with my friends or play basketball." These might be activities that usually give the student joy, but does that mean she'll *always* feel joy while doing them? Has there ever been a time when she felt bored or annoyed with her friends, or nervous when she was playing basketball? If not, is it possible she could feel that way at some point? Is she able to choose to do nothing but spend time with her friends and play basketball? The point of asking questions like these isn't to make students feel depressed about how much of their lives they can't choose; it's to help them distinguish what they *can* choose and to choose according to what matters to them.

Struggle Portfolio

Psychology professor Kelly Wilson (2009) and her collaborator Troy DuFrene explain that "values and vulnerabilities are always poured from the same vessel" (p. 67). The greatest sources of meaning in our lives are also the greatest sources of pain, but if we're willing to explore our struggles, we'll find our values. For this activity, students create portfolios of work products that represent times when they struggled to enact their values as learners. They describe how they can learn from those struggles and enact their values in the future.

> **Suggested duration:** 30 minutes
>
> **When to use:** At the end of a term
>
> **Materials:** Copies of the "Learning Struggles" handout (page 141), a list of values such as the "Examples of Values" handout (page 192), writing supplies

Leading the Activity

The following steps will help you effectively lead the activity.

1. Provide students with a list of values such as the "Examples of Values" handout (page 192). Give them time to silently read over the list and notice which values they feel more drawn to and less drawn to.

2. Ask students to choose three values that are important to them *as learners*. That is, what three qualities do they most want to bring to their work at school?

3. Provide copies of the "Learning Struggles" handout (page 141). Ask students to copy the three values they've just selected into the first column.

4. In the second column, ask students to write specific times during the term when they struggled to enact each value. Encourage them to name particular exercises or assignments (*when we discussed lake stratification*) rather than broad categories (*when we have discussions*).

5. Ask students to look through their files for pieces of work that represent the struggles they described. For example, the student who struggled to be enthusiastic during the lake stratification discussion might find his notes from that class. A student who struggled to be humorous when studying for the lake ecology test might look for her study outline.

6. In the third column, ask students to write ideas for what they can try the next time they do a similar exercise or assignment. Invite students to exchange ideas as they write.

Extending the Work

How students assemble their work into a portfolio will depend on the materials management systems they use. If they do their work using online documents, they could create a document that includes links to each piece of work and brief annotations about how they struggled and what they plan to do in the future. If their work is on paper, they can collect their papers in a folder, along with the "Learning Struggles" handout that explains them. If their work is a physical object that cannot be placed in a folder (such as a piece of art), they could take a photo and either print it to place in their folders or upload it and put a link in their document.

How students use their portfolios will depend on your school's assessment systems. If your school includes students in family conferences—or if you can, even if it's not a schoolwide practice—the portfolios could serve as a catalyst for collaborative discussion. What were some of the student's struggles last term? What values-consistent plans do they have for next term? How can their family, advisor (if they have one), teachers, and friends support them in carrying out those plans? A conversation like this helps students focus less on extrinsic rewards and more on how they can enact their own values, thus creating their own definitions of success.

Alternatively, you could place students into small groups and have them share their portfolios with each other. Each group could talk about how they can support each other in enacting their values next term, and they could share those ideas with the whole class—both to give other groups ideas and to help hold themselves accountable.

If they've built sufficient trust, you could invite students to post some of the work representing their struggles, either on a classroom wall or on a class website. Students could create placards or captions that describe how the work represents a struggle to live by their values and what they learned from that struggle. Usually, student work displays include everyone's work from a particular assignment or only the most excellent examples. Instead of celebrating achievement, a struggle wall or website transforms the meaning of failure from an individual's inadequacy to a feature of our common humanity.

Adjusting the Activity

Instead of asking students to identify values they want to bring to any type of learning, you could ask them to consider one specific learning process, such as writing, problem solving, studying for a test, or collaborating on a project.

Addressing Challenges

As students try to think of times when they struggled, they might say that they couldn't have brought a particular value to a particular situation. For example, a student might say she couldn't have been humorous when she was writing her essay about the Russian Revolution because of the topic's serious nature and that she couldn't have been creative because the teacher's expectations were too rigid. This is a great opportunity to discuss how values, as qualities of action, are always available yet contextually determined.

For example, even if the teacher has rigid rules for the essay, can the student think of a creative argument? Or make creative use of poetic devices in expressing her ideas? If an essay about the Russian Revolution feels like an inappropriate place to use humor, are there other places where she could be humorous? When is it important to her to use humor, when isn't it important, and when does she *not* want to be humorous? You can ask questions like these about any value to help students notice whether, when, and how they want to enact their values.

Failure Timeline

According to psychologist Kristin Neff (2011), self-compassion includes feeling our pain rather than magnifying or ignoring it, treating ourselves with kindness when we're in pain, and noticing how pain unites everyone in a common bond of humanity. This activity gives students an opportunity to practice all three aspects of self-compassion. They list various failures or disappointments in their lives, create timelines of their five or six most significant failures, and discover how those failures can reveal their values and help students connect to each other.

> **Suggested duration:** 45 minutes
>
> **When to use:** Anytime
>
> **Materials:** Copies of the "Failure Timeline Questions" handout (figure 7.2), writing supplies, six sticky notes per student

- What was a time when you worked hard but still failed to accomplish your goal?
- What was a time when you failed to work hard in the first place?
- What's something that seems easy for other people, but you've failed to learn how to do it?

- When did you fail to listen to someone?
- When did you fail to listen to yourself?
- When did you fail to get someone else to listen to you?

- When did you fail to join a group you wanted to be part of?
- When did you quit an activity because you weren't happy with your role?
- When did you quit an activity because you weren't happy with your performance?

- When did you fail to speak up for yourself?
- When did you fail to speak up for someone else?

- What test or project did you get a failing grade on?
- What book did you fail to read?
- What movie or show did you fail to watch?

- When did you fail to do something yourself that you were supposed to do independently?
- When did you fail to collaborate when you were supposed to be part of a team?

- When did you fail to seek help that would have benefited you?
- When did you fail to help someone who needed it?

- When did you miss an opportunity to try something new?
- When did you miss an opportunity to see something special?

- When did you lose a game?
- When did you lose a friend?

- When did you lose an important possession—your own or someone else's?
- When did you lose someone's trust?

- When did you fail to fulfill a family obligation?
- When did you fail to fulfill an academic obligation?

- When did you fail to fulfill a social obligation?
- When did you fail to fulfill an obligation to take care of yourself?

- What information do you always fail to remember?
- What mistake did you fail to learn from?

Figure 7.2: Failure Timeline questions.

*Visit **go.SolutionTree.com/SEL** for a free reproducible version of this figure.*

Leading the Activity

The following steps will help you effectively lead the activity.

1. Provide copies of the "Failure Timeline Questions" handout (figure 7.2, page 131). Ask students to start listing their failures. Tell them you will not collect their papers, they will not share anything they want to keep private, and when they do share, it will only be with one person.

2. To help students continue adding to their lists, ask around twelve of the handout's questions, two or three at a time so students don't feel overwhelmed yet still have some choice as to which questions they answer. (Notice the groupings implied by space in the figure.) Explain that the questions are there to help them think of more failure moments, not to limit what or how much they write. As you ask the questions, write them on a whiteboard or put them on slides so students can come back to questions they skip.

3. Ask students to read over their lists and notice how it feels to do so. Then ask how it feels to notice that everyone in the room *has* a failure list. This question helps them understand failure as part of their common human experience, even if their specific failure experiences are different.

4. Ask students to choose five or six failure moments that they think are significant *and* that they're willing to talk about today with a partner. If the process of choosing significant failures makes them think of more failures they want to add to their lists, they can do so.

5. Provide six sticky notes per student. Ask students to copy their five or six significant failure moments onto them and then arrange the notes in roughly chronological order, resulting in a failure timeline. Figure 7.3 shows the authors' failure timelines.

6. Have students pair up and share their failure timelines with their partners. The first person should share their complete timeline while the second person listens, and then the second person shares their complete timeline.

7. Ask partners to place their timelines so that both people can see them. Ask the following questions to encourage further reflection.

    - "What are some key differences in our failure experiences?"
    - "What are some key similarities in the kinds of failures that matter to us?"
    - "What kinds of failures did neither of us include in our timelines?"

8. Lead a brief discussion, asking some or all of the following questions.

    - "How did it feel to describe your own failure moments?"
    - "How did it feel to hear about your partner's failure moments?"
    - "Notice that everything on your failure timeline happened in the past. If a past failure matters to you, something important was at stake. What can your failure timeline tell you about what's important to you?"
    - "How can you approach those important things, activities, or relationships now?"

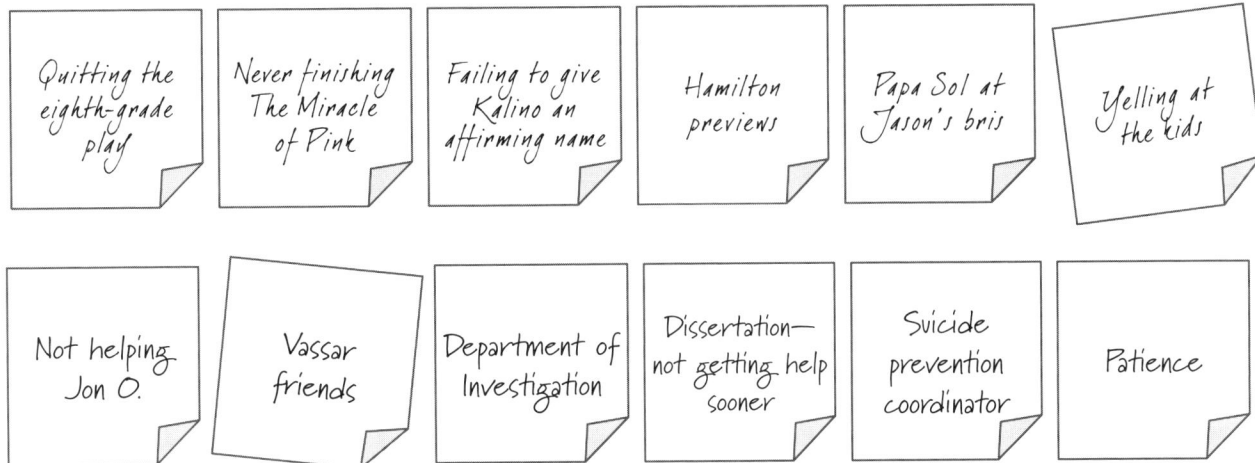

Figure 7.3: The authors' failure timelines.

Extending the Work

This activity helps students notice how their past failures reveal sources of meaning in the present moment and choose how they want to relate to those important people, things, or activities. You could have them write letters to their future selves about what they hope they'll have learned from their failures. Alternatively, you could have them write letters *as* their future selves, offering their present selves words of encouragement.

You could also have students look at a list of values such as the "Examples of Values" handout (page 192) and discuss which values their actions served. Unlike outcomes that we can succeed or fail to achieve, values, as qualities of action, are always available. How can they continue to serve those values, even if they failed to achieve a particular outcome?

Adjusting the Activity

This activity includes several pieces: listing failures, making a failure timeline, sharing that timeline with a partner, connecting with that person based on common experiences, and relating the student's own failures back to sources of meaning in their life. If certain pieces seem like they'd be too much for your students to handle, you can choose the pieces that will work best. You can also select prompts, or write your own, that ask about lower-stakes failures.

Addressing Challenges

As students hear the questions, they might ask if it's OK to write failures that don't quite answer them. For example, on hearing "What test or project did you get a failing grade on," students might ask, "What if I failed an entire class?" or "What if it was a D, not an F, but I consider that a failure?" Other students might want more time to list their failures without responding to the prompts at all. Keep reminding everyone that the prompts are there to help them, not limit them. If they're listing failures, they're doing the activity correctly.

Naming failures can bring up feelings of regret, embarrassment, sadness, guilt, and shame. If you do this activity alongside your students but write your failure list on the board, even though their failure lists are private, your vulnerability will show students how vulnerable they can be if they choose to. You can also narrate your emotions as you list your failures. Saying things like, "This one really hurts to admit," or "I still feel guilty about this one," helps normalize feelings about failure, which creates space for students to have and learn from those feelings.

Even if you're honest and forthcoming about your emotions, some students might avoid their own discomfort by making jokes, calling out each other's failures instead of focusing on themselves, blaming other people for their own failures, or quietly refusing to engage in the activity at all. If possible, try to just notice these reactions and move on. They're a sign that those students are getting close to something that matters to them, which is the whole point of this activity.

Alternatively, some students might say too much about experiences that they'd be better off keeping private, yell, cry, run out of the room, or otherwise exhibit distress. In cases like these, try reminding your students that failure is normal, and the need for other people to bear witness to our stories and emotions is also normal. They can always opt out, but if they do, they'll miss an opportunity to discover something important their strong emotions reveal. Leave the choice to them, and if they choose not to participate, remind them they can always share later with someone they trust and who will honor confidentiality, such as a trusted friend or family member, a school counselor or psychologist, or you.

Self-Care Alerts

This activity helps students build personally meaningful and accessible self-care into their lives. They think of ways they can take care of themselves, choose a self-care action they don't usually do, and set alerts to remind themselves to do it.

> **Suggested duration:** 30 minutes
>
> **When to use:** Anytime, but especially during a stressful time of year
>
> **Materials:** Writing materials, access to their phones (See Adjusting the Activity, page 136, if students don't have phones.)

Leading the Activity

The following steps will help you effectively lead the activity.

1. Lead a brief discussion on the difference between *self-indulgence* and *self-care*. Self-indulgence is giving ourselves something we enjoy in the short term but that might be harmful in the long term, like a brownie sundae or several hours of screen time. Self-care is giving ourselves

something that's helpful in the long term, like a kale salad or an hour at the gym. These might be things we enjoy in the short term, but not necessarily.

2. Ask the students to use the following categories of self-care actions to help them make a list of specific self-care actions they could take. Visit **go.SolutionTree.com/SEL** for a free reproducible version of the list. They should try to include at least one or two concrete, specific actions in each category—although they can put all the actions on one big list.

    - Creating
    - Connecting with loved ones
    - Exercising
    - Being in nature
    - Playing
    - Satisfying the senses
    - Nourishing oneself
    - Practicing mindfulness
    - Resting

3. Invite students to share self-care activities from their lists to give each other ideas to add. Tell them that even if they don't add their classmates' specific activities to their lists, they might get new ideas based on what they hear. For example, after hearing a classmate share songwriting as a creative activity, a student might add "listening to music" as a mindfulness activity.

4. Ask students to look over all the actions on their list, and ask them to circle one new self-care action they're willing to try in the coming week. It should be something they weren't already planning to do. For example, if a student always plays basketball after school, they shouldn't circle "play basketball."

5. Ask students to take out their phones, choose a specific time when they will take the self-care action they just identified, and set an alert so they don't forget. See Adjusting the Activity (page 136) for other options.

6. Invite students to share what self-care actions they chose and why, and when they plan to do them. Sharing could occur with a partner, in a small group, or as a whole class.

Extending the Work

This activity works best if you follow up the next week to ask students if they've completed their self-care actions. For those who did, how did it feel? For those who didn't, what got in the way? Is there a different self-care action they could try?

You can also do this activity repeatedly to help students build patterns of self-care behavior. You could simply do it, as written, over and over. Or you could increase the level of commitment over time. For example, the second time you do this activity, instead of asking students to commit to a self-care action *once*, ask them to choose an action they're willing to do every week for the next month, and to set a repeating alert. The third time, instead of choosing self-care actions to do alone, ask them to choose an action they'd like to invite someone else to do with them and to text that person an invitation.

You might also pair your students up so they can contact each other to ask if they've kept their self-care commitments. If so, they can cheer their partner on, and if not, they can encourage their partner to find a new time or a new action.

Adjusting the Activity

If your students don't have phones or use electronic calendar alerts, have them write their self-care actions in their plan books or make sticky note reminders for themselves—or ask them how they usually remind themselves to do tasks they wouldn't otherwise remember to do.

Addressing Challenges

For some people, self-care has come to mean aromatherapy candles, facial rollers, designer vitamins, and other consumer products. In 2021, the global self-care industry had an estimated value of 1.5 trillion dollars and was still growing (Callaghan, Lösch, Pione, & Teichner, 2021). This activity frames meaningful self-care as *behavior*, but some students might get stuck associating self-care with stuff. If you see that happening, try leading a brief discussion about how self-indulgence is different from self-care. *Self-indulgence* means making ourselves feel good in the short term with no benefit in the long term—and perhaps causing ourselves long-term harm. *Self-care*—despite how the term has been co-opted for profit—might or might not be pleasant in the short term, but it benefits us in the long term.

Some students might need prompts to help them think of specific self-care behaviors. For example, *creating* is a very broad category of behavior, so you can tell them the creation could be art, food, a playlist, a fantasy sports team, a new arrangement for their room, or anything else. If possible, make your own list on the board so students can get their own ideas from yours. Be sure to tell them that your list is exactly that—*your* list of actions that would help *you* take care of *your*self, based on what you need, enjoy, and have access to.

Some students might say they don't have time to take care of themselves in the ways they'd like to or that they can't do some action or other. Instead of arguing the point, try asking questions. Which self-kindness actions on their list can they think of smaller versions of? Would they be willing to try one of those? Are there things—or people—that demand a lot of their attention, and they'd like to save some energy to take care of themselves? How could they set limits in those situations? Who can help?

Another challenge lies in the guilt and shame this activity can stir up. Students might say things like, "Ugh—I really need to get my gross self to the gym," or "I'd *like* to get more rest, but my stupid broken brain makes it really hard to get to sleep." Again, instead of trying to persuade them that they shouldn't feel that way, try asking questions. Do they feel pressured to do some of these actions? Where is that pressure coming from? How are these self-care actions important to *them*?

Your Own Resilience

When the artist Gavin Aung Than heard Neil Gaiman's (2012) University of the Arts graduation speech, Than (2012) was inspired to create a comic version for his website, Zen Pencils (https://zenpencils.com). That was the version Lauren first encountered and the one she searched for a few years later when one of her students—we'll call him Jerome—had committed a harmful act and was asked to leave the school. Lauren was angry about what Jerome had done but even angrier at the school's administrators, who didn't even bother to ask the teachers who know Jerome best what they thought. Jerome was painted as a bad person who didn't deserve to be part of the community, when really he needed his community more than ever.

Lauren saw a Jerome who worked hard to read challenging course texts and to try new writing strategies even though he saw himself as a bad writer. As a child of color adopted into a white family, Jerome was making sense of his identity, and for Lauren's class, he wrote eloquently about how baseball made him feel connected to his birth mother in Colombia *and* to his family in the United States. Jerome often said and did hurtful things, and he didn't always take responsibility for the hurt he caused—which was why he needed his community's support so he could become the person Lauren continues to believe he was trying to be.

After Jerome left, Lauren sent him Gavin Aung Than's (2012) comic of Neil Gaiman's (2012) *Make Good Art* speech, along with the following letter.

> Dear [Jerome],
>
> You and I never talked much about the struggles you went through at [school], but I know you had your share of them. I haven't had the same experiences as you, but I do know what it's like to struggle at [school].
>
> Three years ago, when our assistant principal for academic life was leaving, I applied for the job and didn't get it. I was good at designing curriculum and had worked very hard to make our school a better place. Not getting the job felt like a rejection of everything I'd done. Later, I learned I'd made mistakes in how I related to some of my colleagues—talking when I should have listened, blowing up at small things, letting myself get bullied into bad decisions—and that cost me an opportunity that mattered to me.

> My story is different from yours in lots of ways, but in some ways our stories are the same. We both have skills and talents, we've both worked very hard, and we've both made mistakes and had to suffer the consequences. But for me, that's not the end of the story.
>
> After not getting the job, I recommitted myself to the work I was doing with students. I started developing units that became important parts of the curriculum. I also started creating workshops for teachers and writing about my ideas. I've now given workshops to teachers from all over New York state, published articles in several teaching magazines, and wrote a book on curriculum design that comes out this fall. The most painful failure of my career wasn't an ending. It was a beginning.
>
> Just like I turned my experience of rejection into acts of creativity that served my values, you can take the experiences you had in middle school and turn them into art. I will never forget the power of the vignettes, poems, and other pieces of writing you created for my class. What made your writing so powerful wasn't just the strong imagery and all the other stuff I was teaching about; it's that it was genuine and true. I hope you will keep using writing as a way to transform the negative experiences in your life into something beautiful.
>
> This is your beginning, [Jerome]. Make good art.

Many narratives about resilience are toxic (Del Pozo, 2021; Love, 2019; Schwarz, 2018; Zembylas, 2021). That which does not kill us does *not* necessarily make us stronger. Trauma does *not* build character or turn us into superheroes. People who don't overcome adversity are *not* responsible for their own misfortune. Members of historically marginalized groups should not have to survive oppressive systems in order to succeed. Those who experience harm need care, those who do harm must be held accountable, and we all need to work together to build systems that lead to vitality and liberation for everyone.

Resilience is not about erasing our pain, toughing it out, convincing ourselves that we can do anything if we only work hard enough, or bouncing back so we can live up to someone else's definition of success. Instead, we see resilience as reaffirming our own values so we can choose what we do next. Before we transform our pain into good art or anything else, we need a chance to be *with* that pain.

What values do you want to bring to your teaching? When have you struggled to be that way, and what will you do the next time you teach that lesson or unit? What are some of the failure moments in your teaching practice? How would it feel to share your failure timeline with a trusted colleague? Even if you keep it to yourself, what can your failure timeline tell you about what's important to you? How can you approach those important things, activities, or relationships now?

Most of all, what self-care actions do you want to try? How can you create things, connect with loved ones, exercise, spend time in nature, play, satisfy your senses, get nourishment, practice mindfulness, and rest? Is there a specific self-care action you weren't planning to do anyway and that you're willing to commit to doing in the next few days? Set yourself an alert so you don't forget.

Teaching is hard, even under optimal circumstances, and most of us are dealing with grossly suboptimal circumstances. What if we all took the time and space to feel and honor our pain, notice how that pain reveals what matters to us, connect to each other through the common experience of pain, and give ourselves the care we need to heal?

From Activities to Strategies

This chapter was about how students can use their struggles as opportunities to reaffirm and reconnect with their values. It was the last chapter in part I, which includes activities that empower students to clarify and commit to their values. But empowering students to bring their own values to their learning, work, and relationships requires more than doing an isolated activity here or there. In part II, we'll discover strategies that make EMPOWER work have a greater impact on students, so they can transform school into a source of meaning, vitality, and community in their lives.

Feedback Comic Panels

Learning Struggles

As a learner, I want to be . . .	I struggled to be that way when . . .	Next time I have a similar learning opportunity, I will . . .
1.		
2.		
3.		

PART II

Strategies That Make EMPOWER More Effective

While the activities in part I foster SEL using the elements of EMPOWER, part II offers strategies that will help you integrate EMPOWER work into students' lives. Each chapter is about a different way to do that: as part of a program, with struggling students, and with families.

- **Chapter 8**—"Designing an Empowering Social-Emotional Learning Program"
- **Chapter 9**—"Supporting Students Who Struggle to Enact Their Values"
- **Chapter 10**—"Inviting Families Into Conversations About Student Values"

As any teacher knows, a student can be fully engaged in an activity and seem to have achieved the learning outcome, yet struggle to recruit that learning in a novel context. Just as a student might correct a sentence's subject-verb agreement during a grammar lesson but fail to use that same skill when writing an essay, a student might engage fully in some EMPOWER activities but not others. Another student might tap into his empathy during an EMPOWER activity but not be empathic toward his lab partner in science class.

Such moments don't mean the activity failed; they indicate how powerfully context shapes behavior. As a teacher, you have influence over the context that shapes your students' behavior. You can make EMPOWER activities part of a larger, cohesive SEL program. If you see students avoiding their values, you can talk to them about that avoidance. Because you know that students only see you for part of their day and that you won't be their teacher forever, you can invite families to continue EMPOWER work at home.

As you read the chapters in part II, you might notice the EMPOWER elements—exploration, motivation, participation, openness, willingness, empathy, and resilience—at different points. However, rather than focusing on one element at a time, we'll look at how everyday interactions at school can become opportunities to empower students to live by their values.

Chapter 8

• • • • •

DESIGNING AN EMPOWERING SOCIAL-EMOTIONAL LEARNING PROGRAM

Social-emotional learning has always been important, but it's more important now than ever. In late 2021—the third school year in which the COVID-19 pandemic affected teaching and learning—United States Surgeon General Vivek Murthy issued an advisory that called for "immediate awareness and action" regarding young people's mental health (Office of the Surgeon General, 2021). According to the advisory, feelings of sadness and depression and rates of mental illness and suicidal behavior were up even before students began losing access to supportive school environments and regular routines. Watching pandemic-caused worldwide suffering and death only exacerbated these problems. Among the advisory's many recommendations to address this crisis was expanding SEL programs in schools.

Some schools are answering this call by adding it after so many educators have witnessed and experienced the pandemic's impacts. Other schools were adding SEL long before the pandemic began. In schools that aren't there yet, some educators are carving out time for SEL in their classes. All that is great. At the same time, we worry that SEL can easily become just another box to check. We've seen many school leaders suddenly realize students should be doing SEL, spend a lot of money (hiring expensive consultants, sending teachers to summer institutes, buying T-shirts for the whole student body), and make grand announcements about how important SEL is. But then, after a year or two, the program amounts to a bulletin board here, an activity there, and not much change in students' lives.

Rather than trying to add SEL programs, we can consider how *existing* programs provide a meaningful context for that learning. In this chapter, we identify three contexts in which students think and talk about their identities, relationships, thoughts, feelings, goals, and values: (1) advisory programs,

(2) academic classes, and (3) counseling sessions. These are contexts in which students *already* engage in SEL, even if we don't call it that. We'll see how to integrate opportunities for students to clarify and commit to their values into these programs, so the program becomes more empowering for the student, and the activity helps the program achieve its purpose.

Integrating SEL Into Existing Programs

The *L* in SEL is for *learning*. Although the term *social-emotional learning* and the initialism SEL are relatively recent additions to the educational lexicon, social and emotional learning themselves are as old as human existence. All students have a social experience of school in that they interact with other people, and they all have an emotional experience of school, because being human means constantly having feelings. Students don't leave their thoughts and feelings in their lockers when they go to class, or pull them out like calculators when they seem useful. Even though we use the phrase *social life* to distinguish time spent having fun with friends from other pursuits (academic, athletic, artistic, and so on), the word *social* just means people are together having some sort of effect on each other.

We can build any SEL program or none at all, and students will still have social and emotional experiences and learn to respond in some way. The question for us to consider isn't *where* students should do SEL, because they're already doing it wherever they have social interactions and emotional responses—which is to say, everywhere. Instead, we need to ask ourselves, "*How* can educators foster the sort of SEL our students need?"

We propose three different contexts in which educators can foster SEL: (1) advisory programs, (2) academic classes, and (3) counseling sessions. In an advisory program, SEL is the curriculum: a specific set of habits and skills students need to develop healthy relationships with themselves and others. In an academic class, SEL is a pedagogy: a way of designing academic instruction so that learning tasks become opportunities for students to develop healthy relationships with themselves and others. In counseling sessions, SEL is an intervention: a supportive service for individual students who experience or are at risk of experiencing challenges in relating to themselves or others. EMPOWER, as the name implies, empowers educators to implement SEL in various contexts to enhance learning objectives.

Figure 8.1 summarizes these three approaches to integrating SEL. We're presenting it as a pyramid because only some students receive counseling, which occurs during certain periods; all students participate in advisory programs (at schools that have them), which occur during certain periods; and all students take academic classes, which occur all day long.

EMPOWER as Curriculum

Some schools block out advisory periods during which a group of students meets with a faculty or staff member so they can develop closer relationships. Lauren worked in two different middle schools that had advisory periods; these included some discussions of emotions, goals, identities, relationships, and

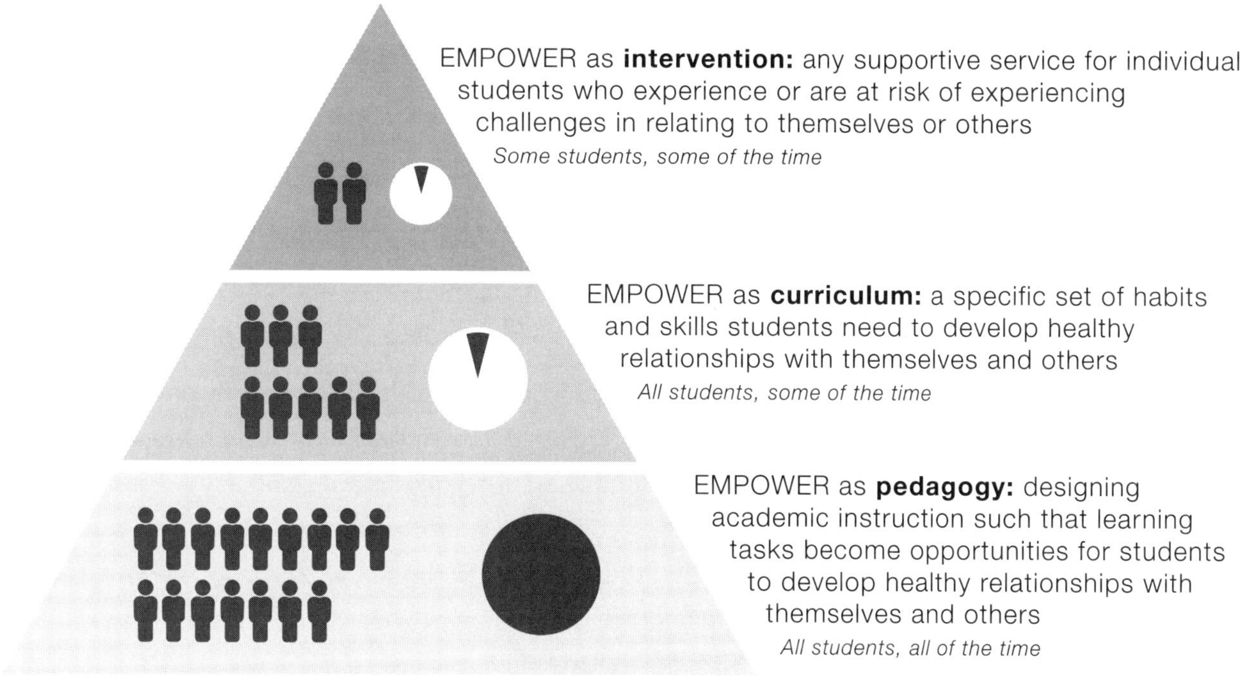

EMPOWER as **intervention:** any supportive service for individual students who experience or are at risk of experiencing challenges in relating to themselves or others
Some students, some of the time

EMPOWER as **curriculum:** a specific set of habits and skills students need to develop healthy relationships with themselves and others
All students, some of the time

EMPOWER as **pedagogy:** designing academic instruction such that learning tasks become opportunities for students to develop healthy relationships with themselves and others
All students, all of the time

Figure 8.1: Approaches to integrating EMPOWER.

*Visit **go.SolutionTree.com/SEL** for a free reproducible version of this figure.*

values—but also included trivia contests, group games, open discussions, holiday-themed activities such as pumpkin painting, and unstructured hanging out. Advisory programs go by different names; Kalino's middle school advisory program was called *Core* and is now called *Keystone* (because relationships are the keystone of successful learning), and eir high school's advisory program is called *Seminar*.

Some advisory programs have students meet several times a week, perhaps for fifteen or twenty minutes, while others have students meet once a week, perhaps for forty-five or fifty minutes, but not necessarily for a full year. Advisory might alternate with assemblies that feature outside speakers or student performances, or advisory might be a half-year course, replaced during the second semester with an extra art class or free period. Whatever name advisory goes by, and whatever amount of time gets allocated to it, EMPOWER activities can constitute its curriculum. You can create that curriculum adaptively, using whatever activities that meet students' needs and interests as they emerge, or you can design a scope and sequence, aligning the activities with planned themes or essential questions.

Responding to Emergent Interests and Needs

One way to use EMPOWER activities as an advisory curriculum is to simply do whatever activity fits students' interests or meets their needs in the moment. For example, if students report high levels of stress, you could do Self-Care Alerts (page 134), or if a traumatic event has occurred and students heard about it in the news, you could use Emotions and Values Audit (page 48) to help them process it. You can also address positive developments. For example, if your students express interest in leadership roles at school, you could do Leading With Values (page 70) to broaden the conversation. Rather than planning weeks in advance, you'd respond to socially and emotionally relevant events in students' lives by helping them bring their values to those moments.

Planning a Scope and Sequence

Another way to build an advisory curriculum is to plan a scope and sequence, just as you would for any course. Ask yourself, "What are the most important SEL topics in this community and during *this* school year? In what order should students consider those topics? Which activities would further that inquiry?"

One way to design an advisory scope and sequence would be to devote a month or two to each EMPOWER element: September is exploration, October is motivation, November and December are participation, and so on. Figure 8.2 shows a sample advisory scope and sequence mapped to the EMPOWER elements. In this scope and sequence, activities slated for earlier in the year tend to invoke less vulnerability than those occurring later. By the springtime, when the advisory group has been together for several months, students might be ready to tell each other more personal stories—and experience the vitality that comes along with connecting on a deeper level.

Month	Theme and Essential Question	EMPOWER Activity
September	Exploration: How do my values show up in my life?	Values Concept Photos (page 20) Our Values in Action (page 22)
October	Motivation: How can I associate my actions with my values?	Values on My To-Do List (page 35) Values on My Device (page 40)
November–December	Participation: How can I create my own ways to enact my values?	Value of the Week (page 61)
January	Openness: How can I share how other people move me toward my values?	The Acknowledgments Section (page 72) Leading With Values (page 70)
February	Willingness: How can I serve my values when it's especially hard?	Guests in Our Houses (page 88) Freak Out, Act Out, Zone Out (page 92)
March–April	Empathy: How can I understand and care about another person's values?	Storytelling Circles (page 106) Common Values and Complementary Strengths (page 108)
May–June	Resilience: How can I turn my struggles into opportunities to reaffirm my values?	Struggle Portfolio (page 128) Failure Timeline (page 130)

Figure 8.2: Sample advisory scope and sequence mapped to the EMPOWER elements.

Another way to create an advisory scope and sequence would be to think about yearly events and plan activities that help students bring their values to those events. Figure 8.3 (page 150) shows a sample advisory scope and sequence mapped to yearly events at the middle school where Lauren used to teach.

In this scope and sequence, some activities are adapted so they apply to students' experiences at a particular time of year. For example, the Four Self Responding protocol (page 37) usually has students consider a specific assignment or performance in terms of values they'll bring to it. However, the activity could also be used at the beginning of the year so students can consider how they'll bring their values to the classes they see on their schedules. Using the activity in this way helps students review their course schedules—which advisors might do with their advisees anyway—while also finding intrinsic motivation to engage in those courses.

Advisory themes can relate to yearly events at that particular school. For example, some of Lauren's English department colleagues decided to host a Valentine's Day poetry reading that they called Love Is Love Is Love. They wanted to counteract messages of heteronormativity, the gender binary, and consumption while getting students to read and listen to poems. Students could come to the academic center during a free period or study hall, or teachers could bring their classes, and students could select from poems about all kinds of love—not just romantic love but love for a family member, friend, pet, place, activity, or oneself—or they could find, write, or improvise their own poems. That month, because students were already having conversations about love, advisory could focus on peer relationships. The activities Bringing Our Full Selves to Our Friendships (page 78) and Common Values and Complementary Strengths (page 108) don't use the word *love* but nevertheless are about how students can show love to one another and to themselves.

Both sample advisory curriculum maps (figure 8.2 and figure 8.3, page 150) are for advisory programs that meet every week, but both maps include only one or two EMPOWER activities per month to leave room for other activities that address emergent concerns, finishing planned activities, or having related discussions. If your students end up not needing the extra time, you can always use the activity extensions, have open discussions, or do something fun. If your school's schedule and priorities accommodate fewer advisory periods, then plan fewer EMPOWER activities—perhaps only one or two per semester. In any case, a scope and sequence doesn't limit you; it reflects your commitment to making your advisory program more meaningful for your students.

EMPOWER as Pedagogy

In an advisory setting, EMPOWER is *curricular content*—what students learn. But in any other class, instead of thinking of EMPOWER as a curriculum, you can think of it as *pedagogy*—how the teacher structures students' engagement with the content and with one another.

For example, a science teacher could use Feedback Comics (page 124) every time she hands back a test or project so her students can notice how they feel and choose what they'll do the next time they have a major assessment task. A history teacher could use Enjoyment and Satisfaction (page 55) whenever he

Month and Event	Essential Question	EMPOWER Activity
September • (Re)orienting to school	Who do I want to be this year in my classes and community?	Shape of My Life Posters (page 16) Four Self Responding (page 37)
October • Seventh-grade trip	What makes school meaningful for me?	Value of the Week (page 61)
November • Finishing first trimester	How do I define success at school?	Assessing My Classes (page 59) Enjoyment and Satisfaction (page 55) regarding a challenging task
December • Home reports • Assessments • Holiday celebrations	How can I take care of myself as school becomes more challenging?	Frustration Coloring Book (page 96) regarding a stressful assessment task Self-Care Alerts (page 134)
January • Resuming classes • Language week	Who helps me accomplish my goals?	The Acknowledgments Section (page 72) to review a key piece of work Leading With Values (page 70)
February • Love Is Love Is Love	How do I want to relate to my peers?	Bringing Our Full Selves to Our Friendships (page 78) Common Values and Complementary Strengths (page 108)
March • Eighth-grade trip • Assessments	How do I want to relate to my struggles?	From Conflict to Connection (page 111)—social struggles Struggle Portfolio (page 128)—academic struggles
April • Student-led conferences	How do I define success at school now?	Assessing My Classes (page 59) Emotions and Values Audit (page 48) to frame conferences
May • Screen-free week	How will I define success online?	Values on My Device (page 40)
June • Assessments • Moving-up ceremony	How can I appreciate others as the school year ends?	Satisfying Our Needs Together (page 76) The Acknowledgments Section (page 72) for important work from throughout the year

Figure 8.3: Sample advisory scope and sequence mapped to yearly events.

wants his students to notice how well their classroom behaviors serve them. A drama teacher could use Common Values and Complementary Strengths (page 108) after assigning scene partners so the two students can appreciate each other and decide how they want to work together.

Values, as qualities of action, can be brought to any task. Students can be creative when solving an algebra problem, responsible when conducting a lab experiment, compassionate when reading history, and respectful when painting a portrait. Arguably, any moment is a potential opportunity for explicit SEL, and any teacher who wants students to reflect on the values they bring (or could bring) to their learning could use an EMPOWER activity to foster that reflection—whether as a regular routine, occasional practice, or one-time occurrence.

That said, EMPOWER activities help students bring their values to various aspects of their lives in school and beyond. Therefore, the activities fit most easily into units or courses that involve behavior change in students' lives beyond the classroom. For example, in health classes, students don't just learn the fundamentals of nutrition; they learn to use those fundamentals by paying attention to media messages about food, reading labels on the foods they buy, and making informed decisions about the foods they eat. In a civic education class, students don't just learn how governments work; they learn how to vote, evaluate candidates' platforms, and advocate for change in their communities. Other courses that foster real-world behavior change include physical education, peer leadership, ethics, home and career skills, and study skills. In such courses, EMPOWER activities can help students bring their values to the actions they're learning to take in their everyday lives.

Figures 8.4 (page 152), 8.5 (page 153), 8.6 (page 154), and 8.7 (page 154) show how teachers might use EMPOWER activities in units on nutrition, leadership, study skills, and the climate crisis, respectively. Even if you don't teach about these specific topics, we hope the unit plans will help you see how EMPOWER activities can be modified to help students apply the content they learn in class to their lives and ultimately build values-consistent behavioral patterns in how they treat their bodies, minds, relationships, and communities.

EMPOWER as Intervention

Some students meet on a scheduled or as-needed basis with a teacher or with a support provider such as a counselor, social worker, psychologist, physical or occupational therapist, administrator, or dean. At our older child's high school, every student meets with their dean in the fall for a progress review conference and in the spring for a course planning conference (replaced by a transition or college planning conference senior year). Our older child also meets with the learning specialist twice a week, and our younger child meets with a psychologist once a week. These meetings are regularly scheduled, but sometimes, a student or an adult sets up a special meeting to address an academic, social, or emotional concern.

At any of these meetings, students might talk about their emotions, thoughts, identities, relationships, goals, and values. Even though we don't usually call these meetings SEL, that's precisely what happens in them—or at least, what *can* happen. If you meet with individual students, you can use EMPOWER

Unit: Nutrition	
Essential Questions: What influences our food decisions? How do our food decisions influence us?	
EMPOWER Activities	**Modifications**
Fun and Important Graphing (page 32)	Instead of considering activities during an upcoming week, students consider the foods they eat. What makes a food fun or painful to eat? What makes a food important or pointless to eat? They think of foods that are fun and important to eat, fun but otherwise pointless to eat, important but painful to eat, and both painful and pointless to eat. Then, they reflect on how they can approach eating decisions in accordance with their values.
Frustration Coloring Book (page 96)	Instead of considering frustrating assignments, students consider frustrating messages or annoying rules about food. They turn those messages or rules into coloring pages that they choose how to fill in. Then, they discuss how it felt to make their coloring pages, choices they made while coloring, things they can add to their eating experiences to make them better, and how they can make their eating experiences personally and culturally affirming.
The Acknowledgments Section (page 72)	Students consider how they get different types of help when nourishing themselves: information about nourishment, exemplars of excellent nourishing food, resources they need to nourish themselves, strategies for keeping themselves properly nourished, feedback on their food decisions, and emotional support when making healthy food decisions. After identifying the kinds of help they need, students write acknowledgments that describe who help them nourish themselves and how.
Four Self Responding (page 37)	Instead of looking at a major assignment, students look at a healthy recipe as their most curious self, grateful self, responsible self, and compassionate self. They listen to what those selves are saying and then consider how they want to approach the task of making this healthy food.

Figure 8.4: Using EMPOWER activities in a nutrition unit.

Unit: Leadership	
Essential Questions: What does good leadership mean? What would it take for me to become a good leader?	
EMPOWER Activities	**Modifications**
Emotions and Values Audit (page 48)	Instead of identifying experiences during the previous week that made them feel various emotions, students identify times when a particular leader's actions made them feel different emotions. Then, after discovering how those emotions reveal what matters to them, they discuss how the things they care about might inform their own actions as leaders.
Leading With Values (page 70)	After completing the activity (by identifying classmates who enact certain values and who support them in bringing those values to their own actions), students have a discussion about leadership. They discuss qualities or actions typically associated with leaders, leaders they've studied or encountered, and different ways to define leadership. Then, they share ideas for how they want to inspire others to enact certain values and support others who are striving to act on their own values.
Guests in Our Houses (page 88)	Instead of thinking of any action they know is important to take, students specifically think about the act of stepping into a leadership role. They consider some of the values they would serve by being leaders, notice mental barriers to taking on a leadership role, and represent those barriers as uninvited houseguests.
Common Values and Complementary Strengths (page 108)	Students do this activity with a potential or actual co-leader. First, they examine the values and strengths they each bring to the leadership role. Then, they discover how their own values align with their co-leader's and how their different strengths can benefit the group or work they're leading together.
Self-Care Alerts (page 134)	Before starting the activity, students discuss how leaders take care of others and why they also need to take care of themselves.

Figure 8.5: Using EMPOWER activities in a leadership unit.

Unit: Study Skills	
Essential Questions: What does it look like to study effectively? How can I study effectively?	
EMPOWER Activities	**Modifications**
Values Concept Photos (page 20)	Instead of choosing only one value to explore, students choose several values they want to bring to the act of studying. They take photos of people bringing those values to studying, places that make it easier for people to enact those values when studying, and objects that symbolize bringing those values to studying.
Values on My Device (page 40)	Students consider how using their devices supports and interferes with values-consistent studying. They add the phrase "When I study" to both questions on their "Enacting My Values When I Use Devices" chart (page 46), so the questions read, "When I study, how do my devices help me be _____?" and "When I study, how do my devices get in the way of my being _____?"
Storytelling Circles (page 106)	Students describe struggles related to studying. Their peers respond with their observations, questions, and interpretations—but no judgment of any kind.
Feedback Comics (page 124)	None needed.

Figure 8.6: Using EMPOWER activities in a study skills unit.

Unit: Climate Crisis	
Essential Questions: Who is responsible for the climate crisis? How can we address the climate crisis?	
EMPOWER Activities	**Modifications**
Our Values in Action (page 22)	Instead of listing parts of their work at school, students list ways to complete the following sentence: As part of caring for the planet, I . . . . Then, they write questions about how they can bring a particular value to the act of caring for the planet. They form groups to discuss their responses to questions the class finds especially interesting and important.
Enjoyment and Satisfaction (page 55)	Instead of reflecting on actions they took while working on a project, students receive a list of actions that harm or heal the planet. They rate how much they enjoy each action, learn how these actions harm or heal the planet, and rate how satisfied they are with each outcome. Then, they discuss ways they can make choices that minimize harm and maximize healing.
From Conflict to Connection (page 111)	Students use this activity to consider a conflict related to the climate crisis.

Figure 8.7: Using EMPOWER activities in a climate crisis unit.

activities to help the student take a more active role in choosing how they approach their learning, work, and relationships at school.

Although some students—and adults—might prefer to have free-flowing conversations (especially outside a classroom setting), there are at least three reasons to consider using EMPOWER activities when meeting with individual students.

1. **EMPOWER activities slow the conversation down so students notice interesting and relevant aspects of their own experience:** When we have a goal—such as helping a friend, studying for a test, or getting out of trouble—we tend to focus narrowly on achieving that goal (Gilbert, 2010; Villatte et al., 2016; Wilson, 2009). To help students observe and describe their lives more fully, the adult needs a way to make the meeting seem less goal oriented. To be clear: any meeting should *have* a goal, but the adult needs a way to help students focus less on that singular goal and more on who they are, what matters to them, and how they want to live.

2. **EMPOWER activities organize the conversation:** Perhaps you've had students come to your classroom or office to receive a particular type of help, but the conversation meandered into half a dozen other topics. Sometimes, you can learn a lot about students this way, but other times, their topic changes are how they avoid the issue they need to address.

3. **EMPOWER activities guide the conversation toward specific details:** Students who are struggling might see that struggle as large, amorphous, and inseparable from who they are (McHugh et al., 2019). "I don't know how to organize my time this week" becomes "I can't get organized," which becomes "I can't do anything." The adult needs a way to break something that looms large in a student's mind into more manageable parts.

Selecting an EMPOWER activity for one student and leading that student through it depend on who the student is and what brought them to you.

Selecting an EMPOWER Activity for One Student

When selecting an EMPOWER activity to use in a one-to-one meeting, first consider the activity's function in the meeting. For example, an assistant principal who attended one of our workshops asked us how she could have conversations with students who'd been sent to her office for a disciplinary referral. These were usually students who knew they were in trouble but barely knew *her*, and she wanted them to know she was there to support them, not punish them. She also didn't want their first real discussion to be about whatever bad thing they'd done. We suggested playing the Values and Questions Card Game (page 24) to show she cares about the student as a person before addressing their wrongdoing.

Figure 8.8 (page 156) provides some guidance in selecting EMPOWER activities for one-to-one meetings. Because you're working with a single student, you can use activities that fit that individual's interests. For example, if you're working with a student who loves art, you could try an activity that involves visually representing psychological experiences, such as Shape of My Life Posters (page 16), Values Concept

156 | EMPOWER MOVES FOR SOCIAL-EMOTIONAL LEARNING

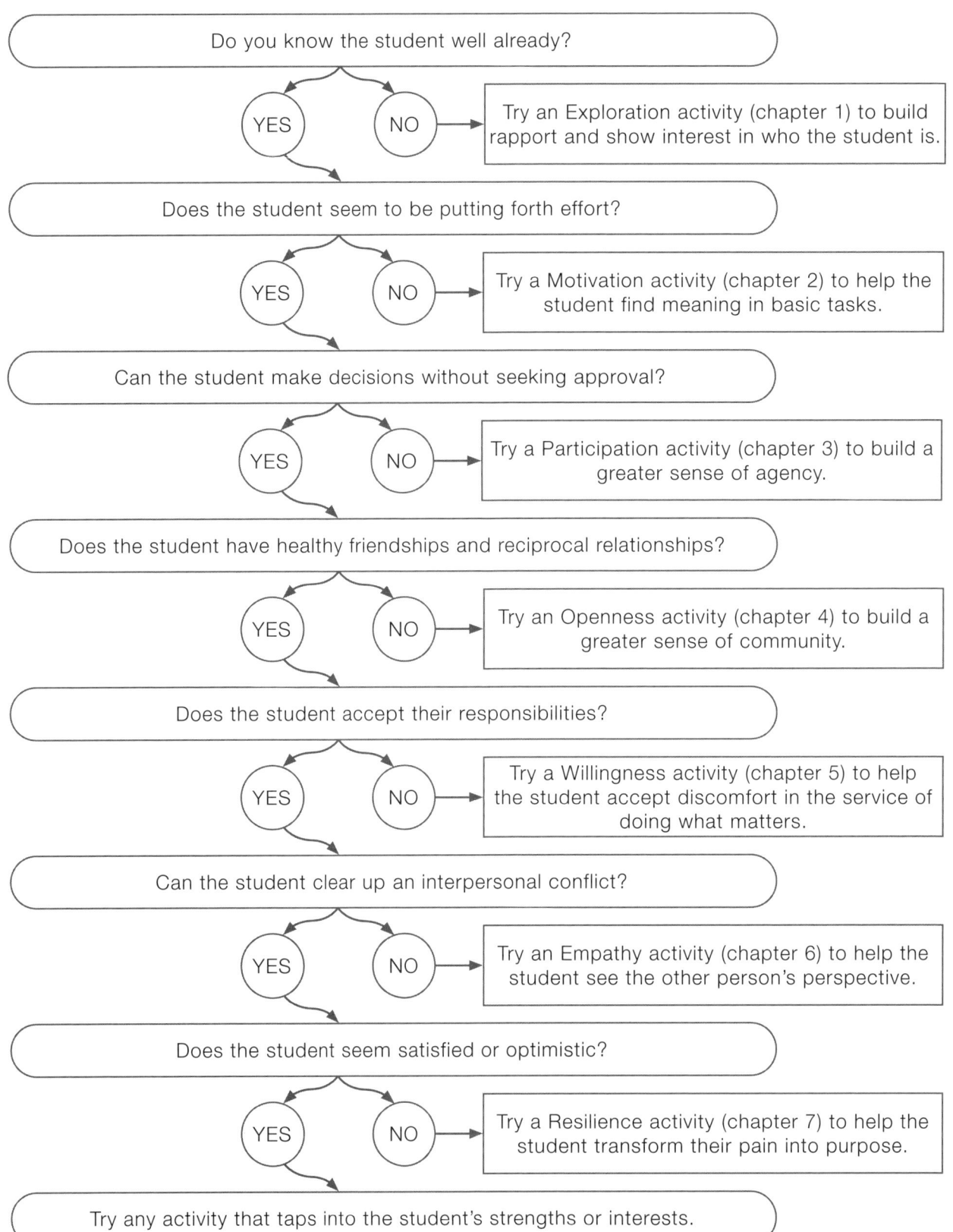

Figure 8.8: Selecting EMPOWER activities for one-to-one meetings.

*Visit **go.SolutionTree.com/SEL** for a free reproducible version of this figure.*

Photos (page 20), or Discovery Drawings (page 97). However, more important than picking an activity you think a student will enjoy is shifting the conversation from deficit correction to values clarification and activation.

Leading One Student Through an EMPOWER Activity

In a one-to-one meeting, EMPOWER activities should feel more like conversation starters and less like . . . well . . . activities. Before starting, give the student a brief synopsis of the activity and its purpose, and ask how they'd feel about trying the first step. Then, check in with them throughout the process by summarizing the steps they have taken so far, describing the next step, and asking if they'd be willing to try it. Your goal isn't necessarily to get through the activity but rather to help the student notice more aspects of their own experience and choose what they want to do next in accordance with their own values.

Many activities involve writing, sometimes in a notebook, and sometimes in a chart or graphic organizer. In classrooms, writing allows everyone to respond at the same time yet keep their thoughts private. In one-to-one meetings, the teacher could take notes while the student speaks freely about their experiences. Ask the student whether they'd prefer to talk while you take notes or write for themselves.

If you're concerned about time, consider asking the student to complete parts of the activity between meetings. Although you might hesitate to add what could feel like homework, some students will welcome the opportunity to think about their values on their own. Others might be less excited, but if the student does the homework assignment, you'll get some insight into how important the work is to them.

Finally, if the student arranged the meeting, just listen to their concerns, and then ask to set up a second meeting to do the EMPOWER activity. Even though all EMPOWER activities invoke the student's own values, the fact that you're suggesting it might make the student feel like you're taking over with your own agenda.

Applying Systems Thinking

Environmental scientist Donella H. Meadows (2008) defines a system as "an interconnected set of elements that is coherently organized in a way that achieves something" (p. 11). An SEL curriculum is a system: its activities are coherently organized to build on each other and toward an outcome—in our case, students finding meaning, vitality, and community in and beyond school. Any other course is a system: its lessons, discussions, and assignments are coherently organized to advance an inquiry and achieve defined learning objectives. Student services are systems: the various programs, policies, and practices are coherently organized to help students succeed at school. We've now seen how to integrate EMPOWER activities into these various systems to help them achieve their intended goals while also helping students achieve their own goals, consistent with their values. Let's now explore ways you can use EMPOWER activities to coherently organize your course or program into a single, composed whole: repeat activities for continuity, diversify activities for balance, and plan flexibly to respond to change.

Repeat Activities for Continuity

Many teachers use classroom routines to provide a sense of continuity. For example, every time Lauren began a new unit in her English class, her students read a summary of their upcoming work and responded to prompts about what they found interesting, challenging, and meaningful. After a few units, just receiving the summary signaled to students that they were transitioning into a new unit, and sometimes a student would say, "Oh, are we doing those three questions?"

Deliberately repeating certain EMPOWER activities, or repeating them with slight changes, turns the activity into a ritual that orients students in their learning and helps them notice new ways to bring their values to that learning. For example, doing the Assessing My Classes activity (page 59) in November and again in April helps students notice how their feelings toward their classes have evolved and how they can keep bringing their values to different classes. Playing the Values and Questions Card Game (page 24) every Friday in advisory reminds students that they've come to the end of another week, and now it's once again time to think about their values as part of a community. Repetition transforms an activity from something we happen to be doing today to something that's part of a purposeful whole.

Diversify Activities for Balance

Some activities are more playful, while others are more serious. Some involve art, while others involve writing or discussion. Some take only fifteen or twenty minutes, while others take an entire class period. Some focus on life at school in the present moment, while others focus on life beyond school or in the future. Some invoke much more vulnerability than others. Some invite students to celebrate their accomplishments, while others invite them to fully feel and stay inside their frustration, anger, disappointment, and sadness. If you use different kinds of activities, students will experience a wide range of emotions together. Also, by engaging in a wide variety of activities, they'll discover multiple ways to bring their values to their actions.

Plan Flexibly to Respond to Change

Making a plan doesn't mean you must rigidly follow it. You might change your mind about which activities you want to use. If a colleague tells you about how well an activity went for her group, you might decide to use it too. Maybe you realize your students aren't quite ready to be as vulnerable as a particular activity calls for, so you pick a psychologically easier one. Or maybe your students built trust more quickly than you'd imagined they would, and they're ready for a psychologically challenging activity you hadn't planned to do until later in the year. Your students might experience some challenge in their lives that a particular activity would help them address. Your students might need much more time than you'd expected to do or debrief an activity. The activity might fail, and then you might decide to try a variation. The activity might succeed, and then you might decide to try an extension. A pandemic might hit, and then you might rethink your entire program. Because so much can change, use your plan flexibly so you don't miss opportunities to help students bring their values to important events that emerge. You can even tell your students about the changes you've made and why those changes matter, thus modeling psychological flexibility in the service of your values.

From Integrated to Responsive SEL

This chapter was about how to integrate EMPOWER activities into various programs and practices. But EMPOWER is not just a set of activities; it's an approach to SEL that helps students bring their values to their learning, work, and relationships. Sometimes, students avoid living by their values, so in the next chapter, we'll discover how to have conversations that help students overcome that avoidance.

Chapter 9

SUPPORTING STUDENTS WHO STRUGGLE TO ENACT THEIR VALUES

When our older child was little, eir favorite books were from the *My Weird School* series (Gutman, 2004–2008), which follows the character A.J. dealing with his teachers in such titles as *Mrs. Yonkers Is Bonkers!* (Gutman, 2007) and *Mr. Hynde Is Out of His Mind!* (Gutman, 2005). Nearly every book opens with the same sentence: "My name is A.J., and I hate school." While the antics at Ella Mentry School are intentionally over the top in order to be funny, author Dan Gutman assumes children will understand hating school, thinking teachers are crazy, and judging peers who like learning (like A.J.'s archnemesis, Andrea).

Even those of us who loved school can probably remember teachers we couldn't stand, assignments that made no sense, and work we found excruciating. Some of us faked the occasional illness, hid out in a bathroom or nurse's office, rushed through homework on the bus or skipped it altogether, doodled, whispered to our friends, read under our desks, or stared at the walls. These are all avoidance moves—ways of disengaging physically or psychologically from experiences that make us uncomfortable (Hayes et al., 2012).

As teachers, we try our best to make our classes warm, inviting, engaging, and positive experiences for our students so they'll want to be in the room, do their work, and learn the material. We also recognize that students sometimes avoid their work—whether that's because they can't do it, won't do it, or prefer to do something else. Depending on the circumstances, we might impose consequences such as a lower grade, a detention, a demotion to a lower-level class, a lecture, a phone call home, or a referral for special services. These consequences might get the student to show up for class and do the work in the future because that becomes the least unpleasant path.

This chapter is about a different way to respond to student avoidance: helping them reframe their actions as inconsistent with their own values and then choose new actions that better align with who they want to be. In order to do that, we need to understand how avoidance functions, be able to identify avoidant behavior, and address any knowledge and access barriers that might prevent students from doing the work even if they want to. At that point, we can shape values-based behavior change. This process requires understanding why suggestions are unhelpful, using open-ended questions and other conversational strategies to evoke change, and making time for those one-to-one conversations.

Understanding How Avoidance Functions

Some people escape school as soon as they can, yet even those of us who pursue advanced degrees and return to school as teachers develop our share of avoidance moves. Jonathan is a prime example. After the typical path through elementary, middle, and high school, Jonathan went through four years of college, got a master's degree in public administration, and did his PhD in clinical psychology. You might think someone who chose all that school would be the last person to avoid engaging with it. You'd be wrong. Jonathan's experiences as a student provide a case study in how avoidance functions.

Jonathan first discovered the art of procrastination at the age of eight. He had a teacher who made a star chart indicating who'd filled in or completed their multiplication tables. The future high school class valedictorian led the pack, having dutifully filled in his chart. One day, the teacher made an announcement that *some* students hadn't even begun theirs, while staring directly in Jonathan's direction. Paralyzed with fear and shame, Jonathan stared back, hoping the moment would pass. He did not attempt to memorize his multiplication tables until the next year. No stars for him! When a task is aversive, students might avoid it even when there are extrinsic positive consequences (in this case, status and approval).

Jonathan's avoidance didn't end in elementary school—nor did it only apply to mandatory assignments. For his senior year of high school, he enrolled in a half-year elective on Russian language and culture taught by the principal and superintendent of his school district. Apart from trying to make up for his uneven performance with French, the only foreign language he'd somewhat learned to date, he wanted to be in that class because it was the closest he could get to a more advanced version of European history. The class only met twice a week and rotated between Russian culture and history, which fascinated him, and the language itself, which sounded kind of cool but also involved memorizing the Cyrillic alphabet—which Jonathan didn't even try to do. Even in situations where a student chooses what they do (such as taking an elective class or picking a research topic), certain components might be aversive, and the student might avoid those components.

Jonathan's highest-achieving classmates made flash cards so they would learn the alphabet. A few even succeeded, and he recalls feeling jealous of their efforts and regretting that he wasted an opportunity. Apart from that awareness, the consequences were laughably inert. Jonathan correctly guessed that his class wouldn't be learning much Russian at all, with only a weekly emphasis on the language over the course of six months. Also, the tests tended to have both topics on them, so Jonathan managed to squeak by with an A- for the part of the academic year that would be relevant to his college applications—and by that time, he'd become quite good at multiple-choice tests. Looking back, he wonders if he might have pursued Russian in college had he managed to care a bit more, but in the moment, he avoided putting in effort. When a task is aversive and avoidance has no consequences, students might avoid the task.

Jonathan's avoidance moves extended to learning activities beyond the classroom, including his participation on the school wrestling team. As a wrestler, he was often in the small, dingy, and loud weight room at Ardsley High School. The paint was peeling, and the room itself was much colder than it should've been. Jonathan can still hear "Paradise City" blasting from someone's boombox and thinking that maybe he didn't like Guns N' Roses after all. The weight room coach was specifically for the football team. He yelled a lot and gave long lectures. The football team all had their own weightlifting belts and were always hogging the equipment, so if Jonathan wanted to get a workout in, he needed to know exactly what he wanted to do, with no hesitation.

Jonathan's senior year of high school wrestling was only his third year on the varsity team and second as a regular starter. If he was going to compensate for his mediocre athletic talents, he needed to get stronger. The thing was, he was too embarrassed to ask for help. Everyone around him seemed to know what they needed to do to work out. He figured a bunch of daily push-ups might help, but that wasn't cutting it, largely because he got bored. Jonathan's brother had bought him a curling bar for his sixteenth birthday, but he needed more weights for it. He also didn't know which exercises to do, the number of repetitions, or the frequency needed for him to reach his goals, which were hazy at best. Jonathan never did figure out what to lift, when, or how. He could've asked his wrestling coach but would have had to do so in person—email didn't exist in those days. Since that time, Jonathan only dabbled with lifting weights until the pandemic hit and he discovered the world of free workout videos. At the time, though, the idea of appearing incapable and weak to his coach and peers outweighed his interest in learning to lift. Students might be interested in the work itself, or at least willing to do it, but aversive social consequences prevent them from engaging.

Jonathan's experiences offer us two important lessons.

1. Even students who do good work, challenge themselves, and reach the highest levels of academic achievement will avoid aversive experiences. Everyone avoids aversive experiences—often with good reason. Researchers Steven Hayes, Stefan Hofmann, and David Sloan Wilson (2020) use the term *adaptive distress* to describe how both physical and psychological pain warn us that something is amiss, and we've evolved to pay attention to pain so we can fix the problem now and avoid it later. The problem is, avoiding short-term distress can cause long-term problems (Hayes et al., 2020; Waltz & Follette, 2009). At school, avoiding uncomfortable feelings such as boredom, frustration, confusion, and embarrassment means also avoiding assignments and interactions that might lead to important learning.

2. Avoidance is not a single behavior; it's a functional class of behaviors (Friman, Hayes, & Wilson, 1998; Rajaraman et al., 2022). That is, there are many different possible behaviors that all serve the same function: helping someone avoid physical or psychological pain. That makes avoidance difficult to identify.

Identifying Avoidance Behaviors

Typically, when teachers say a student is being *avoidant*, it means the student isn't doing the task itself or appears to be putting forth very little effort. Conversely, as long as students do the work—correctly, completely, and to the best of their ability—teachers may think of students as fulfilling the assignment. But just because students have met *our* expectations doesn't mean they've enacted their own values.

Recall the example of Jonathan doing well in his Russian language and culture class: he met enough of his teacher's expectations to get an A-, but he came away from the class feeling like he missed an opportunity to learn the Cyrillic alphabet. Now he wishes he'd learned it because it would help him follow international wrestling and the attack on Ukraine. Although his avoidance behaviors gave him a sense of relief, they were inconsistent with his values.

When we consider that students might not be enacting their own values, we might notice many other forms of avoidance beyond noncompliance, such as the following.

- Choosing a topic that has no emotional stakes
- Choosing a topic another student chose or that the teacher suggested but isn't important to that student
- Hiding knowledge that would expose personal or cultural experiences
- Oversimplifying; refusing to consider additional factors or alternative perspectives
- Overcomplicating; getting bogged down in details
- Refusing to take the work seriously; turning everything into a joke
- Taking the work too seriously; refusing to make it fun or exciting
- Refusing to change or extend the assignment to fit the student's interests, talents, or needs
- Following instructions to the letter without questioning the teacher's intent or the assignment's purpose
- Sticking with a familiar but inapplicable strategy or format (for example, continuing to write five-paragraph essays after learning about more sophisticated essay structures)
- Becoming defensive when offered feedback
- Accepting all suggestions without thinking about how applicable they are
- Refusing support altogether ("No thanks. I'm good.")
- Asking for permission or approval at every turn ("Is this OK?")
- Doing the work without helping anyone else
- Spending more time helping a classmate with their work than doing the student's own
- Excluding a group member the student thinks isn't as strong
- Being perfectionistic; spending too much time getting something right at the expense of other parts of the assignment, work in other classes, or life outside school

As you read through this list of avoidance behaviors, you might think of students who exhibit each one. But any student might display any of these behaviors depending on the context—and in fact, you can probably think of times when you yourself were avoidant in each of these ways.

Also, the list contains only some examples of student behaviors that are less obvious forms of avoidance. You could pick any value—imaginative, inclusive, resourceful, and so on—and ask yourself whether a particular student is bringing this quality to their work or not. You could also ask yourself whether any particular quality of action functions as avoidance for a particular student. For example, doing an assignment *imaginatively* might function as a way for the student to avoid discomfort associated with *carefully* reading instructions and exemplars.

It's hard for us, as teachers, to look at students and decide whether their actions function in the service of their values or as avoidance. That's why, if we suspect avoidance, we need to have conversations with our students to help them observe their actions, decide how well those actions match their values, and make a choice about what they want to do. However, before we initiate conversations with students about avoidance, we need to make sure we've removed any external barriers to success.

Addressing Knowledge and Access Barriers

Just because a student isn't meeting our expectations or serving their own values, it doesn't mean they're being avoidant. The student might need access to certain resources or opportunities to develop certain skills. That is, they might not know how to complete the task, make it appropriately challenging for themselves, collaborate with others without feeling like they're imposing or cheating, take creative risks while adhering to requirements, and so on. Some students might come into your class with these skills; others surely won't.

Other students might have the requisite skills but lack access to the time, tools, and support systems they need to do work they'd otherwise be capable of doing. A student who has a lightning-fast internet connection at home might be able to write her essay easily, while her classmate might share his connection with multiple family members who work from home. He might lose track of his ideas while waiting for his document to autosave. The first student might be able to upload her essay instantaneously; the second might have to build upload time into his work schedule or miss the assignment deadline. That extra labor might seem insignificant for any particular assignment, but over many assignments in many courses over many months of a school year, the added time and frustration can make a very real difference.

Technology concerns are only one access issue. Some students have entire art studios at home; others have an incomplete set of hand-me-down markers or none at all. Some students have a parent who can run to Target on a Thursday night to buy their child a piece of posterboard; others have parents who work at night, who don't have the money for extra supplies, whose physical or mental health conditions would prevent them from taking a quick shopping excursion, who are incarcerated, or who left. Instead of prying into the private details of students' lives, we can provide all necessary materials and time in class.

Before addressing student avoidance, make sure you've provided everything they need to succeed, such as the following.

- A clearly articulated *assignment* so students know exactly what they're supposed to do.
- A list of *expectations* so students know exactly what success means.
- Multiple, diverse *exemplars* so students can visualize what success will look like.
- *Strategy instruction* so students know how to achieve success.
- All *resources and materials* necessary for successful completion.
- *Time* in class to complete the work successfully.
- *Feedback* throughout the work process so students know if they're headed toward success.

Finally, some teachers create unnecessary barriers to success. Kalino had a teacher who sometimes required his students to find a short story on Schoology, annotate it in Notability, write responses in Google Docs, download everything and assemble it into a single PDF, and upload that to Schoology. That's a lot of steps for any child, but particularly for one like ours who struggles with executive functioning—and who usually feels too embarrassed to ask for help. There were assignments Kalino never started because ey felt overwhelmed by all the steps that had nothing to do with becoming a better reader and writer. In addition to ensuring access to success, make sure you aren't creating barriers yourself.

We've now used the word *success* a lot. But how we define success depends on our values. Once your students have everything they need to be successful by your standards, you can have a conversation with students who might not be meeting their own standards for success, based on their own values.

Understanding Why Suggestions Don't Help

As teachers, we're used to correcting our students. A student says the capital of Bosnia is Serbia; we say no, it's Sarajevo. A student misses a step in solving an equation; we point out the error and tell her to try again. A student turns in a poorly organized essay; we show them how to outline. Psychologists William Miller and Stephen Rollnick (2013) call such moves the *righting reflex*, or "the desire to fix what seems wrong with people and set them promptly on a better course, relying in particular on directing" (p. 6). Many, if not most, teachers see righting our students—telling them when they're headed down a bad path and suggesting a better one—as essential to our jobs, and the righting reflex often comes from a place of love.

At the same time, the righting reflex often leads to counterproductive behaviors. Miller and Rollnick (2013) explain why:

> Arguments both for and against change already reside within the ambivalent person. The helper's natural reflex is to take up the "good" side of the

> argument, explaining why change is important and advising how to do it . . . . Chances are, however, that the person has already heard the "good" arguments, not only from others but also from a voice within. Ambivalence is a bit like having a committee inside your mind, with members who disagree on the proper course of action. A helper who follows the righting reflex and argues for change is siding with one voice on the person's internal committee . . . . Argue for one side, and the ambivalent person is likely to take up and defend the opposite. This sometimes gets labeled as "denial" or "resistance" or "being oppositional," but there is nothing pathological about such responses . . . . It's just how people normally respond to the righting reflex, to being told what to do and why and how they should do it. (pp. 7–11)

When we tell an ambivalent person what to do, they begin to talk about reasons *not* to do it—and end up convincing themselves not to. Students aren't necessarily ambivalent, though; if there's a correct or best way to do something, they'll often listen to our suggestions rather than waste their time doing it wrong. However, if there is no one correct way and how they proceed is up to them, students might feel caught between acting on their values and doing whatever feels easy, comfortable, or fun.

For example, imagine that Kalino is learning to play the ukulele, and the strings keep buzzing. The teacher says to put eir fingers between the frets. Kalino isn't going to argue; there's a right and a wrong way to position fingers, and ey wants to do it right. But when the teacher suggests practicing more at home, Kalino is ambivalent. The student knows ey'll improve with practice *and* that ey is tired and would rather watch YouTube. The more the teacher encourages Kalino to practice, the more Kalino will say ey doesn't need to—and will end up convincing emself!

The more we try to convince students to do something, even if that something is consistent with their values, the more they'll convince themselves *not* to do it. We ultimately do the very opposite of what we'd set out to do, which was to help students act in accordance with their values so they can live more meaningful and satisfying lives.

There's another problem with suggesting. Every time we tell our students what they should do and why they should do it, we position ourselves as experts on their experience, judges of their actions, and saviors who can rescue them from themselves. Certainly, there are areas in which a teacher's expertise outstrips a student's, but the student's own life is not one of them. And when it comes to judging how well a past or potential action aligns with students' own values, not only are students best positioned to decide, but their empowerment is in the deciding itself.

So if we see (or at least suspect) that our students are avoiding values-consistent actions, but we can't tell them what to do because either they'll convince themselves to do otherwise or we'll take away their power to choose their own actions, how *can* we help?

Evoking Instead of Suggesting

Psychologists Matthieu Villatte, Jennifer Villatte, and Steven Hayes (2016) explain that in order to change their behavior in accordance with their values, people "need to learn to be good observers of their own inner and outer world and, based on what they see, to derive ideas about what would work" (p. 124). Because our goal is to help students develop these skills—of observing their own experiences and deriving ideas about what works for them—our goal becomes "to *evoke* rather than to provide observations" (Villatte et al., 2016, p. 126, emphasis added).

We can help students become better observers of their own experiences and decide what will work best for them by asking questions that help students do the following (Villatte et al., 2016).

- *Describe* their experiences in their own words (as opposed to telling them what's happening).
- *Assess* their actions according to their own values (as opposed to explaining why their actions are a problem).
- *Imagine* possible actions that are more consistent with their own values (as opposed to convincing them).
- *Choose* values-consistent actions for themselves (as opposed to telling them what to choose).

Evoking Description

Asking students to describe their own experiences is harder than it sounds. If you were right there and saw what they did, asking them to describe events you witnessed can feel a little disingenuous. You also know what was supposed to happen or what you wish had happened. You might have trouble asking questions in an open and curious manner when you feel disappointed. Finally, you might doubt students' abilities to describe their actions fully, accurately, and honestly.

As tempting as it might be to express skepticism ("You're telling me you really didn't have enough time?"), fill in details the students missed ("But you had an entire week to fill in your multiplication tables!"), and use an exasperated tone, these approaches substitute *your* observations for students'. If we want to help our students become better observers of their own experiences so they can choose values-consistent actions, we need to ask open-ended questions that help students notice various aspects of their experiences and describe these experiences in their own words.

If a student omits a key detail, instead of pointing it out, try asking what happened before, during, or after an event the student already described. Let's imagine that Jonathan's third-grade teacher knows he had a full week to complete his multiplication table. She might ask, "After you got the table, where did you put it?" If Jonathan describes putting it in his binder, the teacher could then ask, "What did you do at home that night?" As Jonathan describes doing other assignments and activities, he might realize he actually had plenty of time to complete his multiplication table and then be ready to see time use as a values-conscious choice. The teacher already knows that Jonathan had plenty of time, but she's not a prosecutor trying to get to that truth; she's helping Jonathan observe his actions so he can then decide whether they contribute to the life he wants to build.

Whatever questions you ask, use a tone that makes the student feel safe, not threatened. Psychologist Russell Kolts (2016) describes how to "create feelings of safeness and emotional balance" by engaging "in a compassionately collaborative, warm, nonshaming, and encouraging manner" (pp. 20–21). Although he is describing therapeutic relationships, there is no reason to believe the same isn't true for teachers' relationships with their students—in any context, but especially when we're asking them to be vulnerable in a one-to-one conversation about their struggles to enact their values.

Figure 9.1 (page 170) has general questions you can ask to help students describe their actions. These are not the only questions you can ask, and some don't apply to every assignment. Customize the questions to fit your class and voice. For example, instead of asking, "Can you tell me about your process?" Lauren's biology teacher might say, "So Porosoff, what was going on in lab today?" The teacher might even say, "Start at the beginning: you got out your microscope . . . ." In this case, the teacher does mention a particular detail, but that's just to help the student know where to begin so she can then describe her actions in her own words.

We wouldn't advise asking too many questions, as that can overwhelm the student. Pick out two or three questions to ask, and as the student talks about their experience, ask follow-up questions about what happened before and after, what else was happening, who else was there, and other aspects of the context.

Evoking Assessment

When students do something that goes against their own values—not to mention our expectations—we naturally want to understand why. But if we ask a *why* question, such as, "Why haven't you filled out the multiplication table?" or "If you didn't know how to lift weights, why didn't you just ask me to show you?" they'll often say they don't know.

Asking *why* frames the action as a *cause* of some outcome, and students don't always know what outcome they were after. They haven't learned about common sources of reinforcement such as sensory stimulation, attention, status, and escape. Sometimes they say things like, "I was just bored," which tells us they were looking for stimulation, but that might not be the real reason, or it might only be part of the picture. They also know that whatever explanation they give won't be enough. Being bored isn't a good enough reason to disrupt class, being tired isn't a good enough reason to miss a deadline, and being stressed isn't a good enough reason to exclude a group member. Even if they're aware of the problem they were trying to solve, they already know they had a bad solution and feel embarrassed. That embarrassment will make them less likely to open up.

Finally, while some students will have the language to describe how schoolwork makes them feel (*bored, exhausted, frustrated, annoyed, panicked,* and so on), they might not have the language to describe their social needs. A student might offer "I was bored" as an explanation, but how often do they say, "I was

To help the student...	Ask...
Describe the work process	• "How did you get from having nothing at all to the finished product?" • "How did you choose your topic? What other topics did you consider?" • "How did you come up with your ideas?" • "How did you know what the finished product would look like?" • "What strategies did you use to revise?" • "What feedback did you receive?" • "How did you know you were finished?"
Describe group dynamics	• "How did your group decide how to approach the work?" • "What was each person's role in the group?"
Describe self-organization	• "What happened when you first received the assignment?" • "What was your plan for working on this?" • "How have you used your time? Which parts did you spend the most time on?" • "Can you tell me about your routine when you come home from school?" • "Can you tell me about the space where you do schoolwork?"
Add details	• "What happened right before _____?" • "What happened right after _____?" • "What happened in between _____ and _____?" • "What else was happening in the room when _____?" • "Who else was there when _____?" • "What similar assignments have you done before? How was this one different?" • "How do you think [a classmate or family member] would describe _____?" • "A month from now, when you think back on this, which parts will you remember?"

Figure 9.1: Questions to help students describe their actions in their own words.

lonely," "I was desperate for connection," "I just wanted to feel seen," or the like? As bad as academic inadequacy feels, social inadequacy can feel even worse. Many students aren't used to talking about it and don't have the language to name it. Merely *noticing* it, let alone naming it, might invoke way too much vulnerability.

Instead of asking about the causes of their actions, ask an open-ended question about the effects. For example, Jonathan's Russian teacher might have asked how avoiding learning the Cyrillic alphabet affected his work quality, the amount of time he spends on assignments (and therefore the amount of time he can devote to other pursuits), and his relationships with classmates who do know the Cyrillic alphabet (and therefore might be picking up his slack in group work). Asking how students' actions affected their learning, work, relationships, and out-of-school endeavors helps them assess whether their actions contribute to the kind of life they want for themselves.

Beyond asking about these external effects, you can ask about internal effects of students' actions. What thoughts, emotions, and physical sensations did they experience before, during, and after their avoidance move? For example, the Russian teacher could ask Jonathan how he feels in his body when he sees Cyrillic letters, what emotions come up, and what thoughts he has about them and about himself. Avoiding an action (such as studying) is often a way to avoid unwanted thoughts, emotions, and physical sensations (Hayes et al., 2012).

Other types of helpful questions elicit comparisons between what actually happened and what might have happened, and perspective taking so the student might notice features they wouldn't have otherwise noticed (Villatte et al., 2016). Imagine the Russian teacher had asked Jonathan how the student who sits next to him might feel when Jonathan asks her for answers, or how his grandmother would see his work. In addition to asking about other people's perspectives, you can ask the student to imagine other versions of themselves. If Jonathan imagines his college self, or his adult self in the workplace, why will that future Jonathan be glad he learned the Cyrillic alphabet now? Perspective taking helps students get outside themselves and their immediate surroundings so they see more impacts of their actions (McHugh et al., 2019; Villatte et al., 2016). From there, they might be more willing and able to imagine other actions they could take.

Figure 9.2 (page 172) has general questions that help students identify external and internal effects of their actions, compare their actions to ones they could have taken, and take other perspectives on their actions—all so they can assess those actions according to their own values.

Evoking Imagination

Just as it can be hard not to tell students what *did* happen, it can be hard not to tell them what *should* happen. But again, the goal here is for students to discover for themselves what *could* happen that would be more consistent with their values. If you see a student running toward self-destruction, you always have the power to tell them *no*, *stop*, *don't do that*, or *do something else*. But again, telling your students what to do can get them to argue why they should not do the thing you're suggesting and end up convincing themselves (Miller & Rollnick, 2013). Also, the more you tell your students what to do, the fewer opportunities they have to imagine new possibilities for themselves. Figure 9.3 (page 173) has questions you can ask students to help them imagine actions that are more consistent with their own values.

Evoking Choice

At this point in the conversation, you might see a clear next step for students to take. But the goal is for students to choose a next step that feels meaningful and important to them. Specifying what they'll

To help the student...	Ask...
Identify external effects	• "How did your actions affect your relationship with [*a classmate*]?" • "How did your actions affect your learning?" • "How did your actions affect your work?" • "Did your actions affect any other parts of your life?"
Identify internal effects	• "What did you feel in your body when _____?" • "What emotions came up when _____?" • "What thoughts were you having when _____?" • "How do you feel about yourself as a result of the work you did?"
Make comparisons	• "If you could do this assignment over, what, if anything, would you do differently?" • "What would you do the same?"
Take other perspectives	• "What do you think [*a classmate or group member*] was feeling when _____?" • "When you picture yourself in five years, how will that future you feel about this?" • "How would [*someone they care about*] see your work product?" • "How would [*someone they care about*] see your work process?"

Figure 9.2: Questions to help students assess their actions according to their own values.

do, when, what happens next if they succeed, what else they can try if they fail, and how other people can provide support helps students stay committed—not just to the action itself, but to the values underneath that action (Hayes et al., 2012). Figure 9.4 (page 174) has open-ended questions you can ask to help students choose values-consistent actions.

Using More Strategies to Shape Values-Based Behavior Change

So far, we've focused on how to use open-ended questions to evoke describing, assessing, imagining, and choosing actions. According to Miller and Rollnick (2013), open-ended questions are only one strategy to guide people toward values-based behavior change. Other strategies include *affirmations*, which make the person feel good about acting on their values; *reflections*, which help people clarify what serves their values; and *summaries*, which help the person feel heard so the conversation can move forward (Miller & Rollnick, 2013). Let's look at each of these strategies in a bit more depth.

To help the student...	Ask...
Identify qualities of their work experiences	• "What do you want the experience of working to be like?" • "How could you have made this work more interesting for yourself?" • "How could you have made this work more challenging for yourself?" • "What kinds of experiences does [*someone they care about*] want for you?"
Identify qualities of their work products	• "What do you want your finished work to be like?" • "How could you have made the result of this work more satisfying for yourself?" • "What does [*someone they care about*] want the result of your work to be like?"
Identify qualities of their working relationships	• "Who do you want to be as a classmate?" • "What role do you want to have in future groups or partnerships?" • "What experience do you want other people to have when they work with you?"
Consider next steps	• "What might you try next time you have a similar assignment?" • "What are some specific action steps you can take in the next few days or weeks?" • "What might happen if you don't do that?" • "What might happen if you do?" • "How would doing this be a part of the life you want to build for yourself?" • "What else could you try doing?" • "What would [*someone they care about*] think of these options?" • "How do you feel about yourself as a result of exploring these possibilities?"

Figure 9.3: Questions to help students imagine actions that are more consistent with their values.

Affirming Positive Steps

Acting on our values makes life meaningful and satisfying in the long term, but in the short term, it can be difficult and even painful. You can think of affirmations as a kind of down payment. Students receive some positive feelings now, so when they inevitably struggle later, remembering those positive feelings might help them keep up the effort. Saying things like, "I'm so excited that I get to teach you how to lift weights," "I can't wait to see your finished multiplication table," or just smiling as students describe their next steps can help them feel some of the satisfaction of enacting their values in advance. Even telling them, "I'm so glad we're having this conversation," helps them feel proud of the work they're doing. Eventually, the struggle itself might start to feel satisfying (if not exactly good), because students will know it's part of what it means to live a meaningful life.

To help the student...	Ask...
Choose an action	• "What's your first step?" • "What do you feel in your body as you imagine yourself taking this step?" • "What emotions do you notice?" • "What thoughts or questions are coming up?"
Specify an action	• "When do you plan to start?" • "Do you need to set an alert so you remember to do it?" • "What will it look like when you do it?"
Plan for contingencies	• "How confident are you that you can do this?" • "How confident are you that you will do this?" • "What will be hard about this?" • "Why is it still worthwhile?" • "How will you know whether this is working out the way you want it to?" • "If it works out, what will you do next?" • "If it doesn't work out, what else could you try?" • "Regardless of whether it works out, what might you learn from trying this?"
Identify sources of support	• "How can I support you?" • "Who else can support you? How?"

Figure 9.4: Questions to help students choose values-consistent actions.

Reflecting Back Values

Throughout the conversation, reflect back to students what seems important to them. They might mention a value explicitly, in which case you can simply say it back: "I heard you say you were trying to work carefully, and it seems like that's important to you." More often, you'll need to make explicit what students implied. In that case, try your best not to sound presumptuous, as if you know students' values better than they do. Instead, point out a pattern, make it clear that you're inferring a value from that pattern, and ask them to confirm whether you're right: "*I noticed* that you color-code your notes, make an outline, and then check back to see if there were topics you missed. *It sounds like* you're very thorough. *Would you say* thoroughness is important to you?"

You might also pick up on certain emotions and help students derive their values from them. For example, as Jonathan described the football coach yelling and lecturing, and the football team hogging the equipment, his wrestling coach could say, "That sounds really frustrating. Am I right that you felt frustrated?" If Jonathan says yes, the coach could say, "Usually, frustration tells us we're not getting something that matters to us. It seems like what matters to you is having a fair system for sharing the weights and a peaceful environment to work out in. Does that sound about right?" If Jonathan agrees, both he and his coach now know that fairness and peacefulness are some of his values in this context.

If at any point students tell you your assumption was incorrect, just thank them for clarifying and move on. Jonathan might say something like, "I don't necessarily need peace and quiet—I just want it to be fair." The coach could then say, "Got it. Thanks. So let's focus on fairness. What would be different for you if there were a fair system for sharing the weights?" The coach might think peacefulness truly is one of Jonathan's values, but he shouldn't push. Students will come to their own values when they're ready.

Summarizing What Has Been Said

Recall that your open-ended questions follow a sequence: you're getting students to (1) describe their actions, (2) then assess those actions, (3) then imagine new actions, and (4) then choose an action to try. When it seems like students are ready to move forward to the next stage of the conversation—from describing to assessing their actions, from assessing their past actions to imagining new ones, and from imagining possible actions to choosing what they'll actually do—you can summarize what they have said so far. When students hear your summary, they'll know you heard them. They'll also have a chance to repeat any key details you missed and add any details they left out. A summary is also another opportunity for you to amplify what seems important to students (Miller & Rollnick, 2013) so they can enact their values.

Making Time for One-to-One Conversations

At this point, you might be thinking that these conversations sound great, but when will I ever have time for them? These strategies come from therapeutic models, and therapists have fifty glorious minutes with a single person. How can teachers possibly have such in-depth conversations with students when class periods are barely long enough as it is and two or three dozen other students are in the room clamoring for attention?

We wish we could increase school funding so there could be smaller classes, more support professionals in the building, and larger classrooms with little nooks for meeting with students (not to mention more windows, books, art supplies, and snacks). We wish we could decrease the number of classes we teach so we have more time to meet with students outside class (not to mention prepare for classes, assess student work, meet with colleagues, and engage in professional learning). We'll keep arguing for equitable systemic changes necessary for healthy learning, working, and living.

In the meantime, are there recesses, study periods, or lunch periods when you can meet with students? Can you pull a student aside for a few minutes while other students are working? Can you structure learning so it's inquiry driven and project based, and the rest of your students therefore have plenty to do on their own or in groups while you talk to one student? Could this conversation be part of a family conference or IEP meeting? Could you get out of a faculty meeting to have this conversation with a student? Does it have to be you who has this conversation, or can you read this chapter with a group of colleagues so you're all prepared to have empowering conversations with students? So much of good teaching is doing what we can with what we have.

From Students to Families

This chapter has been about how to have conversations with students who, for one reason or another, are struggling to live by their values. In the next chapter, we'll see how to have conversations with students' families so they're equipped to support their children as they strive to live by their values.

Chapter 10

• • • • •

INVITING FAMILIES INTO CONVERSATIONS ABOUT STUDENT VALUES

Social-emotional learning is an ongoing process, integral to everything students do at school and beyond. As teachers, we have a role in helping our students learn how to clarify and commit to their values, but ultimately, that learning is the student's ongoing work to do.

Even if you know a student very well and develop a close relationship with them, and even if you teach a student for multiple years, their family members usually know them better and have a longer-lasting relationship with them. This chapter is about how to collaborate with parents, guardians, and caregivers in empowering students to become the people they want to be—and to extend that empowerment beyond any one time or place.

Choosing Language to Describe EMPOWER

Some parents resist the very idea of SEL in school. They see school as a place for academic learning, some art and athletics, and perhaps an occasional school-sponsored social event such as a movie night or dance—but learning about relationships? Emotions? Identity? Values? Many parents and caregivers see these topics as exclusively belonging in the home, or perhaps religious and cultural institutions, but not school.

EMPOWER is not about instilling any particular set of values; it's about helping students clarify their values and helping them bring those values to their learning, work, and relationships. Despite that fact, as soon as parents hear the word *values*, some will think you're trying to indoctrinate their children.

If you think the V word will be a distraction—as it often is—don't use it. Talk about *making school meaningful*. Talk about *empowering students*. Talk about *cultivating intrinsic motivation* and *developing the willingness to do what matters*. Parents might not be as put off by words naming the elements of

EMPOWER—exploration, motivation, participation, openness, willingness, empathy, and resilience—as they are by the word *values*.

When you describe EMPOWER activities and strategies to families, use your judgment and talk to your colleagues about your word choices so the message gets across: this work is about empowering students to discover the qualities they want to bring to their actions and interactions at school, so that school becomes a source of meaning, vitality, and community in their lives—and so they can choose to become the people they most want to be. We haven't encountered many parents who don't want that kind of life for their children.

Helping Families Extend EMPOWER Activities at Home

Part I of this book contains twenty-eight different EMPOWER activities designed so students can discover the values they want to live by and bring those values to different parts of their lives. But after the activity ends, you don't know what students will do. Some might keep commitments they made and seek out more ways to live by their values; others might leave the room having done just another activity at school. Parents and caregivers are in an ideal position to help students carry EMPOWER work forward.

If the activity is sufficiently simple—it has few steps, takes a short amount of time, and requires materials families are likely to have on hand—you can send parents and caregivers the instructions and suggest they try the activity themselves. That way, they're equipped to discuss the experience with their child. What did each of them discover in the process of doing the activity? What implications does that learning have for how they might approach different aspects of their lives—at home, at work or school, during the week and on weekends, now and in the future? What commitments might they make? How can they help each other keep those commitments?

Figure 10.1 has a sample letter to family members inviting them to try an EMPOWER activity. It describes the Our Values in Action activity from chapter 1 (page 22). We didn't use the word *values* because we wanted to demonstrate how it's possible to leave out the word but still describe the work. That doesn't mean you should avoid the word—only that you can leave it out if the word will be more distracting than helpful.

If the activity is too long or complex to explain to parents, let alone to ask them to do it on their own, you could summarize the activity and share reflection questions you asked at the end or didn't get a chance to ask. That way, parents are equipped to continue the conversation at home with their children.

Figure 10.2 (page 180) has a sample letter that summarizes an EMPOWER activity for family members and invites them to continue the discussion at home. It describes the Values Concept Photos activity, also from chapter 1 (page 20). This letter does use the word *values*. Again, use your judgment about how to communicate with your students' families.

If you have the time, interest, and funding, you could host evening sessions in which parents engage in the same EMPOWER activities that their children recently did at school. Parents and caregivers can have the

> Dear families,
>
> Today in class, students did an activity to help them imagine positive, meaningful actions that could make school more fulfilling. I'm writing to tell you about the activity and invite you to try a version of it for yourself.
>
> First, students listed ways they could complete the sentence, *As part of my work at school, I . . . .* Then, they received a list of qualities of action that make our lives meaningful. Students chose one quality to explore in greater depth.
>
> Next, the students turned each statement on their lists into a question: How can I be [*the quality they chose*] when I...? For example, a student who chose the quality *generous* might turn the statement "As part of my work at school, I write essays" into the question "How can I be generous when I write essays?" They kept most of their questions private but were given the option to share one, and from these shared questions, the class chose a few to discuss in small groups.
>
> Just as your child did, try spending a few minutes completing the sentence, *As part of being a parent, I . . . .* Then, choose a quality that feels important to you, and turn your statements into questions: How can I be [*the quality you choose*] when I...?
>
> If you made a list of questions, you might wish to share some of them with them and ask your child to share what they wrote with you. It might be interesting to hear which positive quality your child chose (and for them to hear which positive quality you chose) and to look for points of connection between your responses. Regardless of whether you try the activity yourself, I hope you'll ask your child about it—and that you'll ask me any questions you have. Most of all, I hope we'll work together to help your child bring the qualities they find most important to their work at school, so school becomes a source of meaning and vitality in their lives.
>
> Take good care,
>
> *Ms. Porosoff*

Figure 10.1: Sample letter inviting family members to try an EMPOWER activity.

same discussions with one another that students had with their peers, which can be a great way to deepen community. Then, when parents go home, they and their children can discuss how the activity made them feel, what they might do as a result, and how they can support one another in acting on their values.

If you plan programming for parents and caregivers, consider their diverse needs.

- When should the activities occur?
- Should they be in person, virtual, or hybrid?
- In what language should they be delivered?
- Should parents and guardians be grouped based on their children's classes or based on their own interests, identifiers, and needs?

> Dear families,
>
> Today in class, students took photos of people, places, and objects that represent a particular value. I'm writing in the hope that knowing more about the activity might help you have a discussion about it with your child.
>
> First, students received a list of values (see attached), which we defined as qualities of action that make our lives meaningful. Students chose one value to explore in greater depth.
>
> Next, after we discussed how photos of people, places, and objects can represent a particular idea, students took photos that represent their selected values. Their photos could include the following.
>
> - People putting their selected value into action
> - Places that make it easier for people to enact the value
> - Things that symbolize living by the value
>
> Finally, students took turns explaining their photos in small groups, and our class had a great discussion about how different people think about the same values in different ways.
>
> I hope you'll ask your child to show you their photos. You might ask them why they chose that particular value; which photo is their favorite; how they found people, places, and objects to represent the value; and how (if at all) this assignment expanded their thinking about the value. If it feels right for your family, you could even ask your child if they'd like to take more photos at home or in your community to represent that same value, or another value that feels important to them.
>
> Please be in touch with any questions or concerns you have about the activity itself or that come up in your discussion with your child.
>
> Take good care,
>
> *Ms. Porosoff*

Figure 10.2: Sample letter summarizing an EMPOWER activity and inviting families to continue the discussion at home.

There are no right or wrong answers to these questions; what's important is to consider them in designing an SEL curriculum for adults that builds their capacity to continue that work with their children.

Bringing Families Into Conversations About Student Avoidance

Everyone avoids living by their values sometimes, and many instances of student avoidance are, quite literally, nothing to write home about. But if a student's avoidance rises to a level that you're taking time to talk with them about it, their parents need to know about that conversation. Parents, guardians, and caregivers can also help you understand the context around their child's avoidance and support the student in staying committed to the values-consistent behaviors they identified during their conversation with you.

As we mentioned, when Jonathan took Russian civilization in high school, he didn't try to learn the Cyrillic alphabet. His teacher never talked to him about it—perhaps because the teacher never noticed, or perhaps because Jonathan was successful in the course according to the teacher's definition. That is, Jonathan came to class, contributed to discussions, handed in his work, and got good grades. But let's imagine that the teacher did notice Jonathan's avoidance and talked to him about it. Jonathan might have revealed that he always loved history and wanted the opportunity to study it in greater depth. Learning about Russian history matters to Jonathan. Learning the Cyrillic alphabet? Not so much.

At that point, some teachers would express disappointment, explain why it's important for the student to engage in that aspect of the course, and maybe make it impossible for the student to get an A. Any communication with the family would likely just inform them of what's happening—perhaps in an attempt to enlist their help in getting the student to do the work, or perhaps to preempt any complaints about the student's eventual grade.

But imagine that instead, the teacher reaches out to Jonathan's parents to tell them about the conversation and find out if they can add any information. Figure 10.3 is a letter that the Russian civilization teacher could have sent to Jonathan's parents.

Dear Mr. and Mrs. Weinstein,

I hope you're doing well. I am Jonathan's teacher for Russian civilization, and he's doing very well in the class. He comes to class on time and prepared, contributes powerful insights to discussions, turns in his work, and does well on tests. He's clearly very interested in history, and I'd be surprised if his eventual path doesn't involve history in some way.

Precisely because he does so well in class and seems so engaged, I was surprised to discover that Jonathan is not learning the Russian language, which is a key element of this course. I talked to him in an attempt to discover how he might find the language part of the class more meaningful. During our conversation, Jonathan told me that he loves history and was looking for more challenging material. He said the language was less of a draw.

Most students will find some parts of a course more interesting than others. Nevertheless, I was wondering if you'd be willing to set up a time when we can talk about Jonathan's previous experiences learning languages and any other experiences you think might be relevant to helping him find the motivation to learn Russian and make his experience of this class as meaningful and satisfying as it can be for him.

I look forward to hearing from you soon.

Thank you,

Dr. T

Figure 10.3: Sample letter to a family about their child's avoidance.

In the ensuing conversation with Jonathan's parents, the teacher might learn he'd taken and enjoyed French classes and that he'd attended Hebrew school as a child but remembers very little. The teacher decides to ask Jonathan what he found satisfying and dissatisfying about studying these other languages and how satisfied he feels with his knowledge of these languages now.

Maybe Jonathan's parents also share that their ancestors came from Eastern Europe and that even though they weren't directly involved in events the class is studying, those events had an impact on their lives and ultimately on the lives of their descendants, including Jonathan. The teacher realizes he can ask Jonathan perspective-taking questions, such as, "How do you think your ancestors would feel if they knew their great-great-grandson had religious freedom yet chose to master the language of their oppressors?" With the answers to some of these questions in mind, Jonathan could work with his teacher to imagine possible actions and choose one to try.

This story might sound very specific to Jonathan's situation—and that's exactly the point. Every behavior occurs in a context that includes not only the particular teacher, class, and assignment but also the student's family, friends, other classes, extracurricular activities, learning history, cultural background, and values. Jonathan's avoidance move—his not learning the Cyrillic alphabet—occurred in a context. It was different from the context in which Lauren avoided reading for her tenth-grade English class, the context in which Kalino avoided turning in artwork ey'd completed, the context in which Jason avoids speech therapy, and the context in which any student makes any avoidance move.

Back in chapter 9 (page 161), we discussed using open-ended questions to help avoidant students (1) describe their experiences, (2) assess their actions according to their values, (3) imagine other possible actions, and (4) choose a values-consistent action to try. The imagined letter from Jonathan's Russian civilization teacher to his parents in figure 10.3 (page 181) would have occurred after Jonathan described his experiences and assessed his actions according to his values, but before he imagined other possible actions and chose one to try. In asking the parents to describe Jonathan's experiences more fully, the teacher is attempting to gather information that might help him decide what questions to ask Jonathan in the next stage of their conversation.

Depending on when we communicate with families, we can ask them to do the following.

- Fill in details about their child's experiences in the past and present.
- Assess the extent to which their child's actions match values they've developed over time.
- Share which possible actions sound most feasible, given the student's track record, current life situation, and resources.
- Support their child in taking the values-consistent action they chose.

Regardless of when you communicate with parents, that message should serve mostly as an update. What did the student do (or avoid doing) to prompt your attention? What conversations have you had with the student so far? What is the student's plan? What is your plan for supporting the student? These plans might just be waiting and watching or having another conversation, or the plan might include the student taking a specific values-consistent action step and you helping them take it. In that case, you can ask the family to help at home and give them an easy strategy to use, but don't demand additional labor from them or expect them to change their children's behavior. Values-consistent behavior is, by definition, a choice.

Bringing Families Into Conversations About Student Success

Sometimes a parent's or caregiver's definition of success is very different from the teacher's. These adults learned certain skills—how to diagram a sentence, write in cursive, tell time on an analog clock, tie shoelaces, balance a checkbook, touch type—that they see as easy and fundamental, and their children can't do them. Their method for doing division looks nothing like the method their children use. They read certain books in school, and it would be a travesty for their children not to read those same ones. Responding to such complaints can take a lot of time and energy, yet they're often how families express their definitions of success—and their anxiety that their children might not achieve it.

If there's more than one parent or caregiver in the picture, their definitions of success often differ from each other. Our son Jason has various special needs, and for Lauren, his success in school would mean making friends, learning the pragmatic language to express his needs, keeping himself physically safe, fully understanding the concept of consent, liking himself, and one day having the skills to get and keep a job. Jonathan wants all of that too, but also wants Jason to read fluently. For Jason's teachers, success means achieving the goals on Jason's IEP, which mostly describes reading and mathematical skills, along with activities of daily living.

The one person whose definition of success has never figured into any formal or informal conference with Jason's teachers or district representatives is Jason himself. Our typical-developing child, Kalino, has the same experience, and when we were students, so did we. Amid arguments about what students should learn, how they should learn it, and how we should define successful learning, we can easily lose sight of the students themselves.

Just as our definitions of success can exist alongside a student's own definition, a family member's definition of success can exist alongside both. In communicating with families, we don't have to convince them to adopt our definitions of success; we can articulate our definitions of success, encourage them to articulate theirs, and validate both. However, if we're looking to empower students to live by their values, then our communications with families will focus on what matters *to the student*. At that point, our shared goal becomes amplifying any feelings of satisfaction that arise when students do work they find meaningful. The following sections look at four ways families can do that.

1. Seeing the student's work
2. Connecting with the student's ideas
3. Discovering the student's process
4. Extending the student's learning

Seeing the Student's Work: Look At . . .

Just as it's difficult for us as teachers to suspend our judgment and just *see* a student's work, the same is true for family members. Whenever we send work home, we alert parents and caregivers so they know to ask about it and encourage them to spend a few minutes just looking at it and telling the student what they see. When they first look at the work, what do they notice? Which details stand out? When they look again, what *else* do they notice? By taking the time to look and look again, the parent or caregiver devotes their most precious resource—attention—to their child.

For example, our son Jason brought home an informational comic he made about bats. We could easily take note of his spelling errors and graphomotor weaknesses, and the fact that he's a fourth grader who reads at a first-grade level, but instead of seeing deficits as measured according to various extrinsic definitions of success, we can *see* Jason's work. "Look at how you drew the bats sleeping upside-down." "Look at how this bat is flapping its wings, and this other bat has its wings spread." "Look at the little bug the bat is eating" (to which Jason replied, "You mean *insect*"). Parents can learn to see their child's work for what it is, and through that work, they can better see who their child is.

Connecting With the Student's Ideas: This Makes Me Think Of . . .

After taking time to see their child's work, parents and caregivers can find ways to connect with their child's ideas. Jason's bat drawing reminded us of times when we've seen bats, and we had a lively conversation about bats we saw on vacation and at the zoo. We talked about movies with bat characters and remembered books we read as children in which bats featured prominently. Kalino's work has also sparked many lively conversations about topics ey studied—whether we were arguing about how to address fat shaming in a short story ey read, guessing the translations of words on eir Latin quiz, or belting out a soundtrack about a certain historical figure after reading eir Lafayette report (to which Kalino replied, "Mom, you're so cringey!").

Parents and caregivers connect with their child's ideas—and by extension, with their child—by noticing and naming any associations or memories that come to mind as they look at their child's work. If the topic is unfamiliar (as many topics are, especially as students advance in their learning, or if there are linguistic or cultural differences between home and school), parents and caregivers can ask questions—not to test their children's knowledge but to show genuine curiosity and appreciate their children's expertise.

Discovering the Student's Process: How Did You . . . ?

After students complete any piece of work, it's helpful for them to reflect on what they did so they can evaluate which actions led them to be successful. Parents and caregivers can ask questions to raise their child's awareness of their work process and discover which actions were effective, which weren't, and what they might try next time. For example, we might ask Jason why he chose to study bats, how he made his bat comic, and what materials he used. Such questions can help students notice the extent to which their work process matched their values so they can choose similar or different actions next time.

Although we can—and should—ask these questions at school, families can encourage further and deeper reflection at home.

Extending the Student's Learning: Let's . . .

Typically, when a unit ends, we move on to another course topic. After the bat unit, Jason read about weather events, then fire safety, then winter holidays. Reading about a variety of topics is important at school, but at home, we, as Jason's parents, could encourage his interests in bats. We could find books about bats at the library, visit the nocturnal animals exhibit at the zoo, go on a nighttime hike at the nature preserve, and look for movies about bats. If educating a student is like lighting a fire, their families can continue to feed those flames long after the unit, and even the year, is over.

Some parents or caregivers will ask a student how their day was, what they're learning about in school, and what they're working on, but students aren't always forthcoming about the details of school (if they even remember by the time they get home). Some families regularly check their child's schoolwork, but many don't, especially as students get older and more autonomous. Even families who regularly talk about school and look at schoolwork together don't necessarily have conversations about how the student can bring their own values to that work.

At the end of any unit, you can inform families about work their children recently completed and offer them some prompts to help them look at their child's work, connect with their child's ideas, discover their child's processes, and extend their child's learning. Figure 10.4 (page 186) has a sample letter to families after a unit. Empowering parents and caregivers to have meaningful conversations about learning ultimately empowers the student to make their learning meaningful.

Understanding the Qualities of Empowering School-to-Home Communications

Many school-to-home communications are transactional. A teacher or administrator shares information about a past or upcoming event—a lesson, assignment, unit, program, or student behavior—and requests that the parent or caregiver do something. "The winter coat drive begins this Monday. Please drop gently used coats into the collection bins by the front entrance." Or, "Our class will be making maps out of recycled materials. Please send in your empty cereal boxes, magazines, and paper towel rolls by February 9." Or, "Kalino was marked absent from first period biology class on Tuesday. Please let me know if there was a valid reason for this absence."

Empowering school-to-home communications still share information with families and make requests of them, but they frame everything in terms of helping students clarify and commit to their own values. Throughout this chapter, you've seen various example letters to families. While these letters are about different events, they all have the following functions.

> Dear English 6 families,
>
> Today was the last day of our Food Essay unit. First, we read several different essays that connected food stories to the authors' cultural identities. Then, we wrote about our own food memories, connected these to our identities, and found recipes to accompany our essays.
>
> I'm looking forward to reading the essays. In the meantime, I encourage you to ask your child if you can read it, too. Here are some questions that might help you respond.
>
> - *What images or details stand out to you?* Making observations helps your child know you take their work seriously and want to engage with the ideas in it.
>
> - *What does the essay make you think about or remember?* Do you have any similar stories you can tell? How does your identity inform some of those experiences? These might be meaningful conversations, and they'll show your child their work has an impact.
>
> - *What questions do you have about your child's writing process?* You might ask about certain parts of the process (choosing a topic, generating ideas, organizing the essay, or revising), or you could just ask what they did to get from having nothing at all to having a finished essay. Talking about the writing process will help your child notice what's working for them and continue to grow.
>
> - *What might you do as a family to continue your child's learning?* For example, could you make the recipe together? What other activities does the essay inspire you to try? What places might you visit? What movies or shows might you watch? Even though our unit is over, your child can continue to understand how their food experiences connect to their identities.
>
> After I read the essays, I will post my feedback. Remember that all feedback is in one document so your child can notice patterns.
>
> Please reach out at any time with questions. I'd also love to hear about any conversations you had at home.
>
> Thank you, and take good care.
>
> *Ms. Porosoff*

Figure 10.4: Sample letter to families after a unit.

- **Tell families what's happening:** This could be about a unit, lesson, project, discussion, set of behaviors, or other event that students would benefit from their family understanding. Building families' awareness positions them to support their children.

- **Relate the event to what matters to students:** How can students use this experience to understand themselves and enact their values? What's at stake for them? Although you and the family will undoubtedly have your own goals, you're also centering students' experiences and values.

- **Ask families to continue the learning:** While teachers are the education experts, the parent or caregiver is the expert about their child. Honoring that expertise, and remembering that there's so much you *don't* know about your students' homes and family relationships, can help you show you care about making students' learning meaningful without imposing on families.

- **Coach families on specific strategies they can use:** Suggest what parents or caregivers *can* or *might* do, not what they *must* or *should* do. You're defining a role for the parent in this particular learning experience and showing you want to support them.

- **Encourage further collaboration:** You might ask for feedback, concerns, and questions, or you might invite the parent or caregiver to meet with you to show a genuine interest in a relationship with that person.

Taken together, these elements keep the communication's focus on students when inviting families into a collaborative partnership. The shared goal becomes about empowering students to turn school into a source of meaning, vitality, and community by bringing their values to their actions.

From Families to Lifelong Empowerment

This chapter was about how to start meaningful conversations with families so they can continue to empower their children, even after you're no longer their teacher. We started this book with an assumption: the goal of SEL—and really all learning—is to empower students to do meaningful work, develop meaningful relationships, and live meaningful lives. With support from their teachers, families, and communities, students get to define *meaningful* for themselves. SEL, like all learning and like any values-consistent action, is lifelong.

Epologue

• • • • •

MAKING THE PROCESS THE OUTCOME

You've now read about EMPOWER, an approach to SEL that helps students bring their own values to their lives. You've discovered activities, tools, and strategies that help students discover what matters to them, choose to do what matters, and accept the struggle inherent in doing what matters.

At school, we tend to focus on outcomes. Lesson objectives may begin with the words *students will be able to*, and assessments make students' resulting knowledge and skills observable. Of course, it matters what students *will* be able to do as a result of engaging in lessons and assignments. But surely it also matters what students' lives are like *now*—their psychological experience of school in the present moment.

An often-repeated line from a foundational text in contextual psychology, the body of science that informs this book, is that in mental health, the "outcome is the process through which process becomes the outcome" (Hayes, Strosahl, & Wilson, 1999, p. 219). When people see a mental health provider, they often see the desired outcome as feeling better, but the outcome can be the ongoing process of living a meaningful life.

EMPOWER can become the process by which doing school—reading books, having discussions, solving equations, writing essays, conducting experiments, making friends, making art, playing sports, walking down the hallway—becomes a series of opportunities for students to clarify and commit to their values. The process of living a values-guided life becomes the outcome of school itself.

So let's teach students how to notice, name, affirm, honor, and learn from their own emotions, so that instead of teaching them that only calm and happiness are "good" emotional states while all others need to be changed or managed, we honor the full range of emotions as expressions of our common humanity, and we use emotional experiences as opportunities to discover the values underneath.

Let's dedicate time to values exploration and committed action, and let's *also* embed values work into all aspects of learning. Let's turn everything students do at school—including their lessons, assignments, and projects—into opportunities for them to live meaningful lives.

And let's not pretend that SEL, all by itself, can end human suffering and oppression or guarantee human flourishing and liberation. In addition to SEL, students also need sociopolitical learning, multicultural learning, civic learning, artistic learning, physiological learning, and learning in every domain of their lives.

So let's build values-based programs, policies, and practices that enable everyone to contribute meaningfully to the community and benefit from it. Let's make sure our schools become empowering places that truly belong to everyone, where everyone truly belongs.

Appendix

• • • • •

REPRODUCIBLES

Values aren't things; they're qualities people can choose to bring to their actions in a variety of situations. As chosen qualities, our values tell us how we want to *be* in our lives. They might tell us how we want to be in a particular class, how we want to be when we do a particular assignment, how we want to be in our relationships with other people—and more broadly, how we want to *be*, in and beyond school.

Examples of Values

The following list has examples of values: qualities of action that make life meaningful for some people. Which qualities are especially important to you?

Active	Enthusiastic	Intentional	Reasonable
Adventurous	Expressive	Kind	Resourceful
Ambitious	Fair	Knowledgeable	Respectful
Authentic	Flexible	Loyal	Responsible
Bold	Generous	Modest	Reverent
Careful	Graceful	Open-minded	Serious
Compassionate	Grateful	Organized	Skillful
Considerate	Honest	Patient	Spiritual
Cooperative	Honorable	Peaceful	Steady
Courageous	Hopeful	Perceptive	Supportive
Creative	Humble	Persistent	Thorough
Curious	Humorous	Playful	Traditional
Decisive	Imaginative	Practical	Trustworthy
Diligent	Inclusive	Precise	Warm
Efficient	Independent	Productive	Wise

Values and Questions Cards

We recommend printing the cards on two different colors of cardstock to make it easier to tell the decks apart and laminating them for durability. If possible, make enough decks so each group of four or five students has its own. If students can shuffle and deal the cards themselves, the activity will feel less teacher-directed—but making more decks is more work for you.

Values Cards—Backs

VALUES	VALUES	VALUES
VALUES	VALUES	VALUES
VALUES	VALUES	VALUES
VALUES	VALUES	VALUES
VALUES	VALUES	VALUES

Values Cards One

active	careful	creative
adventurous	compassionate	curious
ambitious	considerate	decisive
authentic	cooperative	diligent
bold	courageous	efficient

EMPOWER Moves for Social-Emotional Learning © 2023 Solution Tree Press
SolutionTree.com • Visit **go.SolutionTree.com/SEL** to download this free reproducible.

Values Cards Two

enthusiastic	graceful	humble
expressive	grateful	humorous
fair	honest	imaginative
flexible	honorable	inclusive
generous	hopeful	independent

Values Cards Three

intentional	open-minded	persistent
kind	organized	playful
knowledgeable	patient	practical
loyal	peaceful	precise
modest	perceptive	productive

Values Cards Four

reasonable	serious	thorough
resourceful	skillful	traditional
respectful	spiritual	trustworthy
responsible	steady	warm
reverent	supportive	wise

Questions Cards—Backs

QUESTIONS	QUESTIONS	QUESTIONS
QUESTIONS	QUESTIONS	QUESTIONS
QUESTIONS	QUESTIONS	QUESTIONS
QUESTIONS	QUESTIONS	QUESTIONS
QUESTIONS	QUESTIONS	QUESTIONS

EMPOWER Moves for Social-Emotional Learning © 2023 Solution Tree Press
SolutionTree.com • Visit **go.SolutionTree.com/SEL** to download this free reproducible.

Questions Cards One

When were you _____ today?	What's your least favorite part of a typical week? How can you use that part of your week as an opportunity to practice being _____?	How does technology help you be more _____, and how does it get in the way?
When can you be _____ tomorrow?	Where can you be especially _____? What about that place helps you be that way?	How can you be _____ in virtual iterations?
When is it easiest to be _____, and when is it hardest?	When did you fail to be _____, and what can you learn from that failure?	Do other people judge you, positively or negatively, for how _____ you are?
When does being _____ exhaust you, and when does it energize you?	When did you succeed at being _____, and what can you learn from that success?	Do you ever judge yourself, positively or negatively, for how _____ you are?
If you could be your most _____ self for one whole day, what would that look like?	When you have trouble being _____, what do you do?	How important is it to you to be _____?

Questions Cards Two

Is it worth being _____ even if other people aren't?	What does it mean to be academically _____?	What's an assignment you're working on right now? What would be a _____ way to do this assignment?
Is it possible to be too _____?	What could it mean to be a _____ thinker?	Which school rules make it easier to be _____, and which school rules make it harder?
Does being _____ come naturally to you, or is it something you have to think about in order to do?	How would you set up a classroom space to encourage the people in it to be _____?	What would be a _____ way to spend your lunch period?
How might you be more _____ at school?	What's a skill you're practicing in school right now? How could learning this skill help you be _____?	How could you be _____ during the time between classes?
In which class are you your most _____ self?	What's a topic you're learning about in school right now? How could learning about this topic help you be _____?	What book are you reading right now? How could reading this book help you be _____?

EMPOWER Moves for Social-Emotional Learning © 2023 Solution Tree Press
SolutionTree.com • Visit go.SolutionTree.com/SEL to download this free reproducible.

Questions Cards Three

What could it mean to be artistically _____?	Which of your teachers supports you when you try to be _____?	Who can help you be more _____ at home?
What could it mean to be authentically _____?	Which of your teachers inspires you to be _____ by setting an example?	What does being _____ look like in your family?
What club or extracurricular activity interests you? How could joining this club or doing this activity help you be _____?	How can you support others who try to be _____ at school?	What does being _____ look like in your neighborhood?
Which of your classmates supports you when you try to be _____?	At school, how can you inspire others to be _____ by setting an example?	What does being _____ look like in your culture?
Which of your classmates inspires you to be _____ by setting an example?	How might you be more _____ at home?	How is being _____ a way to honor your ancestors?

Questions Cards Four

How is being _____ a way to create a legacy?	When was a time that you needed others to be _____?	How could you help someone through a struggle by being _____?
Who do you know that cares a lot about being _____? How does this quality affect your relationship with them?	How can you be _____ in a way that benefits your community?	What goal does a close friend or family member currently have? How could your being _____ help this person work toward that goal?
Who is one of the most _____ people you can think of? What questions would you ask this person?	What could it mean to be _____ in taking care of the planet?	What could it mean to take care of yourself in a _____ way?
What fictional character is especially _____? How does this quality affect them?	Who struggles to be _____, and what can you do to help them?	How is being _____ a way to take care of yourself?
Think of someone you've known for a long time. Has that person become more or less _____ over the years, or stayed the same?	When is life hard for people who are _____? How can you help them?	What does it mean to be socially _____?

Questions Cards Five

What could it mean to be a _____ friend?	How (if at all) does gender inform the ways you are _____?	How (if at all) might your ways of being _____ change in the future?
How are your friends' ways of being _____ different from yours?	How (if at all) does money impact the ways people can be _____?	What's an experience that pushed you to become more _____?
How important is it for your friends to be _____?	Are your ways of being _____ typical for your age?	What are some careers that require being _____?
Think of groups you spend time with, such as family, friends, teams, or classes. Does the group of people you're with affect how _____ you are?	What (if anything) does your religion teach about being _____?	What's a goal you have for yourself? How could being _____ help you achieve that goal?
How (if at all) does race inform the ways you are _____?	How (if at all) have your ways of being _____ changed over time?	If you were to be more _____, how might that make your life better?

Questions Cards Six

What could it mean to be a _____ leader?	Is it possible to be _____ when you're worried?	Is it possible to fake being _____?
What's your earliest memory of being _____?	What does being _____ look like at different times of the year?	What are a few small but significant ways to be _____?
What's your earliest memory of someone else being _____?	Are there stereotypes of being _____?	What's an obvious way of being _____, and what's a less obvious way?
Is it possible to be _____ when you're angry?	Can an animal be _____, or is this a quality that only humans can have?	What's the opposite of being _____, and what does it look like when someone acts that way?
Is it possible to be _____ when you're sad?	Can a group be _____, or is this a quality that only individuals can have?	What questions can you ask about being _____?

More Ways to Use the Values and Questions Cards

The following are more ways to use the Values and Questions card decks. Some of these activities are adapted from our Values and Questions card game (Porosoff & Weinstein, 2020b).

Conversation Starter

This game supports two people—you and a student, or a pair of students—to understand their own values and each other. Instead of merely taking turns responding to a given question, players listen to one another and respond to each other's responses. This game is adapted from the Collaborative Conversations protocol in *Two-for-One Teaching* (Porosoff & Weinstein, 2020a), which itself is based on the work of psychologist Jonathan Kanter (2016).

Number of players: 2

Suggested duration: 15 minutes

The following steps will help you effectively lead the activity.

1. Player 1 draws three Values cards and three Questions cards. From these, Player 1 chooses one Values card and one Questions card and responds to the resulting question.
2. Player 2 responds to Player 1's response.
3. Player 2 responds to the same question.
4. Player 1 responds to Player 2's response.
5. Roles reverse: Player 2 draws three Values cards and three Questions cards. From these, Player 2 chooses one Values card and one Questions card and responds to the resulting question.
6. Player 1 responds to Player 2's response.
7. Player 1 responds to the same question.
8. Player 2 responds to Player 1's response.
9. The process repeats if both players wish.

Question Ladder

In this game, either the value or the question will stay the same from round to round, which leaves room for the players to reference each other's ideas and discover interesting similarities and differences between them. Play with any student you want to get to know in a different way, or have students play together if they need to find common ground and appreciate each other.

Number of players: 2–4

Suggested duration: 15 minutes

The following steps will help you effectively lead the activity.

1. Players decide together on a number of rounds.
2. Player 1 turns over the top three Values cards, chooses one, and returns the other two to the bottom of the deck.
3. Player 1 turns over the top three Questions cards, chooses one, and returns the other two to the bottom of the deck. Player 1 fills in the blank with the value and responds to the resulting question.

4. Player 2 now has two choices:
   - Turn over three new Values cards, choose one to put into the blank of Player 1's question, return the other two Values cards to the bottom of its deck, and respond to the resulting question.
   - Turn over three new Questions cards, choose one in which to insert Player 1's value, return the other two Questions cards to the bottom of its deck, and respond to the resulting question.
5. This process continues, with each player turning over three new Values cards or three new Questions cards, selecting from these three, and responding.

Pass the Value

In this game, players choose values to plug into one another's questions. The game works best in a group of people who already know each other to some extent, but want to get to know each other better. You can play too.

Number of players: 3–6

Suggested duration: 30 minutes

The following steps will help you effectively lead the activity.

1. Each player is dealt four Values cards, but Player 1 gets one extra card, for a total of five. Players look at their cards without showing them to each other. The remainder of the Values deck is set aside.
2. Player 1 flips over the top Questions card. Player 1 then chooses a value from their own hand to fill in the blank, resulting in a question for Player 2 to respond to.
3. Player 2 responds to the resulting question and keeps the Values card, which means Player 2 now has five cards.
4. Player 2 flips over the next Questions card and chooses a value from their own hand to fill in the blank, resulting in a question for Player 3 to respond to.
5. This process continues, with players responding to the question they were given and choosing a value for the next player's question, until all players have had a chance to respond to two questions.

Sorting Values and Strengths

This is the only game that has a single player work with all sixty Values cards. The player first sorts the cards based on which qualities are most important to them. Then, the player sorts the cards based on which qualities they consider strengths. Finally, the player responds to questions in order to think more deeply about their values and strengths. Use this game with a student who has shown a need for deeper reflection.

Number of players: 1

Suggested duration: 20 minutes

The following steps will help you effectively lead the activity.

1. The player sorts the Values cards into three piles, each with twenty cards: values they think are most important, least important, and in the middle.

2. The player can choose to share how they decided which cards to put in which pile and anything else they noticed about their process of sorting.

3. The player gathers up the "least important" and "in-the-middle" piles into a single pile and puts the pile aside so that only the twenty "most important" Values cards remain. Using only these, the player sorts them into three piles based on whether the quality is a personal strength, a strength sometimes or to some extent, and not really a strength.

4. The player can again choose to share how they decided which cards to put in which pile and anything else they noticed about their process of sorting.

5. The player responds to the following reflection questions.
   - Choose a value that is also a personal strength. How do you use this strength in different parts of your life?
   - Choose a value that is a strength sometimes or to some extent. When is it a strength? When it isn't, what gets in the way?
   - Choose a value that is not so much of a strength. As you think about your school day—your different classes, and the different places you go—what are some opportunities to practice and develop this strength?

Journal Reflection

Here, students use the questions as prompts for private writing. While this is a less playful way to use the cards, students might be more honest and vulnerable in the privacy of a notebook than in a conversation. Because you won't collect or grade this writing, students might opt out, but even if they do, they'll see that you think exploring their values is worth their time. Whether they agree is up to them.

Number of players: any

Suggested duration: 10 minutes

The following steps will help you effectively lead the activity.

1. Draw a Values card and a Questions card. Fill in the blank with the value, and write the resulting question on the board. Students respond to the resulting question in a private written reflection.

2. Students can choose to share all or part of what they wrote, or choose not to share at all. If the group is large, players can share with partners or in small groups.

References

Kanter, J. (2016, June 19). *Conceptualization of awareness, courage, and love as clinical targets in functional analytic psychotherapy* [Workshop presentation]. ACBS Annual World Conference 14, Seattle, WA.

Porosoff, L., & Weinstein, J. (2020a). *Two-for-one teaching: Connecting instruction to student values*. Bloomington, IN: Solution Tree Press.

Porosoff, L., & Weinstein, J. (2020b). *Values and questions*. Cheltenham, Victoria, Australia: Hawker Brownlow Education.

References & Resources

Alexander, E. (2009). *Praise song for the day: A poem for Barack Obama's presidential inauguration.* Accessed at www.poetryfoundation.org/poems/52141/praise-song-for-the-day on October 17, 2022.

Allison, L., Waters, L., & Kern, M. L. (2021). Flourishing classrooms: Applying a systems-informed approach to positive education. *Contemporary School Psychology, 25,* 395–405.

Assaz, D. A., Roche, B., Kanter, J. W., & Oshiro, C. K. (2018). Cognitive defusion in acceptance and commitment therapy: What are the basic processes of change? *The Psychological Record, 68*(4), 405–418.

Bennett, R., & Oliver, J. E. (2019). *Acceptance and commitment therapy: 100 key points and techniques.* New York: Routledge.

Blackledge, J. T. (2015). *Cognitive defusion in practice: A clinician's guide to assessing, observing, and supporting change in your client.* Oakland, CA: New Harbinger.

Byrd, C. M. (2017). The complexity of school racial climate: Reliability and validity of a new measure for secondary students. *British Journal of Educational Psychology, 87*(4), 700–721.

Callaghan, S., Lösch, M., Pione, A., & Teichner, W. (2021, April 8). *Feeling good: The future of the $1.5 trillion wellness market.* Accessed at www.mckinsey.com/industries/consumer-packaged-goods/our-insights/feeling-good-the-future-of-the-1-5-trillion-wellness-market on June 20, 2022.

Carle, E. (1969). *The very hungry caterpillar.* London: Hamish Hamilton.

Dahl, J. C., Plumb, J. C., Stewart, I., & Lundgren, T. (2009). *The art and science of valuing in psychotherapy: Helping clients discover, explore, and commit to valued action using acceptance and commitment therapy.* Oakland, CA: New Harbinger.

Davies, K., Tropp, L. R., Aron, A., Pettigrew, T. F., & Wright, S. C. (2011). Cross-group friendships and intergroup attitudes: A meta-analytic review. *Personality and Social Psychology Review, 15*(4), 332–351.

Del Pozo, J. (2021, November 27). *The dark side of resilience* [Blog post]. Accessed at www.psychologytoday.com/us/blog/being-awake-better/202111/the-dark-side-resilience on June 20, 2022.

Friman, P. C., Hayes, S. C., & Wilson, K. G. (1998). Why behavior analysts should study emotion: The example of anxiety. *Journal of Applied Behavior Analysis, 31*(1), 137–156.

Gagnon, J., Dionne, F., & Pychyl, T. A. (2016). Committed action: An initial study on its association to procrastination in academic settings. *Journal of Contextual Behavioral Science, 5*(2), 97–102.

Gaiman, N. (2012, May 17). *Keynote address: 134th commencement* [Keynote address]. Accessed at www.uarts.edu/neil-gaiman-keynote-address-2012 on May 22, 2022.

Gilbert, P. (2010). *The compassionate mind: A new approach to life's challenges.* Oakland, CA: New Harbinger.

Gutman, D. (2004–2008). *My weird school* series. New York: HarperCollins.

Gutman, D. (2005). *Mr. Hynde is out of his mind!* New York: HarperCollins.

Gutman, D. (2007). *Mrs. Yonkers is bonkers!* New York: HarperCollins.

Hayes, S. C., Barnes-Holmes, D., & Roche, B. (Eds.). (2001). *Relational frame theory: A post-Skinnerian account of human language and cognition.* New York: Kluwer Academic/Plenum.

Hayes, S. C., Hofmann, S. G., & Wilson, D. S. (2020). Clinical psychology is an applied evolutionary science. *Clinical Psychology Review, 81*, 101892.

Hayes, S. C., Strosahl, K. D., & Wilson, K. G. (1999). *Acceptance and commitment therapy: An experiential approach to behavior change.* New York: Guilford Press.

Hayes, S. C., Strosahl, K. D., & Wilson, K. G. (2012). *Acceptance and commitment therapy: The process and practice of mindful change* (2nd ed.). New York: Guilford Press.

Hebert, E. R., Flynn, M. K., Wilson, K. G., & Kellum, K. K. (2021). Values intervention as an establishing operation for approach in the presence of aversive stimuli. *Journal of Contextual Behavioral Science, 20*, 144–154.

Hersey, J. (1977). *The wall.* New York: Vintage Books.

Holman, G., Kanter, J., Tsai, M., & Kohlenberg, R. (2017). *Functional analytic psychotherapy made simple: A practical guide to therapeutic relationships.* Oakland, CA: New Harbinger.

hooks, b. (1994). *Teaching to transgress: Education as the practice of freedom.* New York: Routledge.

Kaler-Jones, C. (2020, May 7). *When SEL is used as another form of policing.* Accessed at https://medium.com/@justschools/when-sel-is-used-as-another-form-of-policing-fa53cf85dce4 on August 11, 2022.

Kanter, J. (2016, June 19). *Conceptualization of awareness, courage, and love as clinical targets in functional analytic psychotherapy* [Workshop presentation]. ACBS Annual World Conference 14, Seattle, WA.

Kanter, J. W., Kuczynski, A. M., Manbeck, K. E., Corey, M. D., & Wallace, E. C. (2020). An integrative contextual behavioral model of intimate relations. *Journal of Contextual Behavioral Science, 18*, 75–91.

Karabenick, S. A., & Newman, R. S. (Eds.). (2006). *Help seeking in academic settings: Goals, groups, and contexts.* New York: Routledge.

Kimmerer, R. W. (2013). *Braiding sweetgrass: Indigenous wisdom, scientific knowledge, and the teachings of plants.* Minneapolis, MN: Milkweed Editions.

Kolts, R. L. (2016). *CFT made simple: A clinician's guide to practicing compassion-focused therapy.* Oakland, CA: New Harbinger.

Leslie, L. M., Bono, J. E., Kim, Y. S., & Beaver, G. R. (2020). On melting pots and salad bowls: A meta-analysis of the effects of identity-blind and identity-conscious diversity ideologies. *Journal of Applied Psychology, 105*(5), 453–471.

Lewicki, R. J., Polin, B., & Lount, R. B. (2016). An exploration of the structure of effective apologies. *Negotiation and Conflict Management Research, 9*(2), 177–196.

Linehan, M. (2015). *DBT skills training manual* (2nd ed.). New York: Guilford Press.

The Local. (2018, December 7). *German word of the day: Die Gemütlichkeit.* Accessed at www.thelocal.de/20180927/die-gemuetlichkeit on May 22, 2022.

Love, B. L. (2019). *We want to do more than survive: Abolitionist teaching and the pursuit of educational freedom.* Boston: Beacon Press.

Luciano, M. C., Salas, S. V., Martínez, O. G., Ruiz, F. J., & Blarrina, M. P. (2009). Brief acceptance-based protocols applied to the work with adolescents. *International Journal of Psychology and Psychological Therapy, 9*(2), 237–257.

Magill, S. (2019). *German word of the day: Die Sehnsucht.* Accessed at www.thelocal.de/20191111/word-of-the-day-sehnsucht on May 20, 2022.

Mahoney, J. L., Durlak, J. A., & Weissberg, R. P. (2018). An update on social and emotional learning outcome research. *Phi Delta Kappan, 100*(4), 18–23.

Mailer, N. (1948). *The naked and the dead.* New York: Rinehart.

Maitland, D. W. M., Kanter, J. W., Manbeck, K. E., & Kuczynski, A. M. (2017). Relationship science informed clinically relevant behaviors in functional analytic psychotherapy: The Awareness, Courage, and Love model. *Journal of Contextual Behavioral Science, 6*(4), 347–359.

McHugh, L., Stewart, I., & Almada, P. (2019). *A contextual behavioral guide to the self: Theory and practice.* Oakland, CA: Context Press.

Meadows, D. H. (2008). *Thinking in systems: A primer.* White River Junction, VT: Chelsea Green.

Melville, H. (1999). *Moby-Dick.* Ware, England: Wordsworth Editions. (Original work published 1851)

Miller, W. R., & Rollnick, S. (2013). *Motivational interviewing: Helping people change* (3rd ed.). New York: Guilford Press.

Murthy, V. E., Villatte, M., & McHugh, L. (2019). Investigating the effect of conditional vs hierarchical framing on motivation. *Learning and Motivation, 65,* 33–42.

Najavits, L. M. (2002). *Seeking safety: A treatment manual for PTSD and substance abuse.* New York: Guilford Press.

National Governors Association Center for Best Practices & Council of Chief State School Officers. (2010). *Common Core State Standards for English language arts and literacy in history/social studies, science, and technical subjects.* Washington, DC: Authors. Accessed at www.corestandards.org/wp-content/uploads/ELA_Standards1.pdf on April 8, 2022.

Neff, K. (2011). *Self-compassion: The proven power of being kind to yourself.* New York: HarperCollins.

Nellen, T. (n.d.). *I heard, I noticed, I wondered.* Accessed at www.tnellen.com/cybereng/method.html on November 20, 2021.

Office of the Surgeon General. (2021). *Protecting youth mental health: The U.S. surgeon general's advisory.* Accessed at www.hhs.gov/sites/default/files/surgeon-general-youth-mental-health-advisory.pdf on April 8, 2022.

Plaut, V. C., Thomas, K. M., & Goren, M. J. (2009). Is multiculturalism or color blindness better for minorities? *Psychological Science, 20*(4), 444–446.

Plutchik, R. (1980). *Emotion: A psychoevolutionary synthesis.* New York: Harper & Row.

Plutchik, R. (2001). The nature of emotions: Human emotions have deep evolutionary roots, a fact that may explain their complexity and provide tools for clinical practice. *American Scientist, 89*(4), 344–350.

Porosoff, L. (2021). *The PD curator: How to design peer-to-peer professional learning that elevates teachers and teaching.* Alexandria, VA: ASCD.

Porosoff, L., & Weinstein, J. (2018). *EMPOWER your students: Tools to inspire a meaningful school experience, grades 6–12*. Bloomington, IN: Solution Tree Press.

Porosoff, L., & Weinstein, J. (2020a). *Two-for-one teaching: Connecting instruction to student values*. Bloomington, IN: Solution Tree Press.

Porosoff, L., & Weinstein, J. (2020b). *Values and questions*. Cheltenham, Victoria, Australia: Hawker Brownlow Education.

Rajaraman, A., Austin, J. L., Gover, H. C., Cammilleri, A. P., Donnelly, D. R., & Hanley, G. P. (2022). Toward trauma-informed applications of behavior analysis. *Journal of Applied Behavior Analysis, 55*(1), 40–61.

Reynolds, M. (2019). Shifting frames: Pedagogical interventions in colorblind teaching practice. In K. W. Crenshaw, L. C. Harris, D. M. HoSang, & G. Lipsitz (Eds.), *Seeing race again: Countering colorblindness across the disciplines* (pp. 352–374). Oakland, CA: University of California Press.

Robinson, K. (2006). *Do schools kill creativity?* [Video file]. TED Conferences. Accessed at www.ted.com/talks/sir_ken_robinson_do_schools_kill_creativity?language=en on September 23, 2022.

Rumi, J. (2004). *The essential Rumi: New expanded edition* (C. Barks, Trans.). New York: HarperCollins.

Ryan, A. M., Hicks, L., & Midgley, C. (1997). Social goals, academic goals, and avoiding seeking help in the classroom. *The Journal of Early Adolescence, 17*(2), 152–171.

Schwarz, S. (2018). Resilience in psychology: A critical analysis of the concept. *Theory and Psychology, 28*(4), 528–541.

Simmons, D. (2021, March 1). *Why SEL alone isn't enough*. Accessed at www.ascd.org/el/articles/why-sel-alone-isnt-enough on June 2, 2022.

Skinner, B. F. (1964). New methods and new aims in teaching. *New Scientist, 22*(392), 483–484.

Than, G. A. (2012). *Neil Gaiman: Make good art*. Accessed at www.zenpencils.com/comic/50-neil-gaiman-make-good-art on November 27, 2021.

Thoreau, H. D. (1995). *Walden*. Accessed at www.gutenberg.org/files/205/205-h/205-h.htm on May 20, 2022. (Original work published 1854)

Tirch, D., Silberstein, L. R., & Kolts, R. L. (2016). *Buddhist psychology and cognitive-behavioral therapy: A clinician's guide*. New York: Guilford Press.

Tomlinson, E. C., Dineen, B. R., & Lewicki, R. J. (2004). The road to reconciliation: Antecedents of victim willingness to reconcile following a broken promise. *Journal of Management, 30*(2), 165–187.

van der Kolk, B. A. (2014). *The body keeps the score: Brain, mind, and body in the healing of trauma*. New York: Penguin.

van Kleef, G. A., & Fischer, A. H. (2016). Emotional collectives: How groups shape emotions and emotions shape groups. *Cognition and Emotion, 30*(1), 3–19.

Villatte, M., Villatte, J. L., & Hayes, S. C. (2016). *Mastering the clinical conversation: Language as intervention*. New York: Guilford Press.

Waltz, T. J., & Follette, W. C. (2009). Molar functional relations and clinical behavior analysis: Implications for assessment and treatment. *The Behavior Analyst, 32*(1), 51–68.

Wilson, K. G. (2009). *Mindfulness for two: An acceptance and commitment therapy approach to mindfulness in psychotherapy*. Oakland, CA: New Harbinger.

Wilson, K. G., Sandoz, E. K., Kitchens, J., & Roberts, M. (2010). The valued living questionnaire: Defining and measuring valued action within a behavioral framework. *The Psychological Record, 60*(2), 249–272.

Winterson, J. (1999). *The world and other places*. New York: Knopf.

Xiaobao, P., & Jinhan, J. (2017). How different apology components drive trust repair: The moderating effect of social value orientation. *European Journal of Business and Management, 9*(8), 68–83.

Zembylas, M. (2021). Against the psychologization of resilience: Towards an onto-political theorization of the concept and its implications for higher education. *Studies in Higher Education, 46*(9), 1966–1977.

Index

A
abstract representation, 99
academic classes, 146
The Acknowledgments Section activity, 148, 150
activities. *See* EMPOWER activities
adaptive distress, 163
addressing challenges, 12–13
    empathy, 107–110, 113, 116–117
    motivation, 34–35, 36, 39, 41–42
    participation, 54–55, 58, 61, 63
    openness, 72, 75–76, 78, 81–82
    willingness, 91–92, 95–97, 100
    resilience, 127–128, 130, 133–134, 136–137
    exploration, 19–21, 23, 27
adjusting activities, 12
    empathy, 107, 1090–110, 113, 116
    motivation, 34, 36, 39, 41
    participation, 53–54, 57–58, 60, 62–63
    openness, 71, 75, 77–78, 81
    willingness, 91, 95, 97, 100
    resilience, 127, 130, 133, 136
    exploration, 18–19, 21, 23, 27
advisory curriculum
    EMPOWER as, 6
advisory programs, 145–146
affirmations, 172–174
Alexander, E., 31
Almada, P., 58
apologizing, 114–117
applying systems thinking, 157
    diversifying activities for balance, 158
    planning flexibly, 158–159
    repeating activities for continuity, 158
asking for help, 72–76
Assessing My Classes activity, 150, 158
    addressing challenges, 61
    adjusting the activity, 60
    extending the work, 60
    leading the activity, 59–60
    materials, 59
assessment
    evoking, 169–171
associating actions with values, 6, 9, 31–32
    Four Self Responding activity, 37–39
    Fun and Important Graphing activity, 32–35
    Values on My Device, 40–42
    Values on My To-Do List activity, 35–36
    your own motivation, 42
avoidance, 161–162
    evoking instead of suggesting, 168–172
    how it functions, 162–163
    identifying behaviors, 164–165
    knowledge and access barriers, 165–166
    one-to-one conversations, 175–176
    strategies to shape values–based behavior change, 172–175
    talking with families about, 180–183
    why suggestions don't help, 166–167

B
Barks, C., 91
both-and approach to SEL, 6
Braiding Sweetgrass (Kimmerer), 69
Bringing Our Full Selves to Our Friendships activity, 149–150
    addressing challenges, 81–82
    adjusting the activity, 81
    extending the work, 80–81
    leading the activity, 79
    materials, 78
Building an Apology activity, 114
    addressing challenges, 116–117
    adjusting the activity, 116
    extending the work, 115–116
    leading the activity, 114–115
    materials, 114
building interdependence, 76–78

C
challenges. *See* addressing challenges
choice
    evoking, 171–172
choosing an EMPOWER activity for one student, 155–157
climate crisis unit, 154
collaboration, 107–110
commitment statements, 23
Common Values and Complementary Strengths activity, 149–151
    addressing challenges, 110
    adjusting the activity, 109–110
    extending the work, 109
    in a leadership unit, 153
    leading the activity, 108–109
    materials, 108
competence-based violations, 116
conceptual photograph, 20
conflict resolution, 111–113
connecting with students' ideas, 184
consent, 21
conversation starter, 206
conversations
    about student success, 183–186
    guiding, 155
    one-to-one, 175–176
    organizing, 155
    slowing, 155
conveying information, 69
counseling sessions, 146
courage in social situations, 82–83
COVID-19 pandemic, 145
creating ways to enact values, 6, 9, 47–48
    Assessing My Classes activity, 59–61
    Emotions and Values Audit activity, 48–55
    Enjoyment and Satisfaction activity, 55–58
    from participation to openness, 64
    Value of the Week activity, 61–63
    your own participation, 63–64
curriculum, 146–149

D
Dahl, J., 88
deictic framing, 4
description
    evoking, 168–169
designing an SEL program, 143, 145–146
    applying systems thinking, 157–159
    integrating SEL into existing programs, 146–157
discovering how values show up, 6, 9
    activities, 15
    Domains of Life activity, 29
    from exploration to motivation, 28
    Our Values in Action activity, 22–24
    Shape of My Life Posters activity, 16–20
    Values and Questions card game, 24–27
    Values Concept Photos activity, 20–21
    your own, 28
discovering a student's process, 184–185
Discovery Drawings activity, 97–98, 157
    addressing challenges, 100
    adjusting the activity, 100
    extending the work, 100
    leading the activity, 98–99
    materials, 98
    sample four illustrations, 98
diversifying activities for balance, 157–158
diversity, 78–82
dominant cultural ideologies, 3

E
Emotions and Values Audit activity, 9–10, 63, 147, 150
    addressing challenges, 54–55
    adjusting the activity, 53–54
    extending the work, 51–53

in a leadership unit, 153
leading the activity, 48–51
materials, 48
empathy, 9, 105, 148, 156
Building an Apology activity, 114–117
Common Values and Complementary Strengths activity, 108–110
defined, 6
From Conflict to Connection activity, 111–113
from empathy to resilience, 118
Storytelling Circles activity, 106–108
your own, 117–118
EMPOWER activities, 5–7
empathy, 6, 9, 105–121
exploration, 6, 9, 15–29
in a leadership unit, 153
in a nutrition unit, 152
low-, medium-, and high-risk, 10
materials, 11
motivation, 6, 9, 31–46
openness, 6, 9, 69–85
participation, 6, 9, 47–67
resilience, 6, 9, 123–139
SEL activities, 9–11
strategies to implement, 7
suggested duration, 10
when to use, 11
willingness, 6, 9, 87–104
EMPOWER as curriculum, 146–147
planning a scope and sequence, 148–150
responding to emergency interests and needs, 147–148
EMPOWER as intervention, 147, 151–155
choosing an activity for one student, 155–157
leading one student through an activity, 157
EMPOWER as pedagogy, 147, 149–151
EMPOWER model
as a pedagogical approach, 6
as a set of interventions, 6
as an advisory curriculum, 6
defined, 6
EMPOWER Your Students (Porosoff & Weinstein), 10
empowering yourself. *See* your empowerment
Enjoyment and Satisfaction activity, 149–151
addressing challenges, 58
adjusting the activity, 57–58
extending the work, 57
in a climate crisis unit, 154
leading the activity, 55–57
materials, 55
evoking
assessment, 169–171
choice, 171–172
description, 168–169
imagination, 171
instead of suggesting, 168
exploration, 9, 148, 156
activities, 15
defined, 6
Domains of Life activity, 29
from exploration to motivation, 28
Our Values in Action activity, 22–24
Shape of My Life Posters activity, 16–20

to motivation, 28
Values and Questions card game, 24–27
Values Concept Photos activity, 20–21
your own, 28
extending the work, 11–12
empathy, 107, 109, 112, 115–116
exploration, 18, 21, 23, 26–27
motivation, 33–34, 36, 39, 41
openness, 71, 74–75, 77, 80–81
participation, 51–53, 57, 60, 62
resilience, 126, 129–130, 133, 135–136
willingness, 91, 94–95, 97, 100
with families, 186

F

Failure Timeline activity, 10, 148
addressing challenges, 133–134
adjusting the activity, 133
extending the work, 133
leading the activity, 132
materials, 130
questions, 131
families
choosing language to describe EMPOWER, 177–178
empowering school-to-home communications, 185–187
extending activities at home, 178–180
inviting into conversation
sample letters to, 179–181
talking about student success, 183–186
talking with about avoidance, 180–183
Feedback Comics activity, 149
addressing challenges, 127–128
adjusting the activity, 127
extending the work, 126
in a study skills unit, 154
leading the activity, 124–126
materials, 124
504 plans, 11
Four Self Responding activity, 9, 149–150, 152
addressing challenges, 39
adjusting the activity, 39
extending the work, 39
leading the activity, 37–39
materials, 37
Freak Out, Act Out, Zone Out activity, 148
addressing challenges, 95–96
adjusting the activity, 95
example of getting back in, 94
example of three kinds of out, 95
extending the activity, 94–95
leading the activity, 92–94
materials, 92
friendships, 77–82
From Conflict to Connection activity, 111
addressing challenges, 113
adjusting the activity, 113
extending the work, 112
in a climate crisis unit, 154
leading the activity, 111–112
materials, 111, 150
Frustration Coloring Book activity, 10, 150
addressing challenges, 97
adjusting the activity, 97
extending the work, 97

in a nutrition unit, 152
leading the activity, 96–97
materials, 96
Fun and Important Graphing activity, 32
addressing challenges, 34–35
adjusting the activity, 34
extending the work, 33–34
in a nutrition unit, 152
leading the activity, 32–33
materials, 32
suggested duration, 32
when to use, 32

G

Gaiman, M., 123–124, 137
gemütlichkeit, 52
Google Docs, 166
green-gender identity poster, 80
"The Guest House" (Rumi), 91
Guests in Our Houses activity, 148
addressing challenges, 91–92
adjusting the activity, 91
extending the work, 91
in a leadership unit, 153
leading the activity, 88–90
materials, 88
Gutman, D., 161

H

Handouts; *see* reproducibles
Hayes, S., 47–48, 163, 168
high-risk activities, 10
Hofman, S., 163
Holman, G., 82
hooks, b., 13
hyperbolic drawing, 99

I

I, here, now, 4
imagination
evoking, 171
in lak'ech hala ken, 105
individualized education plans (IEPs), 11
integrating SEL into existing programs, 145–146, 159
approaches to, 147
EMPOWER as curriculum, 146–149
EMPOWER as intervention, 151–157
EMPOWER as pedagogy, 149–151
integrity-based violations, 116
intervention, 147, 151–155
choosing an activity for one student, 155–157
leading one student through an activity, 157
EMPOWER as, 6

J

journal reflection, 208

K

Kaler-Jones, C., 3
Kanter, J., 82, 206, 208
Kimmerer, R. W., 69
Kitchens, J., 16
knowledge and access barriers, 165–166
Kohlenberg, R., 82
Kolts, R., 169

Index | 217

L
leadership
    as a values-consistent action, 70–72
    unit, 153
leading activities, 11
    empathy, 106, 108–109, 111–112, 114–115
    exploration, 16–17, 20–21, 22–23, 24–26
    motivation, 32–33, 40–41, 35–39
    openness, 70–74, 76–77, 79
    participation, 48–51, 55–57, 59–60, 61–62
    resilience, 124–126, 128–129, 132, 134–135
    willingness, 88–90, 92–94, 96–99
    with one student, 157
Leading With Values activity, 148, 150
    addressing challenges, 72
    adjusting the activity, 71
    extending the work, 71
    in a leadership unit, 153
    leading the activity, 70–71
    materials, 70
Lewicki, R., 116
living by values, 2
    values are chosen, 3–4
    values are consequences of experiences, 2–3
    values are not preferences, 4–5
    values are qualities of action, 5
living deliberately, 15
low-risk activities, 10

M
Make Good Art (Gaiman), 137–138
making an argument, 69
making EMPOWER more effective
    designing a SEL program
    family participation
    supporting students who struggle
materials, 11
    empathy, 106, 108, 111, 114
    exploration activities, 16, 20, 22, 24
    motivation, 32, 36, 40
    openness, 70, 72, 76, 78
    participation, 48, 55, 59, 61
    resilience, 124, 128, 130, 134
    willingness, 88, 92, 96, 98
McHugh, L., 58
Meadows, D. H., 157
medium-risk activities, 10
metaphysical representation, 99
Miller, W., 55, 166–167, 172
The Moth, 107
motivation, 6, 9, 31–32, 148, 156
    defined, 6
    Four Self Responding activity, 37–39
    Fun and Important Graphing activity, 32–35
    to participation, 43
    Values on My Device activity, 40–42
    Values on My To-Do List activity, 35–36
    your own motivation, 42
Mr. Hynde Is Out of His Mind! (Gutman), 161
Mrs. Yonkers Is Bonkers! (Gutman), 161
Murthy, V., 145
My Weird School series (Gutman), 161

N
namaste, 105
narrating a series of events, 69
notability, 166
nutrition unit, 152

O
Obama, B., 31
one-to-one conversations, 156, 175–176
openness, 9, 69–70, 148, 156
    The Acknowledgments Section activity, 72–76
    Bringing Our Full Selves to Our Friendships activity, 78–82
    defined, 6
    from openness to willingness, 83
    Leading With Values activity, 70–72
    Satisfying Our Needs Together activity, 76–78
    your own openness, 82–83
Our Values in Action activity, 148
    addressing challenges, 23
    adjusting the activity, 23
    extending the work, 23
    in a climate crisis unit, 154
    leading the activity, 22–23
    materials, 22

P
participation, 148, 156
    Assessing My Classes activity, 59–61
    defined, 6, 9, 47–48
    Emotions and Values Audit activity, 48–55
    Enjoyment and Satisfaction activity, 55–58
    from participation to openness, 64
    Value of the Week activity, 61–63
    your own, 63–64
pass the value, 207
pedagogy, 6, 147, 149–151
planning a scope and sequence, 148–149
    sample, 148
planning flexibly to respond to change, 157–159
Porosoff, L., 3–4, 10, 17, 19, 24, 54, 105, 137–138, 105–106, 137–138, 149, 169, 183, 208
"Praise Song for the Day" (Alexander), 31
preferences vs. values, 4–5
prevention programming, 91
privacy, 21
Project LIT Community, 78

Q
qualities of action
    values as, 5
question ladders, 206–207
questions
    to help students assess their actions, 172
    to help students choose values-consistent actions, 174
    to help students describe their actions, 170
    to help students imagine actions, 173

R
realistic drawing, 99
reducing prejudice, 78–82
reflections, 172, 174–175
repeating activities for continuity, 157–158
reproducibles
    About Emotions, 49
    Barriers to Enacting Values, 89
    Choice Reflection, 56, 66
    Class Assessment, 67
    Compassionate Responding, 120
    Domains of Life, 29
    Emotions Reveal What Matters to Us, 52
    Enacting My Values When I Use Devices, 46
    Examples of Values, 192
    Failure Timeline, 131, 133
    Feedback Comic Panels, 125, 140
    Four Illustrations, 98, 104
    Four Self Responses, 38
    Fun and Important Graph, 32
    Getting Back In, 94, 103
    Learning Struggles, 141
    more ways to use Values and Questions cards, 27, 206
    Noticing My Emotions, 50, 65
    People I'm Close To, 85
    Six Parts of an Apology, 121
    Things I Need to Do This Week, 44
    Three Kinds of Out, 95, 102
    Types of Help, 73
    Values and Questions cards, 193–205
    Values and Strengths Self-Assessment, 110, 119
    Values Leaders, 84
resilience, 9, 123–124, 148, 156
    defined, 6
    Failure Timeline activity, 130–134
    Feedback Comics activity, 124–128
    Self-Care Alerts activity, 134–137
    Struggle Portfolio activity, 128–130
    your own, 137–139
resistance. *See* addressing challenges
responding to emergency interests and needs, 147–148
righting reflex, 166
Roberts, M., 16
Robinson, K., 1
Rollnick, S., 55, 166–167
Rubric Response protocol, 9
Rumi, 91

S
Sandoz, E., 16
Satisfying Our Needs Together activity, 76
    addressing challenges, 78
    adjusting the activity, 77–78
    extending the work, 77
    leading the activity, 76–77
    materials, 76, 150
Schoology, 166
school-to-home communications, 186–186
    sample letter, 186
seeing students' work, 184
Sehnsucht, 52
Self-Care Alerts activity, 10, 147, 150
    addressing challenges, 136–137
    adjusting the activity, 136
    extending the work, 135–136
    in a leadership unit, 153

leading the activity, 134–135
materials, 134
self-kindness gift cards, 10
self-labeling, 58
serving values when it's hard, 6, 9, 87–88
    Discovery Drawings activity, 97–100
    Freak Out, Act Out, Zone Out activity, 92–96
    from willingness to empathy, 101
    Frustration Coloring Book activity, 96–97
    Guests in Our Houses activity, 88–92
    your own willingness, 100–101
Shape of My Life Posters activity, 10, 17, 150, 155
    addressing challenges, 19–20
    adjusting the activity, 18–19
    extending the work, 18
    leading the activity, 16–17
    materials, 16
sharing how others impact values, 6, 9, 69–70
    The Acknowledgments Section activity, 72–76 Bringing Our full Selves to Our Friendships activity, 78–82
    from openness to willingness, 83
    Leading With Values activity, 70–72
    Satisfying Our Needs Together activity, 76–78
    your own openness, 82–83
sharing struggles, 97–100
Simmons, D., 3
social-emotional learning (SEL), 6–7
    activities that EMPOWER students, 9–14
    applying systems thinking, 157–159
    beyond as a distinct entity, 5–6
    both-and approach, 6
    designing a program, 143, 145–146
    empowering students to live by their values, 2–5
    empowering students, 1
    implementing, 7
    integrating into existing programs, 145–157
    visualizing, 7
sorting values and strengths, 207–208
Steward, I., 58
StoryCorps, 107
Storytelling Circles activity, 148
    addressing challenges, 107–108
    adjusting the activity, 107
    extending the work, 107
    in a study skills unit, 154
    leading the activity, 106
    materials, 106
strategies to implement EMPOWER, 7
    designing an SEL program, 143, 145–159
    inviting families into conversations, 143, 177–187
    supporting students who struggle, 143, 161–176
Struggle Portfolio activity, 148, 150
    addressing challenges, 130
    adjusting the activity, 130
    extending the work, 129–130
    leading the activity, 128–129
    materials, 128
students of color
    dominant cultural ideologies, 3
study skills unit, 154
suggestions
    don't help, 166–167
    evoking instead, 168–169
summaries, 172, 175
supporting students who struggle, 143, 161–162
    evoking instead of suggesting, 168–172
    how avoidance functions, 162–163
    identifying avoidance behaviors, 164–165
    knowledge and access barriers, 165–166
    one-to-one conversations, 175–176
    strategies to shape values-based behavior change, 172–175
    why suggestions don't help, 166–167
systems thinking
    applying, 157–159
    defined, 157

T

technology access, 165–166
Than, G. A., 137
Thoreau, H. D., 15
Tsai, M., 82
turning struggles into opportunities, 6, 9, 123–124
    Failure Timeline activity, 130–134
    Feedback Comics activity, 124–128
    from activities to strategies, 139
    Self-Care Alerts activity, 134–137
    Struggle Portfolio activity, 128–130
    your own resilience, 137–139
Two-for-One Teaching (Porosoff & Weinstein), 9–10, 54, 206

U

understanding and caring about others' values, 6, 9, 105
    Building an Apology activity, 114–117
    Common Values and Complementary Strengths activity, 108–110
    defined, 6
    From Conflict to Connection activity, 111–113
    from empathy to resilience, 118
    Storytelling Circles activity, 106–108
    your own, 117–118

V

V'ahavta l'reacha kamocha, 105
Value of the Week activity, 148
    addressing challenges, 63
    adjusting the activity, 62–63
    extending the work, 62
    leading the activity, 61–62
    materials, 61
Valued Living Questionnaire (Wilson et. al), 16
values
    are chosen, 2–4
    are consequences of experience, 2–3
    are not preferences, 2, 4–5
    are qualities of action, 2, 5
    empowering students to live by, 2
Values and Questions card game, 12, 155, 158
    addressing challenges, 27
    adjusting the activity, 27
    deck, 61, 63, 109, 117
    extending the work, 26–27
    leading the activity, 24–26
    materials, 24
    setup, 25–26
Values Concept Photos activity, 148, 155–157
    addressing challenges, 21
    adjusting the activity, 21
    extending the work, 21
    in a study skills unit, 154
    leading the activity, 20–21
    materials, 20
Values on My Device activity, 148, 150
    addressing challenges, 41–42
    adjusting the activity, 41
    extending the work, 41
    in a study skills unit, 154
    leading the activity, 40–41
    materials, 40
Values on My To-Do List activity, 148
    addressing challenges, 36
    adjusting activities, 36
    extending the work, 36
    leading the activity, 35–36
    materials, 35
values-based behavior change, 172–173
    affirming positive steps, 173–174
    reflecting back values, 174–175
    summarizing what has been said, 175
values-consistent actions, 4–5
The Very Hungry Caterpillar by Eric Carle, 76
Villatte, J., 47–48, 168
Villatte, M., 47–48, 168

W

Walden (Thoreau), 15
We Need Diverse Books, 78
Weinstein, J., 2–4, 10, 24, 54, 162–164, 168–169, 171, 174–175, 181–182, 206, 208
when to use EMPOWER activities, 11
white supremacy with a hug," 3
willingness, 9, 87–88, 148, 156
    defined, 6
    Discovery Drawings activity, 97–100
    Freak Out, Act Out, Zone Out activity, 92–96
    from willingness to empathy, 101
    Frustration Coloring Book activity, 96–97
    Guests in Our Houses activity, 88–92
    your own willingness, 100–101
Wilson, D. S., 163
Wilson, K., 2, 16
Winterson, J., 47
"The World and Other Places" (Winterson), 47

Y

your empowerment, 13–14
    empathy, 117–118
    exploration, 28
    motivation, 42
    openness, 82–83
    participation, 63–64
    resilience, 137–139
    willingness, 100–101

Z

Zen Pencils, 137

EMPOWER Your Students
Lauren Porosoff and Jonathan Weinstein
Discover how to use the elements of EMPOWER—exploration, motivation, participation, openness, willingness, empathy, and resilience—to make school a positive, meaningful experience in your students' lives. This highly practical resource offers enjoyable, engaging classroom activities, as well as strategies for refining teaching practices, incorporating student values into course content, and deeply connecting with learners.
BKF791

Two-for-One Teaching
Lauren Porosoff and Jonathan Weinstein
Empower your students to make school a source of meaning, vitality, and community. *Two-for-One Teaching* offers 30 protocols, derived from contextual behavioral science, that embed student-centered, equity-driven social-emotional learning into every stage of an academic unit. Transform students' psychological experience of school by turning their lessons, assignments, and assessments into opportunities for them to explore and enact the values they want to live by.
BKF923

Building Blocks for Social-Emotional Learning
Tracey A. Hulen and Ann-Bailey Lipsett
Support the growth of your students with meaningful, effective social-emotional learning. Full of resources, tools, and planning templates, this comprehensive guide provides everything you need to embed SEL practices within your daily work. You'll engage in deep reflection and discover ways to refine instruction, lesson planning, and assessment; promote whole-child development; and foster a productive learning environment for all.
BKG019

The School Wellness Wheel
Mike Ruyle, Libby Child, and Nancy Dome
Your school can evolve to address trauma, promote well-being, and elevate learning. *The School Wellness Wheel* will show you how. Backed by educational, psychological, and medical research, the resource introduces a comprehensive framework for supporting students' cognitive, social, and emotional needs. Each chapter contains vignettes, examples, and advice from educators who are actively engaged in transforming their schools into centers of healing and resilience.
BKL064

The Identity-Conscious Educator
Liza A. Talusan
Learn powerful, practical strategies for creating an inclusive school community. *The Identity-Conscious Educator* provides a framework for building awareness and understanding of five identity categories: race, social class, gender, sexual orientation, and disability. Connect with vignettes and personal stories from the author that illuminate how to address identity topics in your personal and professional life. Then, develop skills in engaging in meaningful interactions with students and peers.
BKG031

Visit SolutionTree.com or call 800.733.6786 to order.

Global PD teams
Collaborative Learning for School Improvement

Quality team learning **from authors you trust**

Global PD Teams is the first-ever **online professional development resource designed to support your entire faculty on your learning journey.** This convenient tool offers daily access to videos, mini-courses, eBooks, articles, and more packed with insights and research-backed strategies you can use immediately.

GET STARTED
SolutionTree.com/**GlobalPDTeams**
800.733.6786